MW01252771

Who Gets What?

Analysing Economic Inequality in Australia

Why have the incomes of corporate executives dramatically outstripped those of other workers? Do people's income and wealth reflect differences in their contributions to the Australian economy? Do big economic inequalities damage productivity and social cohesion? Why isn't Australia a more egalitarian society?

Who Gets What? explores questions like these. It looks at recent trends in income and wealth in Australia and examines the economic evidence in a way that makes fascinating reading for both general and specialist audiences.

The book looks at who is rich and who in Australia still lives in poverty – and why. It explores the causes of economic inequality and the possibility of making our society more equal. Ultimately, the authors offer their own solution to these problems, with policies which could redistribute income and wealth more equitably.

FRANK STILWELL is Professor of Political Economy at the University of Sydney.

KIRRILY JORDAN is a research assistant in political economy at the University of Sydney.

Who Gets What?
Analysing Economic Inequality in Australia

FRANK STILWELL AND KIRRILY JORDAN

CAMBRIDGE
UNIVERSITY PRESS

CAMBRIDGE UNIVERSITY PRESS
Cambridge, New York, Melbourne, Madrid, Cape Town,
Singapore, São Paulo, Delhi, Mexico City

Cambridge University Press
The Edinburgh Building, Cambridge CB2 8RU, UK

Published in the United States of America by Cambridge University Press, New York

www.cambridge.org
Information on this title: www.cambridge.org/9780521700320

First published 2007

A catalogue record for this publication is available from the British Library

National Library of Australia Cataloguing in Publication data
Stilwell, Frank J B
Who GetsWhat?: Analysing Economic Inequality in Australia.
Bibliography.
Includes index.
ISBN-13 978-0-52170-032-0 paperback
ISBN-10 0-52170-032-9 paperback
1. Income distribution – Australia. 2.Wealth – Moral and ethical aspects – Australia.
3. Australia – Economic conditions – 2001 – Regional disparities. I. Jordan, Kirrily.
II. Title.
339.220994

ISBN 978-0-521-70032-0 Paperback

CONTENTS

LIST OF FIGURES

LIST OF TABLES

ACKNOWLEDGEMENTS

Research in the social sciences has an inherently collective character. Individual researchers compile and interpret information about patterns and processes, as we have done in this study, drawing on previous knowledge developed by other researchers. This is both inevitable and desirable. In developing this analysis of economic inequality we have built on a wide array of previously published research, as well as official data from the Australian Bureau of Statistics. These sources are carefully acknowledged in the text and in the comprehensive bibliography.

We would also like to acknowledge the direct assistance of other researchers. Bill Pritchard commented on an earlier draft of chapter 6, Elizabeth Hill made helpful suggestions about chapter 7 and Phil Raskall helped clarify the relationship between economic inequality and the balance of payments that is considered in chapter 10. Three anonymous referees also provided comments on an earlier draft of the whole volume; their work had a major influence on the revisions we made for the final version.

Makiz Ansari provided valuable research assistance at an early stage in the project. Eleanor Armstrong did much of the word processing. Kim Armitage from Cambridge University Press buoyed our spirits with her enthusiasm for publishing the volume, and Kate Indigo steered it through the production process. Sandra Goldbloom Zurbo was an excellent copy editor and Neale Towart efficiently compiled the index.

The veracity of the published work and its value for future researchers and policy-makers, as well as students of the social sciences, is our own joint responsibility, of course. We hope it helps to inform and to make a difference.

Frank Stilwell
Kirrily Jordan
February 2007

x

Chapter One

INEQUALITY

Dramatic economic and social inequalities have become a feature of modern Australia. As the society as a whole has become more wealthy the wealth has been spread very unevenly. Yet there is still a widespread, lingering attachment to egalitarian ideals. This interesting situation requires careful analysis.

Some people have huge incomes, most notably the corporate executives whose prodigious remuneration packages now sometimes exceed $20 million annually. Others, including members of some well-known family dynasties, have vast accumulated wealth: the assets of the richest two hundred wealth holders currently range from $196 million to $7.1 billion. Regularly celebrating these concentrations of wealth, magazines such as *Business Review Weekly* and *Wealth Creators* illustrate the media's tendency to identify success in terms of material prosperity. The conspicuously luxurious lifestyles of the wealthy shape broader social aspirations, often engendering feelings of personal deprivation among people with incomes that, in much of the rest of the world, would also be regarded as affluent.

Other Australians face more tangible economic hardships and insecurity. Many are struggling to meet their expenditure commitments, particularly because housing costs have risen rapidly in the last two decades. Industrial relations policies have increased the downward pressure on the wages of the less well-organised sections of the workforce. Having a job is no longer sufficient to escape the risk of sliding into poverty. Those who are reliant on social security payments as the principal source of their income have also been subjected to particular stresses, as governments embracing neoliberal ideology have implemented policies to reduce what they refer to as welfare dependency. So poverty persists – at least relative to the general standard of living – despite the greater affluence of society as a whole. Indeed, it seems that growing wealth and persistent poverty are two sides of the same coin.

Should this gulf between rich and poor be a matter of public concern? Some say not. These are either the complacent or the committed. Those who are complacent accept whatever *is* as natural and therefore not something to be challenged, even if it is a source of anxiety or regret. The committed have a more assertive ideological stance. These are the proponents of 'incentivation'. They argue that, in general, people receive rewards in proportion to their productivity. So a steep gradient between low and high incomes is a necessary incentive for the efforts that create a thriving economy. This view – that economic inequality is conducive to overall economic prosperity – has been very influential in the realm of public policy during the last two decades, when neoliberalism has been the dominant discourse. Neoliberal beliefs generally lead to a *laissez-faire* attitude to inequality, in effect accepting any distribution of incomes and wealth that is generated by a market economy. More audaciously, neoliberal policies, such as cutting income taxes more for the rich than for the poor, directly intensify economic inequalities.

Meanwhile, critics of economic inequality warn of the consequences of a more divided society. They challenge the notion that differential rewards reflect productivity differences, pointing out that, in practice, class-based power relationships significantly determine the distribution of income and wealth. On this reasoning, the gulf between rich and poor has less defensible economic and ethical justifications. It also has some dangerous social consequences. Since problems such as violence and crime tend to intensify in an unequal society, more and more resources need to be allocated to social control. Wealthy suburbs and gated communities coexist with disadvantaged areas in an increasingly tense and unstable mix. Concerns for social cohesion in these circumstances fuel demands for a more egalitarian society.

A cautious, intermediate view between the committed and critical perspectives stresses the desirability of creating equality of opportunity rather than equality of outcome. From this meritocratic perspective, the gulf between high incomes and low incomes does not particularly matter. Rather, the issue is whether everyone has an equal opportunity to attain the high incomes. Concern with social mobility thereby takes precedence over concern with economic inequality. It is the sort of view that has also been promoted by politicians claiming to cater for aspirational voters – those who are concerned with their own personal advancement rather than any general egalitarian goals. Such reasoning and political focus are compatible with an increasingly unequal society. So, notwithstanding the inherent appeal of the notion of equality of opportunity (who would seriously argue against it?), it is not a position that challenges big inequalities in the distribution of income and wealth.

Downplaying the importance of economic inequality has also become a feature of some otherwise challenging, progressive social commentary. The writings of Clive Hamilton, executive director of The Australia Institute, are particularly important in this context. Hamilton considers inequality a less central issue than affluence. In publications such as his recent *Quarterly Essay, What's Left? The Death of Social Democracy*, he argues that the political Left has overemphasised problems of inequality, leading to insufficient attention being paid to the social consequences of 'affluenza'. According to Hamilton, it is the excesses of affluence and the continual quest by those who want to be wealthier that are more fundamentally problematic. On this reading, the problems of injustice in modern Australian society are focused on just three groups: people in poverty, Indigenous Australians and people with physical disabilities. Beyond that, Hamilton says 'the defining problem of modern industrial society is not injustice but alienation, and the central task of progressive politics today is to achieve not equality, but liberation' (Hamilton 2006: 32). There is merit in this viewpoint, but it is important to recognise the central role that economic inequality plays in contemporary social problems, including the very affluenza that Hamilton emphasises. Affluenza is fuelled by the gap between rich and poor and is manifest in the concerns of the latter to emulate the former. Without redressing economic inequality it is hard to see the problems that Hamilton rightly emphasises ever being resolved. Yet Hamilton's intervention in public debate is significant in demonstrating that views on inequality now no longer align neatly with other issues on which the political Left and Right disagree.

Economic inequality is evidently a contentious issue. If we are to understand the possibility and desirability of its redress we need an analysis of its causes and consequences. First and foremost we need a clear picture of the facts of the matter – who gets what?

Wide disparities

Australian society has always had marked economic inequalities. Some indication of their current extent can be gauged by looking at the official Australian Bureau of Statistics (ABS) data on the distribution of household incomes, which include income from all sources, such as wages, rents, dividends, interest and social security payments. Dividing the whole population into five groups, or quintiles, and ranking them from richest to poorest gives an initial summary of the overall disparities. Households in the top quintile in 2003–4 had an average after-tax income of $1027 per week, whereas the bottom quintile received an average of only $226. So the former group had average incomes more than four times those of the latter. Over the period since 1994–5 the real income of people in the top quintile rose by an average of $166 per week, while those in the lowest quintile received an average increase of $45 per week. Again, the ratio was about four to one. Of course, those broad categories mask some enormous variations in the incomes of particular groups within Australian society. To take an extreme case, the spectacular remuneration packages enjoyed by senior corporate managers not only dwarf the incomes of the bulk of the population (even dwarfing the average incomes of those in the top quintile identified by the ABS), but they have also been growing dramatically faster. By 2005, the average annual remuneration of chief executives in the top fifty-one companies who are members of the Business Council of Australia had risen to sixty-three times the average annual earnings of full-time Australian workers – up from twenty times the average in 1992 (Shields 2005: 302).

A rather different way of looking at income distribution is in terms of the relative size of incomes received as wages or profits. This shows the shares of labour and capital in the national income. In 2003–4, wages comprised 53.1 per cent of the total, while profits formed 26.7 per cent. This profit share was the highest share recorded since 1959–60. A class dimension is embedded in this way of looking at inequality because the shares of wages and profits reflect the relative power of labour and capital – or, broadly speaking, employees and employers. A shift from wages to profits – which has been the dominant trend since the 1970s – predictably feeds into more inequality in the distribution of household incomes. The correlation is not perfect because some of the profits flow as dividend payments to so-called mum and dad shareholders. But the overall distribution of shareholdings is heavily skewed towards the richest households who have been the principal beneficiaries of tax concessions such as dividend imputation and reductions in capital gains tax during the last decade.

Even more striking than the disparities in income are the inequalities in the distribution of wealth – the financial and physical assets, such as cash, shares and real estate, that households own. The wealthiest 10 per cent of the Australian population owns about 45 per cent of the total wealth. The top 50 per cent owns over 90 per cent of the wealth, leaving the people in the other half of Australian society with less than 10 per cent of the national wealth between them (Harding 2002: 11; Headey *et al.* 2005: 159). Not surprisingly, households in the wealthier groups also hold more of their wealth in income-generating forms, such as shares and property. This wealth inequality thereby significantly impacts on income inequalities. Those in the top fifth of the wealth distribution increased their wealth by an average of around $250 000 in the ten years to 2004, two-thirds of which resulted from gains in the real estate property market. In contrast, the least wealthy fifth of the population increased their wealth by only about $3000 in the period, half of which derived from their small superannuation entitlements (Button and Stevenson 2004). Evidently, who gets what depends significantly on who owns what.

At the top of the tree is a tiny elite of extraordinarily wealthy people. According to *Business Review Weekly*, the total amount of wealth held by the richest 200 Australians surpassed $117 billion in 2006. The amount of wealth necessary to just scrape into this 'rich 200' list has more than tripled since the mid 1990s, even accounting for inflation. A chasm separates wealthy individuals such as these from most of Australian society. The sources of their wealth are also distinctive. Among the top wealth holders, the owner-ship and development of property features particularly prominently, with manufacturing, retail development and media interests also significant. Four of the richest ten Australians in 2006 started their careers through family inheritances, although these inheritances were only a fraction of their current wealth.

At the other end of the scale, the incidence of poverty has proved remarkably persistent. According to a study undertaken for the National Centre for Social and Economic Modelling (NATSEM), if the poverty line is set at half the average family income, about 11 per cent (or one in nine Australians) are living in poverty (Lloyd *et al.* 2004a). Those most at risk include young people in the 15–24 year age bracket, single people, sole parents, Indigenous Australians, recently arrived migrants, refugees and people with disabilities. The 41 per cent poverty rate among the unemployed is the highest of all, being almost four times the national average (Lloyd *et al.* 2004a: 14). But poverty is also evident among those in full-time and part-time work, indicating that a problem of the so-called working poor now exists in the Australian economy, albeit not yet on the same scale as in the USA. Full-time and part-time workers make up more than one-quarter of all Australians living in poverty (Lloyd *et al.* 2004a: 15). Poverty, at least in relative terms, is inseparable from the more general forces reproducing economic inequality.

Does inequality matter?

The predictably divergent views about the pros and cons of economic inequality have their roots in distinctive political economic judgements. The concentration of incomes and wealth is sometimes defended on the grounds that it creates a trickle-down effect. On this reasoning, society as a whole benefits from the presence of very wealthy people because of the employment they create through their business activities, the economic stimulus that results from their consumer spending and the tax contributions they make to government revenues. However, there is a difference between the case for accumulation of wealth in general and for the concentration of that wealth in a few hands. The positive effects of capital accumulation on employment, consumption and tax revenues are not contingent on its concentrated ownership, and may even be impaired by it. In other words, a broader spread of income and wealth could be quite compatible with equally strong national economic performance.

The big political economic question is whether there is a trade-off between equity and efficiency. In other words, would sharing incomes and wealth more equitably reduce the total amount to be shared? If that were the case – if a more equitable society were necessarily a poorer society – then egalitarian sentiments and policies would certainly have less general appeal. In practice, the evidence of any such trade-off between equity and efficiency is quite inconclusive. More equitable societies, such as the Scandinavian nations and Japan, are not notably less economically prosperous than other, more unequal, ones. And, within individual nations, economic efficiency evidently has only a weak connection with reward. The remuneration of different occupations, typically, has more to do with bargaining power than any objective measure of efficiency or labour productivity. Incomes from inheritance, to take the extreme case, have nothing to do with the productivity of the recipients. Even in business, the relationship between productivity and economic rewards is dubious: as research undertaken by the author of the study of executive remuneration cited earlier shows, there is no clear overall correlation between executives' incomes and the performance of the companies they manage (Shields *et al.* 2003).

Scepticism about the commonly asserted relationship between material rewards and economic contributions is appropriate. Much depends on the nature of this relationship in practice. If the markedly uneven distribution of income and wealth *were* the product of productivity differentials we might be more inclined to accept it as legitimate – as the logical outcome of a capitalist market system in which people derive rewards according to their economic contributions. Those, such as prominent Australian businessman and Liberal parliamentarian Malcolm Turnbull, who have been arguing for cutting the top rate of income tax in Australia implicitly make that assumption (Turnbull and Temple 2005). Hence the claim that allowing the rich to retain more of their incomes after tax would generate more productive effort, benefiting society as a whole. On similar reasoning, the poor should be encouraged to shift from welfare to work by removing social security payments, which, according to this argument, encourage idleness. But the connection between rewards and productivity is, in practice, ill-defined. Productivity is often hard to measure, particularly in service industries, where most Australians now work. Power relationships, deriving from organisational strengths and monopoly positions, are often more decisive than productivity differences in shaping actual incomes (Stilwell 2006: ch. 22). Moreover, as political economist J. K. Galbraith once noted, to justify increased economic inequality on the grounds of 'incentivation' makes an odd behavioural assumption – that the rich will work harder if their incomes are increased whereas the poor will work harder if theirs are reduced (Davidson 1987).

Even if some economic inequality is conducive to the creation of economic incentives, it is important to ask just how much is necessary in practice. On the United Nations league-table of economic inequality, Australia is a middling nation with a ratio of around 12.5:1 between the average incomes of the richest 10 per cent of households and the poorest 10 per cent (United Nations 2004). Would a much lower ratio of, say, 5:1 or 6:1 between high and low incomes be sufficient to maintain economic incentives? In Norway, Sweden and Denmark the ratio is typically of that magnitude, and those nations face no obvious problem of economic stagnation arising from a lack of material incentive. In modern economies there are always going to be some rich people and some poor people, but there are major variations between nations in the extent of that inequality. There is evidently significant scope for different distributions of income and wealth: an element of political choice is inescapable.

Are inequalities consistently conducive to more impressive economic outcomes anyway? There are good grounds for doubt. Big inequalities – or certainly the perception of unwarranted inequalities – can generate quite perverse economic effects in practice. Among any group of people, cooperative and productive relationships usually depend on the expectation of reasonably fair shares in the distribution of the fruits of that cooperation. Casual empiricism suggests that is generally true for households, sporting teams and small businesses, for example, even for universities. One may reasonably expect the same to apply to nations. A high incidence of property crime, violence and other social pathologies is a predictable outcome if some broadly acceptable degree of distributional equity is not ensured. It is not just the facts of inequality that matter, but also beliefs about whether the inequalities are justifiable in terms of differential effort or merit.

Then there is the even more fundamental question about whether the drive for income and wealth produces more personal contentment. Does the relentless pursuit of income and wealth make us happier, individually and collectively? Evidently not, according to a range of social surveys that show only a weak correlation between material wealth and self-reported happiness in different societies (see Frey and Stutzer 2002; Saunders 2002; Frank 1999; Hamilton 2003a; Hamilton and Denniss 2005). It also seems that the citizens of societies in which economic inequality is greatest generally report lower levels of personal satisfaction (Layard 2003b, 2005). This is not surprising because, if our wellbeing is assessed in relative terms, a wide gulf between rich and poor tends to intensify the latter's feelings of relative deprivation. Social cohesion can be threatened in these circumstances. This has led to a growing concern, internationally as well as in Australia, that economic growth accompanied by increased inequality may have no net social benefit, and may indeed have negative effects on the overall wellbeing of society.

Logged in or logged out?

Income inequality is strongly correlated with the digital divide – the gulf between those who have ready access to the internet and those who do not. Between 1998–9 and 2004–5, the proportion of Australian homes with computers connected to the internet more than trebled – from 16 per cent to 56 per cent. However, there are striking differences between wealthy and poor households. According to unpublished ABS statistics analysed by Steve Burrell and Anna Patty (2006), households with incomes of $100 000 per annum or more are nearly three and a half times more likely to be connected to the internet than are households with incomes below $25 000 (86 per cent in the former group have internet access, compared with only 26 per cent in the latter). Between these two extremes the digital divide widens consistently. Of households with annual incomes in the $75 000–100 000 range 74 per cent had home internet access, as did 66 per cent of households in the $50 000–75 000 range and 38 per cent in the $25 000–50 000 range.

Why does this variation in internet access matter? It certainly provides a striking illustration of how the economic inequality that pervades Australian society shapes access to resources and social opportunities. Moreover, internet access is particularly important because information flows are increasingly computer-based. So being income poor tends to go hand in hand with being information disadvantaged. The problem is most acute in regard to children because information disadvantage affects their educational experiences and the intergenerational transmission of inequality.

Overall, internet access is significantly higher for households with children under fifteen than for households without children – 70 per cent compared with 49 per cent. But the bias according to household income is evident here, too. Ninety-four per cent of households with children and an annual income of $120 000 or more had internet access in 2004–5, but only 50 per cent of households with children and incomes of less than $40 000 did so. Educational success depends on much more than home internet access, of course, but educational specialists (quoted by Burrell and Patty 2006: 30) emphasise the importance of the internet today in coping with areas of knowledge that are rapidly changing, and in developing young people's ability to deal with that knowledge in a more interactive manner than conventional textbooks permit.

Internet access is strongly correlated with the employment status of parents, too. The same study shows only 30 per cent of adults not in the workforce as having home internet access, compared with 64 per cent of those with jobs. In one-parent families where the parent is unemployed the rate was a mere 28 per cent (Burrell and Patty 2006: 29). The relative disadvantages of children in the less well-resourced households can be ameliorated by more universal access to computer facilities in schools, by better provision through public libraries and by programs such as that offered by the Smith Family to teach disadvantaged children internet skills. Even so, there is a strong inbuilt socioeconomic bias to overcome.

Children in families with working parents who have high incomes have traditionally experienced the advantages of private study space, ready access to books and (sometimes, but not always) greater encouragement to educational achievement, so the gulf between haves and have nots in the educational process is nothing new. Nor has it proved insuperable, especially where parental or teacher encouragement more than compensates for material disadvantage. But the prospect of a 'cyber underclass' poses new challenges for those concerned with equality of educational opportunity.

Class, status, power

Underlying much discussion of inequality is the notion of class, a term that often makes Australians uneasy. Indeed, part of the appeal for many people of a relatively 'new' society (such as Australia following European occupation) is that it is not saddled with the social divisions of old societies, such as the UK, with their inherited traditions of class differentiation. Yet the evidence on income inequalities, for example, suggests that there may be little difference in practice. International league-tables of income inequality show Australia and the UK occupying quite similar positions – more equal than the USA but less so than Japan, Germany and the Scandinavian nations. So, if class is a matter of economic inequalities rather than social mannerisms, Australians cannot readily shrug it off as irrelevant.

Variations in attitude are, nonetheless, important. The egalitarian sentiment in Australia certainly affects how we relate to the existence of major economic inequalities. As historian Humphrey McQueen put it over thirty years ago:

> It is the absence of feudal hangovers in Australia which impresses people. In most European societies the bourgeoisie managed to acquire at least some of the accoutrements of rank and style. The best Australia can manage are double knighthoods for prodigious wealth, and services to tax-deductible sport. Very schematically the position could be put as follows: although Australia is a class society in terms of property ownership it is a classless society in terms of lifestyle and aspiration (McQueen 1974).

Or, to quote contemporary social commentator Craig McGregor:

> I suppose that's how most Australians feel about class: class equals snobbery,
> and it's stupid. Especially if you're on the blunt end of it. I've always liked
> the way Australians tend to think of class distinction as a sort of Pommy
> hangover which someone else is guilty of. Class? In Australia? Isn't this place
> classless? (McGregor 1997: 1)

Analytically, it is useful to distinguish between class, status and power. Class
concerns people's relationship to the means of production – whether as
a wage worker, a self-employed person, small-business owner or captain
of industry. Status relates to social esteem and may involve differentiation
between blue- and white-collar workers, between people who live in different
localities or between people who engage in different patterns of consumption, even when they earn similar incomes. Power derives primarily from
command over resources, particularly where that affects other people's economic opportunities – such as the power of business executives to hire or
fire or the power of politicians and judges to set the rules of the game in
society. The three dimensions of inequality – class, status and power – may
be broadly correlated, but are usually less than completely so. Therein lies
considerable social complexity, and also much scope for confusion about
what class means in practice.

According to sociologists who stress the complexity of modern society,
identity has become the subjective lens through which the inequalities of
class, status and power are related. Identity also reflects other bases of social
differentiation, such as gender, ethnicity and sexual preference. It may – and,
typically, does – embrace identification with locality, too, and with particular
patterns of social activity and consumerist behaviour. The result is a highly
differentiated set of outcomes. A person whose self-identity is primarily
as a surfer from Bondi, for example, may be affluent or poor: their class
position does not determine their personal identity. Similarly, a resident
of Bankstown may self-identify as female of Greek descent, a follower of
the Sydney Bulldogs and a listener to radio station 2WS, as well as being
a hairdresser who aspires to own her own salon. Any coherent notion of
class seems to sink in the swamp of subjectivity and individual choice. The
challenge for social science is to balance this complexity with analysis of the

broader structural factors that continue to shape people's actual life chances. Personal identity is important because it does have a bearing on people's behaviour – on their economic, social and political actions. Indeed, how we variously respond to evidence about inequalities of class, status and power is strongly influenced by our subjective identity. We have to find some way of reconciling these subjective elements with the objective characteristics of economic inequality that are evident in the distribution of income, wealth and life chances.

The propensity of the bulk of people to self-identify as middle class is perhaps the clearest illustration of the ambivalence about class in modern Australian society. In part, this may represent false consciousness – to use the traditional Marxian terminology. The majority of people identifying as middle class derive their income primarily from the sale of their labour or capacity to work and, as such, they are working class. To limit the term 'working class' to traditional blue-collar jobs is hopelessly restrictive in an era in which service industries employ over two-thirds of the workforce. Yet the preference for identifying as middle class may also have a significant material base – reflecting ownership of some capital, whether in the form of shares, superannuation or maybe an investment property or two in addition to an owner-occupied house. The number of people who derive some income from both labour and capital has grown steadily throughout the last half century. As Gibson-Graham, Resnick and Wolff (2001: 17) note, if 'class analysis involves sorting individuals into mutually exclusive class categories [it is] often a frustrating analytical project'. Class has to be treated as being about processes, not positions – in this case, the processes that shape the economic opportunities and rewards within Australian society.

The issue of social mobility also warrants consideration in this context. People are much less likely to be comfortable about the concept of class where they perceive opportunities for social mobility to be extensive. Formally, it is possible to differentiate the two phenomena – identifying the class inequalities that exist at a point of time, and the extent to which social mobility allows some repositioning over time. Social mobility injects rather more flexibility into the issue of who gets what, without necessarily reducing the extent of economic inequalities that exist. However, in practice, people are evidently less troubled by inequalities if they perceive society is sufficiently open to allow upwardly mobile individuals to reap the rewards of their own efforts (or luck).

In all these respects, it is perceptions that matter – the perceptions that underpin people's class identity, if any, and the beliefs about social mobility that shape their views about the extent to which income and wealth inequalities are regarded as just. Not surprisingly, the result is a wide array of attitudes to economic inequality. Some say 'Good luck to rich people, they've earned what they've got', while others take the view that the presence and reproduction of an affluent elite limits other people's economic opportunities and destroys the foundations for a more cohesive society. Such popular perceptions can, and do, coexist.

Although perceptions matter, an objective material basis for class inequality remains. As various contributors to a recent book, *Class and Struggle in Australia*, emphasise, fundamental differences in economic circumstances underpin a wide array of social and modern political tensions and conflicts (Kuhn 2005). Similarly, as the contributors to another book, *Ruling Australia*, show, the processes of power, privilege and politics continue to have systematic class dimensions, pervading all aspects of Australian society (Hollier 2004). The industrial relations reforms introduced by the federal government in 2005 are a particularly striking illustration of the continuing relevance of class in public policy, because they have radically restructured the power relationship between the class of employers and the class of employees (see, for example, King and Stilwell 2005). The economics editor of the *Sydney Morning Herald* – not generally noted for his recourse to class analysis – summarised the changes as being 'more about class war than economics' (Gittins 2005a).

Attitudes to inequality

There is evidence that egalitarian sentiments are alive and well among the Australian people. It seems that most would prefer a more egalitarian distribution of income. The basis for this claim is the Australian Survey of Social Attitudes that was conducted in 2005 (Wilson *et al.* 2006). Just under 4000 respondents answered a wide range of questions, one set of which probed attitudes to the distribution of income and the role of government in pursuing more egalitarian outcomes. The responses (more details about which are provided in Appendix A) show remarkable evidence of the widespread nature of egalitarian attitudes.

When asked whether the gap between high incomes and low incomes is currently too large or too small, just under 82 per cent of those surveyed said it is too large. Less than 1 per cent said it is too small. Twelve per cent said it was about right and about 6 per cent of respondents were undecided. Predictably, the pattern of responses varies according to income, but even among the upper-income groups an egalitarian sentiment was dominant. In the top-income category, comprising people with annual incomes over $78 000, almost 60 per cent considered the distribution of income to be too unequal.

When asked to respond to the further proposition that 'ordinary working people do not get a fair share of the nation's wealth', an overall 61 per cent of those surveyed agreed. Only 15 per cent disagreed with the proposition, the remaining 24 per cent taking a neutral position or not being able to choose. Here is further evidence of widespread belief that economic inequality has become too pronounced. It is notable that this question, referring explicitly to 'ordinary working people' and 'a fair share', elicited a rather more mixed response than the first question about the extent of inequality – not surprisingly, because some sort of class identity is thereby implied. Yet the dominant response clearly demonstrates the widespread disquiet about whether the current distributional patterns are socially just.

The same survey also posed another question: whether government should be pursuing policies of income redistribution. The responses to this were much more mixed. Overall around 39 per cent thought that government should redistribute income, just under 33 per cent thought that it should not, 24 per cent neither agreed nor disagreed and a little over 4 per cent were undecided. Predictably, the strongest support for redistributive policies came from among the lower-income group; but there was significant support among the top income recipients, too.

One-quarter of those in the top group, with incomes over $78 000, favoured a redistributive role for government (Wilson *et al.* 2006). These were people who could be expected themselves to be net losers from a policy of redistribution, so self-interest evidently did not wholly determine these responses.

Analysing economic inequality

All of us are affected by the extent of economic inequality. It shapes our individual options and choices. It sets the character of society as a whole. So it is properly of central concern for social scientists. Indeed, it is a concern that has been reflected in a steady trickle of research publications and books on the topic in recent years (for example, Fincher and Saunders 2001; Saunders 2002; Peel 2003; Greig *et al.* 2003; Hollier 2004; Kuhn 2005; Argy 2006). However, it being a trickle rather than a flood is indicative of the tendency for distributional issues to be marginalised in contemporary discourse. Economists usually subordinate distributional issues to macroeconomic considerations, implicitly assuming that 'a rising tide lifts all boats'.[1] Sociologists – or at least those of a poststructuralist inclination – tend to regard a concern with the economic roots of inequality as reflecting an old analytical tradition, preferring to focus now on the relationship of self to society and on cultural rather than economic considerations. And political scientists tend to emphasise attitudinal and electoral issues rather than the material conditions shaping the production and distribution of income and wealth. Questions about political economic power and inequality are not at the top of these agendas.

It was not ever thus. A great tradition of analysis, research and advocacy in social science has been centred on who gets what. The classical political

---

[1] There have been honourable exceptions. Internationally, Amartya Sen (1985, 1997) and A. B. Atkinson (1972, 1983, 2004) spring to mind as economists prioritising the study of economic inequality. Distributional concerns have also figured, theoretically although not much empirically, in post-Keynesian economics, following the seminal work by Nicholas Kaldor (1955–6). In the modern Australian context, Peter Saunders and Ann Harding are clear examples of economists turning their attention to distributional and equity issues: subsequent chapters draw significantly on their valuable contributions.

economist David Ricardo (1817) considered the distribution of income among social classes to be 'the principal problem in political economy'. Later in the nineteenth century the distinguished liberal political economist John Stuart Mill (1848) argued that the pattern of income distribution was essentially a political choice, largely independent of the economic principles that shape the production of economic wealth. In the twentieth century, economists such as Gunnar Myrdal, Joan Robinson and J. K. Galbraith – as well as social theorists and policy analysts such as R. H. Tawney, Richard Titmuss, Peter Townsend and William Beveridge – were proponents of public policies with egalitarian intentions (see also Baker 1987). Even Lord J. M. Keynes, the father of modern macroeconomics, acknowledged that the distribution of income and wealth matters, not least because of its impact on overall levels of consumption, output and employment. In his own words:

> I believe that there is social and psychological justification for significant inequalities of income and wealth, but not for such large disparities as exist today . . . Much lower stakes will serve the purpose equally well as soon as the players are accustomed to them (Keynes 1951: 374).

The call for a more egalitarian society has been taken up more or less vigorously by numerous political activists concerned with issues of social justice. Socialists have rubbed shoulders with small 'l' liberals in advocating and developing labour market institutions, regulatory arrangements, taxation structures and welfare state provisions to give practical effect to the quest for more equitable outcomes.

Reclaiming, reinvigorating and extending that tradition in the Australian context is the principal aim of this book. It seeks to illumine the complex issues associated with economic inequality in Australian society. The principal dimensions of these disparities are illustrated by the data presented in subsequent chapters. The analysis simultaneously raises many questions. What determines the extent of economic inequality? How has it been changing over time? Does it matter? Is inequality a good thing, creating desirable incentives, or a source of discord, undermining cooperative economic relationships and social cohesion? What should, and could, be done about it? In exploring these questions, and more, the book presents an array of information about incomes and wealth, the rich and the poor, the advantaged and the disadvantaged. It challenges the notion that Australia is an egalitarian society. It considers the social and political implications of economic inequality and it presents some proposals for a way forward.

The method of analysis is characteristic of the institutional tradition within modern political economy. It has a strong empirical foundation, based on the compilation and analysis of descriptive economic statistics that gives a picture of the principal dimensions of economic inequality. Where appropriate, international comparisons are made, situating the Australian experience in a broader context. These empirical data are linked to discussion of causal factors, emphasising relations of economic power between capital and labour and between different subgroups of income recipients, and to consideration of the government's role in redistributing incomes and shaping the rules of the game. These linkages are explored in a qualitative manner, emphasising the complex judgements that have to be made. Emphasis is also placed on the effects of inequality, including the social, environmental and political consequences, as well as the more narrowly economic aspects. Supplementary evidence is drawn from the emerging field of what is called happiness research to see why increasing economic inequality can have perverse outcomes and undermine the individual and collective actions that could actually contribute to human betterment. This normative analysis is then linked to policy prescription, based on the belief that the ultimate purpose of political economy is to generate guidelines for what is to be done in striving for more progressive social change.

This approach to the issue of economic inequality is rather different from previous social and historical studies of Australian egalitarianism, such as the contribution by Elaine Thompson (1994) and the recent reflections by Don Aitkin (2005) on the reshaping of Australia during the last half century. Egalitarianism has been an influential set of beliefs, shaping Australian society and behaviour – for better or worse. As Aitkin notes (p. 255), 'Australia pays a good deal of lip-service to egalitarian ideals'. The notion of mateship is widely regarded as the distinctive local expression of these ideals, one to which Prime Minister John Howard has made recurrent appeals. However, as Thompson demonstrates, 'egalitarianism as sameness' is the implicit view that has commonly led to exclusionary policies and practices, based on race and gender for example. In this sense it sits awkwardly with popular folksy attitudes about 'a fair go' and 'Jack is as good as his master' (or Jill, for that matter). It is important to acknowledge these tensions, not least because an appeal to egalitarian principles is seldom free of contradictions. Narrowing the focus to economic inequalities cuts through this complexity to a considerable extent and provides a means of exploring the material base underpinning concerns about equity, social cohesion and sustainability. Asking who gets what thereby directs our attention to specific political economic concerns and policy issues.

Conclusion

As a society we seem to be at a crossroads in terms of economic inequality. Deep disparities dominate and divide. Yet collective remedies are not commonly sought. The prevailing public policies accommodate, even accentuate, the trend towards inegalitarian outcomes. The individualistic ethos of neoliberalism is more conducive to people seeking their own personal advancement rather than broader political economic reform. Most people, understandably, would wish to be wealthier. However, it is not clear that there is any reliably strong connection between income and happiness, or between inequality and overall national economic performance. Survey evidence also suggests that egalitarian sentiments remain widespread in Australian society, although many people simultaneously hold relatively cautious views about whether governments should act as agents of redistribution.

So it is important to analyse the causes and consequences of the current distribution of income and wealth. It is also important to carefully consider alternative responses and policies that could produce different outcomes, thereby exploring the possibility of a different direction for public policy and social change. There is an essentially normative dimension to an analysis such as this. It leads us to reflect on the big question we all face – 'In what sort of economy and society do we want to live?' A society in which high incomes and wealth are relentlessly sought and celebrated? A society in which incomes and wealth are more evenly redistributed? Or a society which starts to question material affluence as the primary indicator of success? These are the aspects of public debate that this book seeks to stimulate and to which it seeks to contribute.

Chapter Two

INCOMES

First the evidence. We need to build an understanding of the principal dimensions of economic inequality in Australia. Looking at the distribution of income is the obvious starting point. Income is the most obvious indicator of the standard of living that people experience, so using it as the primary measure of economic inequality needs little supporting argument. What is important to note is that income can derive from various activities – from waged work, interest payments on savings, dividends on shares, rents on property or government transfer payments, for example. It is the aggregation of all such current income flows that is the prime determinant of a person's economic wellbeing. It is the unevenness in the distribution of these incomes that is the principal indicator of the degree of inequality within the whole society.

This chapter looks at recent evidence on the extent of income inequality. It examines the relationship between the incomes derived from labour and those derived from capital, and the variations in wage rates between occupations, before turning to look at perhaps the most spectacular income recipients, the chief executive officers (CEOs) of large corporations. It then investigates how overall income inequality can be assessed, how it has changed over the last couple of decades and how it compares internationally. In this way we construct a clear picture of who gets what.

Capital versus labour

The distribution of national income as wages, profits and other types of payment is sometimes called 'the functional distribution of income'. In orthodox economic terms, it shows the relative rewards of the different factors of production that contribute to generating the national income. A political economic class dimension is also evident in this functional distribution to the extent that the shares of wages and profits reflect the relative power between labour and capital. In practice this is complicated by the fact that not all the income from capital goes to what would generally be considered as the capitalist class. Some goes in the form of dividend payments to small shareholders who have a stake in the income from capital. Many workers also receive interest payments on their bank deposits. Though relatively small in volume, such incomes from the ownership of capital tend to blur class divisions, so care must be exercised in equating the functional distribution of income with what goes to particular subsets of the population. Nevertheless, in broad terms, it is an indicator of how the fruits of economic activity are shared between those who derive their income principally from wage labour and those who derive their income from owning capital assets.

In Australia since the mid 1970s the evidence suggests that there has been a long-term redistribution of income away from labour and towards capital. Figures 2.1 and 2.2 on the next page, based on data from the Australian Bureau of Statistics (ABS), show that labour was increasing its share in the 1960s and 1970s, but that redistribution towards profits has been the dominant trend during the last quarter of a century.

The wages figures shown in figure 2.1 refer to income received before personal income tax is taken into account. The rest of the national income is called 'the gross operating surplus'. This mainly comprises profits, rents and interest payments. Trends in the gross operating surplus exactly mirror movements in the wages share of total income – rising when the wages share falls and falling when the wages share rises. Profits are the single largest component in this gross operating surplus; figure 2.2 shows the relentless growth in its share since 1975–6, interrupted only for short periods such as the economic recession in 1990–1.

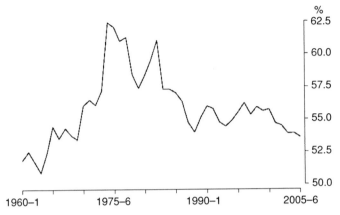

Figure 2.1 Wages share of total income, 1960–1 to 2005–6
Source: ABS 2006a: 9.

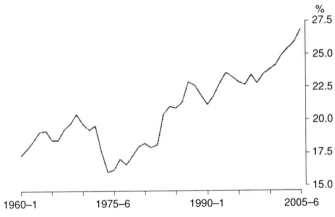

Figure 2.2 Profits share of total income, 1960–1 to 2005–6
Source: ABS 2006a: 9.

As these figures show, a major redistribution of national income has taken place. Indeed, there is some evidence of acceleration in this redistribution since the late 1990s. The 26.9 per cent profit share in 2005–6 was its highest recorded level since 1959–60, while the wage share has significantly declined since 1996–7, as it did in the late 1970s and for much of the 1980s. Labour's relative gains in the 1960s and early 1970s have been effectively obliterated by these reversals. Sociologist Michael Pusey argues that such trends represent 'a clear shift in the distribution of income from wage and salary earners to corporations' (Pusey 2003: 6). He suggests that 'for corporations, this represents the benefits of greater labour productivity. But in the absence of effective redistribution (through taxes and other channels) for wage and salary earners and their dependants, it means more work for (relatively) less pay' (Pusey 2003: 6–7).

The inegalitarian effects of the redistribution of income from labour to capital become more apparent when viewed in conjunction with figures on the concentration of ownership of capital. Share ownership is particularly important in this respect. A recent study carried out by the Australian Stock Exchange (ASX) found that, while 44 per cent of the Australian population directly owned shares in 2004, this figure fell to 20 per cent for households with incomes under $20 000 per year, and rose to 68 per cent for households with annual incomes over $100 000. The value of shares owned is also markedly unequal. Only 10.6 per cent of the Australian population held more than $100 000 in direct share ownership, with 27.7 per cent holding more than $10 000. Fifty-six per cent were holding none and therefore received no income from this form of capital (ASX 2005). So, to the extent that the share of profits in the national income was distributed to households in the form of dividend payments, its impact was highly skewed towards the already richest households.

The spread of wage incomes

The variation in the rewards that different groups of wage earners receive for their labour also affects economic inequality. Wages are markedly uneven across occupations. Table 2.1 on the following page shows illustrative data for nine broad occupational groups, looking at the distribution of earnings between those on the lowest incomes (under $200 per week) and those on the highest incomes (over $2000 per week). In each occupational group there is a significant internal spread of earnings, but equally noteworthy are the striking patterns of inequality between the occupational groups. For employees in the first occupational

Table 2.1 Total weekly earnings by occupation, percentage of employees in each income range, 2005

Occupation	$1–200	$200–399	$400–599	$600–799	$800–999	$1000–1499	$1500–1999	$2000+	Total
Managers and administrators	0.5	2.3	6.7	8.1	11.4	32.4	20.0	18.7	100
Professionals	4.9	6.2	10.0	15.4	21.2	32.0	6.7	3.5	100
Associate professionals	4.1	7.3	13.8	22.8	19.5	25.0	4.9	2.6	100
Tradespeople and related workers	3.2	11.2	15.3	26.9	17.7	19.7	4.4	1.6	100
Advanced clerical, sales and service workers	5.9	12.3	19.5	26.1	22.0	12.5	1.3	0.3	100
Intermediate clerical, sales and service workers	11.1	17.7	24.4	27	13.5	5.7	0.6	0.1	100
Intermediate production and transport workers	6.9	8.5	19.5	26.4	14.9	17.9	4.4	1.4	100
Elementary clerical, sales and service workers	31.7	24.7	22.7	13.5	5.0	2.2	0.1	0.1	100
Labourers and related workers	19.1	18.0	24.4	21.3	9.1	5.6	1.9	0.4	100
All occupations	10.5	12.7	17.7	20.8	14.7	16.7	4.2	2.5	100

Note: The few very small figures (for example, under 0.5) in this table should be treated with caution due to higher relative standard errors.

Source: ABS 2005b: table 5.

category – managers and administrators – a remarkable 18.7 per cent are in the top income bracket. Members of the second category – professionals, such as teachers, doctors and lawyers – are quite a long way behind, with only 3.5 per cent in the top income group. At the other extreme, elementary sales, clerical and service workers cluster in the low-pay ranges, with almost 32 per cent receiving less than $200 per week and just over 56 per cent receiving less than $400 per week. Labourers and related workers are also strongly represented in these lower ranges.

Interestingly, these earnings inequalities also exhibit significantly different profiles over the lifecycle. Younger workers, typically, have lower earnings than older workers, at least up to middle age, but the patterns vary significantly between occupations. A 2006 *Sydney Morning Herald* report presented the latest data: among 15–19 year olds, police officers receive the sixth-highest average wages of any occupational group; transport workers and bank workers also rate within the top 10. However, as university graduates enter full-time work, these groups move out of the top ten rankings in the older age groups. Among workers aged above 20, dentists, medical practitioners, economists and lawyers feature among the most highly paid groups. Interestingly, in all but the 20–24 year age group, those employed in the production and distribution of chemicals, petrol and gas come in as the most highly paid wage earners, and among that age bracket rank second only to dentists. Miners, steel construction workers and engineers are also commonly ranked among the top 10 (O'Malley 2006: 3). The figures on which these rankings are based are average wages within occupational and age groups. Notably, the highest average wage taken home by any of these groups is the $2074 per week received by workers aged over 45 in the chemical, petrol and gas industries. While these are high incomes, when compared to the incomes of Australia's top business managers they look almost trifling.

Nice work if you can get it

The rapid acceleration of the top incomes in recent years is well documented. As A. B. Atkinson and Andrew Leigh note in a research paper from the Australian National University, 'At the start of the twenty-first century, the income share of the richest 1 per cent of Australians was higher than it had been at any point since 1951, while the share of the richest 10 per cent was higher than it had been since 1949' (2006: 12).

If one asks, 'Who's doing particularly well?', the group that springs immediately to mind is corporate executives. So it is pertinent to take these as a case study, notwithstanding the tendency for full details of their remuneration arrangements to be concealed, even from the shareholders of the companies for whom they work (Washington 2006; O'Sullivan and Askew 2006). A 2003 newspaper report on the incomes of senior executives for the top 150 Australian companies, based on what information was then publicly available, showed that before-tax incomes were then, typically, in the range between $2 million and $6 million annually. Topping the list were Peter Chernin and Rupert Murdoch of News Corporation, with total remuneration packages of $28.6 million and $24 million respectively. The biggest package paid to an Australian resident was the $13.4 million received by Frank Lowy of Westfield Holdings (*Sydney Morning Herald*, 2003).

These senior executive incomes have continued to rise since then, with the popular press regularly commenting on particularly spectacular cases. Macquarie Bank's CEO Allan Moss, for example, has overtaken Frank Lowy's position as Australia's most highly remunerated resident, receiving an annual pay of $21.2 million in 2005. This is equivalent to about $400 000 per week. It includes a pay rise of $3 million (or 14 per cent) since the previous year. Macquarie's head of investment banking, Nicholas Moore, enjoyed a 13 per cent pay rise to take home $20.6 million (Geoghegan 2006). The top seven executives at Macquarie received $94.3 million between them (Murray 2006: 2). Notably, few women are included among the high fliers receiving exceptional executive payments. Dawn Robertson made the news in 2006 for securing $18 million in salary, bonuses and share options as managing director of retail giant Coles Myer but this was paid over three and a half years, putting her annual remuneration at a little under $6 million, making it look rather modest beside the payments to the men at the top (McMahon 2006).

Not only are the corporate executives rewarding themselves handsomely, but their incomes have also rapidly outpaced increases in average earnings for all employees since the early 1980s. This is demonstrated in a

Table 2.2 BCA CEO total cash remuneration and adult earnings; trend comparisons 1990–2005

Year	No. firms in sample	Average CEO total cash remuneration ($A million, unadjusted)	Full-time adult total earnings, private sector[1] ($A, unadjusted)	Ratio CEO remuneration to average earnings (A ÷ B)
1989–90	30	514 433	29 198	18:1
1990–1	30	560 667	30 040	19:1
1991–2	35	597 857	31 184	19:1
1992–3	33	631 364	31 798	20:1
1993–4	31	934 355	33 067	28:1
1994–5	34	1 008 735	34 928	29:1
1995–6	34	1 148 421	36 494	31:1
1996–7	38	1 234 625	37 170	33:1
1997–8	39	1 363 144	38 745	35:1
1998–9	47	1 464 324	39 816	37:1
1999–2000	45	1 744 988	41 371	42:1
2000–1	42	2 041 921	43 414	47:1
2001–2	46	2 363 594	45 087	52:1
2002–3	45	2 343 796	48 896	48:1
2003–4	46	2 813 377	50 393	56:1
2004–5	49	3 420 507	54 080	63:1

Note: [1] May quarter, seasonally adjusted and annualised.
Source: Shields, 2005: 302.

recent study by John Shields, a labour market researcher at the University of Sydney, that examines the growth in the incomes of Australia's CEOs over the period 1989–90 to 2004–5. Shields' research analyses CEO remuneration in the fifty-one companies listed on the ASX who are members of the Business Council of Australia (BCA), the nation's peak business lobby group. He compares the CEO remuneration trends to changes in average adult full-time earnings. Table 2.2, based on his findings, shows that the cash component of executive remuneration (including base salaries and cash incentives) rose by a massive 564 per cent over the sixteen year period, compared with an increase of only 85 per cent for the wages of full-time adult employees (Shields 2005: 302). Viewed another way, while the average pay of Australia's top CEOs was eighteen times average adult full-time earnings in 1990, it had grown to 63 times average adult full-time earnings by 2005 (Shields 2005: 302). By then the average annual cash remuneration of CEOs in the sample had reached $3.4 million, an average of $65 700 per week. By comparison, the average annual income of full-time adult employees was just over $54 000 per year (Shields 2005: 301–2). So senior executives were receiving more per week than most workers receive per year.

The evident success of corporate executives in increasing their incomes is of particular interest from a political economic perspective because this group appears, in some respects, to be between capital and labour. Its members wield the power of capital, although they themselves are formally salaried employees of their companies. In a recent article, the distinguished social scientist Hugh Stretton has noted the historical rise to power of these corporate executives and directors. As he points out, in earlier stages of capitalist development large corporations were often owned by individuals and families but, by the 1930s, individual ownership had declined and most of industry was owned by shareholders. Directors now exercise most of the power within firms, including 'the power to hire and fire each other and determine each others' pay' (Stretton 2006). Stretton notes that, while some aspects of corporate law have sought to require directors to serve shareholder and community interests, in practice corporate managers have tended towards self-interest and 'rising executive plunder', particularly within the last few decades. They certainly have been rewarding themselves handsomely.

The incomes of CEOs have become increasingly linked to returns from capital. The 1990s saw the start of a particularly pronounced shift away from a reliance on base salaries towards 'executive option packages', including share option entitlements and other long-term incentives, such as share bonuses and share purchase plans. From 1990 to 2004, such long-term incentives increased from an estimated 13 per cent to 39 per cent of CEO pay in Australia. Over the same period, the contribution of cash bonuses to CEO remuneration increased from 5 per cent to 21 per cent, while the contribution of 'fixed pay' fell from 82 per cent to only 40 per cent (Shields 2005: 306). Similar patterns have occurred in the remuneration of other levels of executives (Shields *et al.* 2003: 4). So the growth in corporate executive salaries, while prodigious on its own, has been dwarfed by the massive increases in wealth that have derived from share and option packages. In 2001–2, for example, the largest 100 executive positions[1] in listed Australian companies received an annual average cash component of remuneration of $2.6 million, compared to an estimated average gross value of share options of $11.9 million and an estimated $160 million in market value of shares (Shields *et al.* 2003: 4).

This trend towards share and options packages forming a growing proportion of executive remuneration stalled after there was a slump in share values in 2002. However, while some of these option plans have been replaced by cash bonuses, the major change within the firms in the BCA sample has been the move to more sophisticated equity plans, most of which require CEOs to meet market or financial performance targets. While this may appear to tighten remuneration standards, such performance targets are often manipulated by company executives to their advantage. Positive earnings forecasts, for example, may be withheld until after the option grant date, or announcements of staff cutbacks may be carefully timed to provide a stimulus to share prices. In addition, CEOs may accept disguised income that is independent of their effectiveness in the job, such as sign-on payments or consultancy fees, or cajole the boards of the companies for whom they work into renegotiating performance standards (Shields 2005: 316).

In Australia, despite the shift towards remuneration packages that are ostensibly linked to performance, CEO earnings have continued to outpace share prices. In terms of cash remuneration, for example, the average pay of CEOs in Shields' study doubled since 1999, while shareholder returns increased by less than 60 per cent over the same period (Shields 2005: 304). So the self-interested claim that the prodigious executive incomes are justified because of their link to increasing shareholder value is not borne out by the evidence.

---

[1] The study by Shields *et al.* (2003) uses *Australian Financial Review* data which categorise chief executive officer and equivalent positions according to their size. The largest positions are those associated with the largest publicly listed companies, taking market capitalisation as an indication of organisational size.

Performance targets and tighter reporting standards have also had a somewhat paradoxical effect. As Shields suggests, rather than ensuring that CEO remuneration is kept under check, CEOs have used them as justifications for the continued growth in their pay. Former Wesfarmers CEO Michael Chaney, for example, reportedly sought to justify a recent round of increases in CEO remuneration by claiming that the growing demand for CEOs to be publicly accountable has increased their personal burden, for which they should be recompensed (Shields 2005: 314). Of course, it is not only CEOs who face workplace stresses because of the pressures of personal accountability. The more basic difference between CEOs and other employees is that the former have considerable influence in setting the performance standards and determining their own pay. The spectacular income levels of the top managers are, in effect, the product of a process that operates within an elite group that sets its own rules and its own rewards.

Current income distribution

Having looked at the shares of labour and capital in the national income, the spread of wage incomes and the distinctive case of corporate CEOs, it is now pertinent to examine the overall distribution of household incomes. This means looking at who gets what, irrespective of whether the incomes come in the form of wages, managerial salaries, profits, rent or interest. It also means bringing government into the picture – taking account of pensions and other welfare payments that for many households are a significant income source, sometimes the sole source.[2]

The Australian Bureau of Statistics carries out regular surveys of the personal income distribution across Australia, with the most recent data available being for the year 2003–4. The published ABS data on gross household

[2] An earlier publication of the ABS, looking at how government taxes and expenditures impact on the distribution of disposable income, showed that 72% of households in the lowest quintile and 55% in the second quintile relied on government pensions and allowances as their principal source of income in 1998–9. These payments boosted the average weekly household incomes from $15 to $156 for the lowest quintile and from $216 to $411 for the second quintile (ABS 2001b, table 1). Unfortunately, this set of calculations had not been updated by the ABS when this book was published.

Table 2.3 Number of Australian households, by income range, 2003–4

Gross household income per week	Number of households (thousands)
$4000 or more	107.4
$2000–3999	892.5
$1000–1999	2539.0
$500–999	2050.8
$300–499	1166.2
Under $300	979.8
All households	7735.8

Source: ABS, 2005a: table 2.

incomes are summarised in table 2.3. These data give a good, down-to-earth feel for household income inequalities in Australia. They show that, in 2003–4, nearly 1 million Australian households had a gross weekly income in excess of $2000 per week, while almost the same number had to get by on less than $300 per week. Between these extremes lie the other 5.7 million households, over 2.5 million of which have gross incomes in the range between $1000 and $2000 per week, but over 1 million of which lie in the weekly income range of only $300–499.

The reliability of the ABS personal income distribution data depends on people telling the truth when responding to the official survey. There are good grounds for scepticism. Understating personal income is quite understandable where there is a fear of being exposed as a tax evader, notwithstanding official assurances that survey data will not be used for that purpose, and the existence of penalties for supplying inaccurate information. One may also infer that any such tendency to understatement would be positively correlated with income, in which case a conservative bias would pervade the official data on the extent of economic inequality. However, even as a conservative underestimate, the ABS evidence reveals some quite dramatic inequalities, as shown in table 2.3.

It is also necessary to take account of how much of these recorded gross incomes constitute actual disposable household incomes. The ABS derives such estimates by deducting estimates of personal income tax and the Medicare levy from gross incomes. It also adjusts for differences in household composition in order to get estimates of equivalised disposable income (as described in the note below table 2.4). According to these estimates of equivalised household disposable income, the mean income of households in the lowest income quintile was, in 2003–4, $226 per week after tax, whereas the mean weekly income of those in the highest income quintile was $1027 (ABS, 2005a: table 1).[3] In other words, the richest 20 per cent of households, on average, receive about four and a half times as much as the poorest 20 per cent of households.

Table 2.4 expresses this information in a rather different way by looking at how much of the total household income goes to different income groups. It shows that the poorest 20 per cent of households (the lowest income quintile) received only 8.2 per cent of the national income in 2003–4, while the richest 20 per cent (the highest income quintile) received 37.4 per cent of the total (ABS 2005a: table 1). Again, there is a ratio of roughly four and a half to one between the top 20 per cent and bottom 20 per cent.

Income inequality can be measured in other ways too. The spread of incomes across a population is commonly represented by a percentile ratio known as the P90:P10 ratio that is calculated by dividing the income of the household at the top of the ninetieth percentile (P90) by the income of the household at the top of the tenth percentile (P10). In other words, if all households are ranked from the richest to the poorest, the P90/P10 ratio shows the income of the household 10 per cent from the top relative to the

---

[3] Unless otherwise stated, the discussion in this chapter uses data from the ABS *Household Income and Income Distribution* survey and refers to distribution across all ten income deciles. In its own discussion of the survey results the ABS excludes the bottom income decile. This has the effect of evening out the picture of income disparity by ignoring the lower extreme. Peter Saunders [CIS] (2002a) argues that the decision not to include the lowest decile in analysis is justifiable because data at this end of the spectrum are unreliable due to possible underreporting of incomes. As the ABS notes, some households in the bottom income decile may have expenditure levels 'comparable to those of households with higher income levels', so that their standard of living may be higher than suggested by their income (ABS 2005a). However, the result of ignoring the bottom decile is that the official analysis does not reflect the circumstances of the poorest households. By contrast, this chapter's inclusion of the bottom decile (combined with the decile immediately above it) is based on the view that underreporting of incomes is just as likely to occur in higher income deciles, and that the ability of households in the bottom decile to maintain expenditure above their income (such as by drawing down on assets) may only be possible in the short term. In any case, in a consideration of income distribution the full set of figures should be included in the analysis.

Table 2.4 Income shares of the Australian population, 2003–4

Income group	Income share (%)
Richest 20%	37.4
Second quintile	23.3
Third quintile	17.9
Fourth quintile	13.1
Poorest 20%	8.2

Note: The ABS *Household Income and Income Distribution* survey, on which this table is based, presents figures on equivalised disposable household income. This refers to disposable income (after deduction of personal income tax and the Medicare levy), and allows a comparison of households of different size and composition. For any household this equivalised income is expressed as the amount of disposable income that a single-person household would require to maintain the same standard of living as the household in question. This calculation takes account of the fact that larger households normally require a greater income to maintain the same material standard of living as smaller households, and that the needs of adults are normally greater than the needs of children, while also accounting for the economies of scale that arise from sharing dwellings. The figures are person weighted to indicate the disposable income available to each member of the household (ABS 2005a).
Source: ABS, 2005a: table 1.

income of the household 10 per cent from the bottom. A ratio of 1.00 would represent equal incomes in those two households. In practice, the ABS data for Australian households indicate that P90 was $912 per week in 2003–4 and P10 was $246 per week, giving a P90/P10 ratio of 3.70 (ABS 2005a: table 1). The relativity in this case is a little below four to one.

The ABS data also highlight the different characteristics of households at different levels of income. In general, the lowest average weekly incomes are found among the elderly (couples or lone person households where the reference person is over 65) and households comprising a single parent with dependent children (ABS 2005a: table 2.5). Along with couples aged 55–64, these groups are also the most likely to depend on government benefits as their principal source of income. On the other hand, young couples with no children and couples with non-dependent children had the highest average weekly incomes (ABS 2005a: table 12).

Significant variations are also apparent between and within the various states and territories.[4] According to the ABS data, Tasmania's mean weekly income is the lowest in the country, 13 per cent below the national average. South Australia, Western Australia, Queensland and Victoria also record mean weekly incomes a little below the national average. The Australian Capital Territory (ACT) has the highest mean income, 22 per cent above the national average, in part reflecting the relatively high proportion of its population who are of working age (ABS 2005a: table 16). There are also significant spatial inequalities within each of the states. Capital cities in each state and territory have uniformly higher mean incomes than the rest of the states' and territories' populations. The biggest gap is in New South Wales, where Sydney's mean income is 26 per cent higher than the average for the rest of that state (ABS 2005a: tables 14, 15). Disaggregating further, yet more striking inequalities are evident between suburbs in the metropolitan areas. Chapter 6 of this book considers this spatial dimension of who gets what in more detail. The equally important dimension to which we now turn is temporal – the big issue of whether income inequalities are decreasing, constant or increasing.

Changes in income inequality

The distribution of incomes tends to change most during periods of rapid structural economic change. Historically, significant shifts occurred in the years of the Great Depression and during the long postwar boom, as studies by several economists and economic historians have shown (Atkinson and Leigh 2006; Butlin 1983; Jackson 1992; Jones 1975; Maddock *et al.* 1984; McLean and Richardson 1986; Saunders 1993; Leigh 2005). Economic inequality increased during the Great Depression but diminished in the long boom. The last two decades, during which Australia has become more closely

---

[4] The ABS data exclude the sparsely settled areas of the Northern Territory. While this is not likely to have a substantial impact on the overall national results, it should be acknowledged that proportionally more Indigenous than non-Indigenous Australians live in these areas. In 2001, only 2 per cent of non-Indigenous Australians lived in 'remote' or 'very remote' regions, compared with 26 per cent of Indigenous Australians. Over half of these were in the Northern Territory (ABS 2003a). The ABS survey therefore excludes some of the country's most impoverished communities.

integrated into the international economy and an array of neoliberal policies have been implemented, is another such period of significant structural change. In terms of distributional consequences it seems more akin to the Great Depression than the long postwar boom, at least to the extent of putting more major obstacles in the way of movement towards a more egalitarian society.

Using a common measure of inequality known as the Gini coefficient, table 2.5 summarises the evidence on how income distribution has changed since the 1970s. This is a useful summary statistic for comparing distributions at different times and in different places, although, as a report by the Economic Planning Advisory Commission (EPAC) cautioned, all statistical measures of distributional changes need to be considered in social and economic context (EPAC 1995: 41). An earlier study, based on data from Australian Household Expenditure Surveys, shows that the Gini coefficient of inequality rose in Australia from 0.295 to 0.311 between 1988–9 and 1998–9 (Harding 2002: 2). The alternative data source, on which table 2.5 is based, is the income surveys conducted by the ABS. The second column of the table shows the Gini coefficient when calculated according to gross household income. This is the measure used by the ABS until 1999–2000. It shows a long-term trend towards increasing income inequality, with the coefficient rising from 0.390 in 1978–9 to 0.448 in 1999–2000.

Discerning the trend since the turn of the millennium is harder. It cannot be determined from the gross household income data because they are no longer published in a comparable form by the ABS. So we have to rely on an alternative measure of 'equivalised disposable income', defined earlier in this chapter. The final column shows the Gini coefficient when calculated according to this alternative measure. It indicates a peak in income inequality between 1999–2000 and 2002–3, with the Gini coefficient falling a little in 2003–4 (ABS 2005a: table 1). So these are rather mixed signals about whether the long-term trend towards a more unequal distribution is continuing.

A similar picture emerges from other measures of temporal changes in income inequality. As discussed earlier, one such measure is the P90/P10 ratio, which shows how much greater is the income of the household at the ninetieth income percentile in comparison with the income of the

Table 2.5 Income inequality in Australia, as shown by the Gini coefficient,
1978–9 to 2003–4 (available years)

Year	Gini coefficient of inequality (gross household income)	Gini coefficient of inequality (equivalised disposable household income)
1978–9	0.390	
1981–2	0.400	
1986*	0.410	
1990*	0.420	
1994–5	0.443	0.302
1995–6	0.444	0.296
1996–7	0.437	0.292
1997–8	0.446	0.303
1999–2000	0.448	0.310
2000–1		0.311
2002–3		0.309
2003–4		0.294

* Data calculated for calendar years.
Note: The Gini coefficient varies from 0 (when income is equally distributed)
to 1 (when one household has all the income). The data gaps result from the
change in the way in which the ABS calculates the Gini coefficient.
Source: ABS, 6523.0, various years.

household at the tenth percentile. In effect, it compares the incomes of
the quite rich with those of the quite poor. Table 2.6 presents the evidence.
In 1994–5 the P90/P10 ratio for Australia was 3.77. Between 1997–8 and
2002–3 the ratio rose steadily to 4.00, indicating a significant increase in
income inequality. In 2003–4 the P90/P10 ratio fell back to 3.70 (ABS 2005a:
table 1).

The changes in the shares of total income received by different income
groups are illustrated rather differently in table 2.7. Here, the focus is on
the share of the total national income that goes to the bottom 20 per cent
of households and to the top 20 per cent. The income share of the former
group (the lowest quintile) fell from 7.9 per cent of total income in 1994–5
to 7.7 per cent in 2002–3, despite rising to a peak of 8.3 per cent in 1996–7.
In 2003–4, the income share of the lowest quintile increased again to 8.2 per
cent. In almost a mirror image of this trend, the income share of the latter

Table 2.6 Income inequality in Australia, as shown by the P90/P10 ratio, 1994–5 to 2003–4

Year	P90/P10
1994–5	3.77
1995–6	3.73
1996–7	3.66
1997–8	3.77
1998–9	–
1999–2000	3.89
2000–1	3.98
2001–2	–
2002–3	4.00
2003–4	3.70

– Data not available.
Note: This table uses data on equivalised disposable household income, as defined in the notes to table 2.4. The P90/P10 ratio compares the incomes of households at the ninetieth and tenth percentiles in the overall distribution.
Source: ABS, 2005a: table 1.

Table 2.7 Income share of different income groups, Australia, 1994–5 to 2003–4

Year	Share of total income (%)	
	Lowest quintile	Highest quintile
1994–5	7.9	37.8
1995–6	8.1	37.3
1996–7	8.3	37.1
1997–8	7.9	37.9
1998–9	–	–
1999–2000	7.7	38.4
2000–1	7.7	38.5
2001–2	–	–
2002–3	7.7	38.3
2003–4	8.2	37.4

– Data not available.
Note: Data on equivalised disposable household income, as defined in note to table 2.4.
Source: ABS, 2005a: table 1.

group (the highest quintile) rose from 37.8 per cent in 1994–5 to 38.3 per cent in 2002–3, despite a dip to its lowest point in the period in 1996–7. In 2003–4 the share of the highest quintile fell, this time to 37.4 per cent (ABS 2005a: table 1).

Yet another way to examine trends in income inequality is to look at the changes in average incomes for different groups. Here, the evidence shows a dominant inegalitarian trend but, again, with some evidence of a recent plateau. Between 1994–5 and 2002–3, the incomes of those in the highest-income quintile grew at a much faster rate than those in the bottom quintile. In 2002–3, those in the lowest quintile received an average of $18 a week more than they received in 1994–5 (a 10 per cent increase in real terms), while those in the highest quintile received an average of $135 more (a 16 per cent increase). In absolute terms, the top-income group received additional income that was seven and a half times greater than that received by the lowest-income group. The latest year shown in table 2.7 indicates some reversal of this trend though. Between 2002–3 and 2003–4, the average weekly incomes of households in the lowest-income group increased by 13 per cent. They received an average of $26 in additional income every week, the biggest absolute increase over the whole period from 1994–5 to 2003–4. In the same year, the average weekly incomes of those in the highest group grew by less than 3 per cent, an absolute increase of $28 (ABS 2005a: table 1).

Is the tide turning?

Income inequality in Australian society has increased in the last decade. Peter Saunders, director of the Social Policy Research Centre at the University of New South Wales, has argued, the changing income shares of the highest and lowest income quintiles between 1996 and 1997 and 2002 and 2003 (shown in table 2.7) indicated a significant shift towards greater income inequality, particularly following the election of the Howard government in 1996. Income inequality had increased during the 1980s, but Saunders concludes that the increase in inequality in the period 1996–7 to 2000–1 was 'at least as great, probably greater than that experienced over similar time periods in the 1980s' (Saunders 2003: 16).

Recent evidence published by the ABS has led some commentators to infer that this trend towards greater economic inequality has halted, even gone into reverse gear. 'Poor outpace the rich in income gains' trumpeted one newspaper headline in mid 2005 (Irvine 2005). Identifying turning points in economic and social trends is always important, of course, so this recent evidence, along with the evidence already reviewed in this chapter – in tables 2.5, 2.6 and 2.7 in particular – needs careful consideration.

In 2003–4 the weekly income of the lowest quintile (the poorest 20 per cent) of households averaged $226, up from $200 the year before. The income of the highest quintile (the richest 20 per cent) averaged $1027, up from $999 the year before. In terms of income shares, this meant that the proportion of the total income going to the lowest quintile of households rose from 7.7 per cent to 8.2 per cent, while that going to the highest quintile fell from 38.3 per cent to 37.4 per cent. A similar narrowing of relativities was evident in the P90/P10 ratio (as defined earlier in this chapter), falling from 4.0 to 3.7 between the two years. The Gini coefficient of inequality, based on equivalised disposable household incomes (also defined earlier in this chapter), dipped a little too, falling from 0.309 to 0.294. This, in a nutshell, is the evidence supporting the claim that the tide of economic inequality has turned.

A more cautious interpretation is probably appropriate because of four other considerations. First, the income gap has not fallen in absolute terms. According to the ABS data, the difference between the average weekly incomes of the lowest quintile and the highest quintile increased just a little over the two years, from $799 to $801. This is a statistically insignificant amount, so the appropriate inference is that the gulf between the rich and poor did not change in those years. Second, different measures of inequality produce different results: the P20/P50 ratio (showing how the income of a household 20 per cent up the income distribution scale compared to the median income) actually fell a little in 2003–4, for example, suggesting a widening gap in that low to middle income range. Third, the apparent improvement in the P90/P10 ratio only returns the figure to that prevailing in the mid 1990s, and the 2003–4 figure is actually still a little above the 1996–7 figure. The same is true of the Gini coefficient. Not surprisingly, short-term fluctuations are dependent on the state of the macroeconomy: it is the long-term trends that matter. Finally, it is important to note that the ABS has modified its methodology for imputing business and investment incomes, so there is a problem of interpreting intertemporal trends in its income distribution data for this particular period. As the ABS itself concedes, if the former method had been continued for 2003–4, the Gini coefficient would have been about 1 per cent higher (ABS 2005a). So the apparent reduction of inequality may be at least partly a product of the change in statistical methods.

The safest inference is that only time will tell. This vapid conclusion can be augmented by noting the important effect of policy changes, particularly those directly affecting income transfers. The federal government's 2004–5 budget, for example, in a pre-election context, significantly raised one-off payments to families and carers. Certainly, many beneficiaries were low-income households, but the Family Tax Benefit Part B – of up to $65 per week – also went to 38 500 families with an annual income of $100 000 or more. The beneficiaries included seventy-six single-income, two-parent families earning more than $1 million per year (*Sydney Morning Herald* 15 August 2005). The same budget also introduced substantial income tax cuts, skewed dramatically in favour of high-income households. Taxpayers with an annual income of $10 000 received an average cut of $80 from their 2005–6 tax bill, while those on $70 000 received a tax cut of $1752 and those on $130 000 received a tax cut of $4502. By any standards these were markedly regressive changes. It is how these sort of policies flow through into the distribution of incomes in the medium term that will determine in which direction the tide is turning.

International comparison

How does the Australian situation compare internationally? All societies are unequal, but not equally unequal. We can compare their economic inequalities by looking at three similar measures that we have already applied to the study of Australian income inequality – the ratio of the income of the top 10 per cent of households to the poorest 10 per cent of households, the ratio

Table 2.8 International comparison of income inequality, selected countries

Country	Richest 10% to poorest 10%	Richest 20% to poorest 20%	Gini coefficient
Japan	4.5	3.4	0.249
Finland	5.6	3.8	0.269
Norway	6.1	3.9	0.258
Sweden	6.2	4.0	0.250
Germany	6.9	4.3	0.283
Denmark	8.1	4.3	0.247
France	9.1	5.6	0.327
Canada	9.4	5.8	0.331
Australia	12.5	7.0	0.352
UK	13.8	7.2	0.360
USA	15.9	8.4	0.408
South Africa	33.1	17.9	0.578
Brazil	57.8	23.7	0.580
Colombia	63.8	25.3	0.586

Source: United Nations *Human Development Report 2006:* table 15.

of the top 20 per cent to the bottom 20 per cent and the Gini coefficient of income inequality. Table 2.8 above provides an international comparison according to these measures, based on the latest data gathered and published by the United Nations.

Unfortunately, as the income inequality data used for Australia in the latest United Nations analysis relate to 1994, they are quite outdated. More recent data are available from the ABS, but the UN seems remarkably slow in updating, perhaps because of a concern to use only those data that are on a comparable basis with other countries. Because, as table 2.5 shows, inequality in Australia was a little greater in 1994 than in 2003–4, table 2.8 probably places Australia a little lower on the league-table of income inequality than would be the case were more recent ABS figures used. Using the most recent Gini coefficient calculated by the ABS as an indication of Australia's current position would shift Australia up two spots to sit somewhere in between Denmark and France. However, any direct comparison between the most recent ABS data and the data for other countries shown in table 2.8 should be treated cautiously, as the methods of measurement may differ and the extent of income inequality in the other countries may also have changed in the intervening years.

All we can properly infer from the UN data are broad international comparisons. The first column of table 2.8, for example, shows that the most affluent 10 per cent of Australian households enjoyed incomes on average 12.5 times higher than the poorest 10 per cent of households. This degree of inequality is similar to the more traditionally class-divided UK, rather less than in the USA where the ratio is nearly 16:1, but very much higher than the ratio in Japan, which has historically had the most equal distribution of household incomes among the advanced capitalist countries, and in the Scandinavian nations (Sweden, Norway, Finland, Denmark), where social democratic parties have had more influence on the redistributive role of government. In those countries the corresponding ratios range from around 6:1 to 8:1. At the other extreme, the ratio is almost 58:1 for Brazil and 64:1 for Colombia – grossly unequal societies in which an affluent elite coexists with masses of people living in abject poverty (United Nations 2006). What these figures illustrate is that, even within the contours of capitalism, strikingly diverse distributional patterns prevail. Among the set of nations considered in table 2.8, Australia looks generally middle-ranking.

Limiting the comparisons to the advanced industrial nations who are members of the OECD, Australia's ranking in terms of income inequality looks rather more distinctive. It is the sixth most unequal society among the thirty OECD nations, sharing this position with New Zealand. Its 12.5:1 ratio between the incomes of the richest 10 per cent and poorest 10 per cent of households puts it only behind Mexico (24.6), Turkey (16.8), the USA (15.9), Portugal (15.0) and the UK (13.8) in this international ranking (United Nations 2006: 335–6). The popular image of Australia as a relatively egalitarian society sits awkwardly with these facts about the economic inequalities that exist in practice.

Conclusion

Capitalism is a system based on the distinctive class relationships in the production of goods and services, and in the distribution of the income that is generated through these productive activities. So exploring the question

'Who gets what?' is a recurrent theme in political economic analyses of capitalist economies. The question is particularly pertinent to Australia in the current period because significant redistributions of income have evidently been accompanying rapid structural economic change. Many of the rich have got much richer, benefiting from the high returns to the ownership of capital and from the redistribution of income shares from labour to capital that has accompanied economic growth in the last two decades. At the other extreme, the trickle down from the economic prosperity has been modest, at best.

The evidence on the distribution of incomes in Australia, although involving somewhat complicated interpretations of recent statistical data, illustrates what Fred Argy (2003) calls 'Australian egalitarianism under threat'. A general trend towards greater inequalities is evident, albeit with some ambiguity about whether this has continued consistently during all years in the current decade. Certainly, subgroups such as the CEOs of large corporations have done extraordinarily well over the last two decades. The gulf between their incomes and those in the middle and lower ranges of the income distribution scale has widened substantially. It is not surprising in these circumstances that the distribution of income is such a contentious – and politically sensitive – matter. So, too, is the distribution of wealth, because inequality in the ownership of assets commonly underpins the income disparities. Recognising this connection turns our attention from 'Who gets what?' to 'Who owns what?'

Chapter Three

WEALTH

Imagine watching a march-past of the whole Australian population. It lasts a hundred minutes. The people file past your vantage point in order of their wealth, starting with the poorest and ending with the richest. Each household is represented by one individual whose height is proportional to the total wealth of that household in the year 2002 – one centimetre for every thousand dollars.

For the first few minutes there is absolutely nothing to be seen. The people marching past are, in effect, burrowing under the ground. These are the 4 per cent of Australian households whose debts are bigger than their assets. They have negative net wealth. Some are households headed by young adults with few assets but with liabilities such as HECS debt or outstanding credit card balances. Others are businesspeople who have got into difficulties or have rearranged their financial affairs to take advantage of bankruptcy laws or favourable tax arrangements.

After four minutes some tiny figures start to appear. After ten minutes they are still only 4 centimetres high. As the parade continues the average height slowly and steadily increases. However, at the thirty-minute mark the marchers' height is still only just over 80 centimetres. It is starting to look like an endless parade of dwarfs.

At the fifty-minute mark, exactly half way through the parade, the height of the marchers has risen to nearly 2.2 metres. These households represent middle Australia. Typically, their home is the bulk of their wealth, although some also have rental investment properties, some are mum and dad shareholders and nearly all have wealth tied up in superannuation funds.

At the seventy-minute mark the marchers are over 4.2 metres tall. The contrast with the height of those earlier in the parade is becoming quite dramatic now. Then, during the last twenty minutes of the parade, really huge people come into view. At the ninety-minute mark the average height is nearly 9.4 metres. With each minute the average height rises by more than the total increase in height that had occurred in the whole of the first half of the parade. Then, in the last minute, giants appear, all over 100 metres high.

Right at the end come people who are really gigantic, even by the standards of giants. These are the wealthiest 200 Australians. Any onlooker who blinks might miss seeing them because they comprise only the last sixth of a second in the 100-minute parade. The shortest of this elite group is 930 metres tall, which is about five times taller than the loftiest skyscrapers in Australian CBDs. The people in the very last sixtieth of a second average 13 kilometres tall, most of their bodies being hidden from view among clouds. Bringing up the rear is a veritable colossus: all that can be seen are his feet and ankles because, at nearly 60 kilometres tall, his body and head puncture the stratosphere. That colossus was Kerry Packer, who died in late 2005, and whose position in the parade has since been taken by his son James, marching on in his father's footsteps in much the same way Kerry had begun – with a business empire inherited from *his* father, Sir Frank Packer.

This parade of dwarfs and giants is a dramatic way of describing the overall distribution of wealth. The form of the presentation is not novel, having been pioneered by Jan Pen (1971) and previously used by Stilwell (1993, 2001) to describe the personal distribution of incomes. Applying it to accumulated wealth rather than current incomes is more unusual, but is useful in introducing this different dimension of economic inequality. The information on which the description is based comes from a survey of the assets and liabilities of Australian households, analysed in a report by the Reserve Bank of Australia released in April 2004, and from data in the *Business Review Weekly* 'Rich 200' publication of 2004. Other evidence on the distribution of wealth in Australia is also explored in this chapter. The primary focus is on the overall volume of wealth, how concentrated is its ownership and the principal forms in which it is held – bank deposits, shares, superannuation and real estate. Attention then turns to the effect of inheritance – a gentle reminder of the importance of choosing your parents wisely – before a note on debt (as the other side of wealth) and some concluding comments on other factors that influence inequality of asset ownership.

Analysing the wealth of the nation

Who owns what is a fundamental concern in the analysis of economic inequality. What income a household receives depends significantly on what, if any, assets it owns. Assets in this general sense may include elements of human capital developed through education and training, for example, but also include physical assets such as land, houses, commercial property, shares in businesses, works of art, jewellery, gold or other valuable items, plus savings held as cash, bank deposits or in the form of superannuation entitlements. It is these physical and financial elements on which the current analysis focuses. In other words, the emphasis is on the capacity to derive income from the ownership of assets without the need to work for other people. It is this aspect of wealth that is the most visible economic marker of class.

While it is quite easy to obtain data on the overall distribution of income (as described in the preceding chapter), reasonably reliable wealth data are more elusive. Whereas income is a flow (over time), wealth is a stock (at a point of time). The personal holdings of that wealth are often hard to estimate. Because there is no general wealth tax in Australia, no information on the distribution of wealth is generated as a by-product of the taxation system, as is the case with incomes liable to income tax, and no question on total wealth has been asked in a national census since 1915. Australian governments have shied away from conducting any similarly systematic survey for nearly a century. The Left faction within the ALP has periodically advocated setting up an inquiry into the distribution of wealth, but when Labor was last in federal government it declined to bite the bullet. Meanwhile, successive Liberal–National Coalition governments, not surprisingly, have not sought to draw attention to this or any other aspect of the economic inequalities to which their policies have contributed.

In the past we have had to rely on indirect estimates of the wealth distribution, such as the pioneering studies by Podder and Kakwani (1976), Raskall (1978) and subsequent research by Piggott (1987) and Dilnot (1990). Radical critic Laurie Aarons (1999) drew on some of these sources in writing a lively polemic on the topic, as well as making his own observations about the political economic forces contributing to the inequalities of wealth that divide Australian society. A little more recently, researchers at the ABS (Northwood, *et al.* 2002) used a range of data sources to develop experimental estimates of wealth distribution, while economist Michael Schneider (2004) situated the Australian evidence in the context of a broader international study. However, we now have better, more up-to-date sources of information. The federal Treasury has recently made estimates of wealth in Australia that can be used to discern how its volume and distribution have been changing. Estimates of who owns what have also been made by the Reserve Bank of Australia (RBA), the University of Canberra's National Centre for Social and Economic Modelling (NATSEM) and, most recently, by the ABS.

The Treasury estimates reveal a dramatic increase in private sector wealth over the last decade, doubling during the decade to reach a record high of $6.2 trillion in June 2005 (Federal Treasury 2006: 90). The previous doubling had taken thirty-five years. More wealth was accumulated in the six years to June 2005 than in the previous thirty-nine years. This phenomenal surge was driven largely by the combined effect of the boom in housing prices and share-market values (Garnaut 2006). Treasury's 2004 wealth study found that, in that year, 63 per cent of Australia's net private sector wealth was held in the form of land and houses. The growth in the value of those dwelling assets accounted for about two-thirds of the growth in total private sector wealth over the previous year (Federal Treasury 2004: 89). In 2005, dwelling assets contributed just under one-third of the growth in private sector wealth. The remainder of the growth resulted largely from an increase in the value of business assets – in line with the rapid gains in share prices. However, the wealth held in land and houses still accounts for 58 per cent of net private sector wealth, significantly overshadowing business assets at 33 per cent of the total. Other forms of wealth include consumer durables (3 per cent of the total), government securities (2 per cent) and money (1 per cent) (Federal Treasury 2005: 91–2).

Overall ownership of wealth

Who has this wealth, and how unevenly is it distributed? The NATSEM study, based on a specified set of assets (including housing, shares, rental property, superannuation and savings deposits), showed that, in June 2002, the average household in Australia owned net wealth of about $280 000. The variation around that average was huge, the wealthiest fifth of households having average assets of more than $750 000 and the bottom fifth having an average of only $18 000. So, according to these estimates, the former households were more than forty times wealthier than the latter (Kelly 2002).

The 2002 *Household, Income and Labour Dynamics (HILDA) Survey* reveals an even starker picture than the NATSEM data.[1] The *HILDA Survey*, reported by the Reserve Bank of Australia, included a sample of 7245 households. It found that the average net wealth was $404 300 (Kohler *et al.* 2004: 7). This figure was skewed upwards by a small number of very wealthy households at the top of the distribution. Calculating the median gives a better indication of the typical household, which had a net worth of around $218 000 (Headey *et al.* 2005: 163). The wealthiest fifth of households had an average wealth of $1 276 000, this being 284 times the average wealth of the least wealthy fifth, whose assets averaged only $4500 (Kohler *et al.* 2004: 7).

The most recent data come from the *ABS Survey of Income and Housing* (SIH), which surveyed over 11 000 households in 2003–4. According to these figures, the average Australian household has a net worth of about $468 000, with the wealthiest fifth of households having an average wealth of around $1.38 million and the bottom fifth having an average of $24 332. This means the wealthiest fifth of households were more than fifty-six times wealthier than the least wealthy fifth (ABS 2006b), an estimate that provides something of a middle ground between the NATSEM and HILDA estimates. The SIH

---

[1] Headey *et al.* (2005) argue that the HILDA Survey probably understates the value of both household assets and debts. They note that measuring wealth in surveys is, typically, associated with underestimates of national wealth due to the underrepresentation of very wealthy households, who own a markedly disproportionate share of national wealth, and due to problems of under-reporting. By comparing the results of the HILDA survey with other wealth data, they conclude that under-reporting in this survey is most concentrated among the most wealthy households, but that over the rest of the wealth distribution the survey data are likely to provide a reasonably good representation.

data show Sydney's households having an average net worth of $641 000, 27 per cent higher than the capital city average of $504 000 and almost double the Tasmanian average of $325 000. Nationwide, owner-occupied dwellings comprise 46 per cent of the value of total household assets.

How concentrated is wealth?

All of the recent studies of wealth in Australia show a striking picture of wealth disparities. The NATSEM study suggests that the top 10 per cent of the population has 45 per cent of the total household wealth, with the top half having over 90 per cent. This leaves the bottom 50 per cent of Australians holding less than 10 per cent of the national wealth (Harding 2002: 11; Headey *et al.* 2005: 159). The ABS data show wealth inequalities of similar magnitude, with the wealthiest 20 per cent of households owning 59 per cent of total wealth and the bottom 40 per cent of households owning only 7 per cent of the wealth between them (ABS 2006b: 11). Researchers at NATSEM suggest that wealth inequalities have had roughly these dimensions since the mid 1980s (Headey *et al.* 2005: 161).

The ABS and HILDA surveys also confirm that the distribution of wealth is more unequal than the distribution of income. Not surprisingly, there is a rough correlation between households according to their wealth and income, with higher-income households usually also having higher wealth. According to the most recent ABS data, the before-tax income of the household at the eightieth percentile of income distribution is 4.2 times greater than the income of the household at the twentieth percentile, while the household at the eightieth wealth percentile owns 10.4 times the wealth of the household at the twentieth percentile (ABS 2006b: 11). Comparing the Gini coefficients for wealth and income distribution, Headey *et al.* (2005) found that the coefficient for household net worth in 2001–2 was 0.61, significantly higher than the coefficient for gross household income at 0.43 (2005: 164). In other words, wealth inequalities are substantially greater than income inequalities.

Wealth is also unevenly distributed between different types of household. The age profile is particularly distinctive. Both the 2002 NATSEM study and the HILDA survey found that the average wealth of households correlated positively with the age of the household reference person up until the 55–64 years age bracket, after which it declined slowly (Kelly 2002: 8; Headey *et al.* 2005: 166). This is not surprising, reflecting normal patterns whereby people accumulate assets until retirement, and then subsequently draw down on them (for example, by selling the family home in order to pay nursing home bills). However, the disparities in wealth are much greater within age groups than between them, indicating that wealth inequalities are not simply a function of the tendency to accumulate wealth through the lifecycle (Headey *et al.* 2005: 172). Wealth inequalities within age groups tend to decline with age (Headey *et al.* 2005: 167).

In addition, while a wealth margin between the younger and older age groups is to be expected, that margin has grown over time. A 2006 *Sydney Morning Herald* report suggests that this gap has reached unprecedented levels, noting that the half of Australia's adult population aged over 45 owns over three-quarters of the nation's household wealth – up from 70 per cent in 1986. This has prompted Chris Richardson, director of economic consultancy group Access Economics, to label Australia a 'gerontocracy', with the increasing concentration of wealth among the older generations 'excessive even by world standards' (Wade and Cubby 2006: 25).

The primary cause of this growing disparity in the ownership of wealth has been the rapid inflation in property prices, particularly during the two housing booms of the late 1980s and from the late 1990s until 2003. The 2002 NATSEM wealth study identified the substantial intergenerational redistribution occurring during this latter boom. In 2002, households in the 25–34 age bracket were less wealthy in real terms than the equivalent households had been nine years earlier, largely as a result of a decline in home equity. Households in this group had accumulated 39 per cent less wealth than households in the same age bracket in 1993. Conversely, households that had entered the housing market in the early 1990s enjoyed the benefits of rising house values, with the average home equity of those in the 45–54 year age group increasing 42 per cent over the nine years to 2002, after adjusting for the effects of inflation (Kelly 2002: 15). Rising property values have evidently strongly advantaged existing owner-occupiers and other landowners, with the younger generations increasingly excluded from owning this form of wealth.

There is also an unequal distribution of wealth according to household composition, with both the ABS and NATSEM studies finding that households containing a couple tend to accumulate more wealth than those comprising a single person or sole parent. The ABS survey, for example, found that, in households where the reference person is under 35, couples tend to have slightly more than twice the wealth of those living alone (ABS 2006b: 6). Single people aged under 35 and sole parent households had the lowest average wealth, averaging $94 000 and $158 000 respectively (ABS 2006b: 6). The NATSEM study found the combination of these factors to be particularly problematic, with a decrease in wealth for sole parent households in the 25–34 age group generating a persistent wealth gap in later years (Kelly 2002: 12). According to that same study, over the period 1993 to 2002 the wealth of sole parent households grew at less than half the rate of other household types (Kelly 2002: 15). Such sole parent households are nearly all headed by women (Headey *et al.* 2005: 169). The ABS data show that the wealthiest households on average are those containing a couple and no dependent children where the reference person is aged between 55 and 64 (ABS 2006b: 6).

The HILDA survey also allows a comparison of household wealth according to the education of the household head. It shows that education significantly influences wealth, although to a lesser degree than it impacts on income. The wealthiest households have tended to be those headed by Australian-born males with parents from high educational status backgrounds (Headey *et al.* 2005: 169). Among working-age households, those in which the household head had completed a university degree were 35 per cent wealthier on average than those who had schooling only to Year 12; households in which the head had not completed Year 12 were substantially less wealthy still (Headey *et al.* 2005: 169).

The range of assets held by different types of households also shows some clear patterns. The HILDA survey confirmed the Treasury study, to which reference has already been made, in showing that the majority of wealth is held in housing, followed by equities and superannuation. In most households, the value of non-financial assets is much greater than the value of financial assets, indicating that most households have relatively little cash or liquid assets to draw on if their normal access to income is interrupted. As a result, many of these households would have little economic buffer

Table 3.1 Wealth held in bank deposits, 2002

Households' percentile of net worth	Percentage of households holding asset	Median value of holdings ($000)
Less than 20	93	1
20–39.9	97	3
40–59.9	97	5
60–79.9	98	9
80–100	99	21
All households	97	5

Source: Kohler *et al.* 2004.

against the effect of a sudden drop in income, such as that resulting from redundancy, and would therefore commonly have no alternative to reliance on social security payments (Headey *et al.* 2005: 164).

It's in the bank

Bank deposits are the most liquid form of wealth. Table 3.1, based on the results of the HILDA survey, shows that 97 per cent of all households were holding some financial assets in the form of bank deposits at the time of the survey, although, at only $5000, the median balance in these accounts was fairly low. Perhaps more tellingly, while the median balance of these financial assets increases rapidly with the total wealth of households, their relative importance as a proportion of total wealth declines as wealth increases (Kohler *et al.* 2004: 3). In other words, wealthy people have more assets held in bank deposits but these usually comprise a smaller proportion of their total assets than is the case for poorer people. The ownership of assets in bank deposits has a Gini coefficient of 0.78, indicating a very high degree of inequality between households (Headey *et al.* 2005: 165).

Wealth in shares, not sharing wealth

Share ownership is even more unequal than bank deposits. Of course, substantial share ownership has traditionally been regarded as a strong indicator, perhaps the primary measure, of class position. Owning and controlling business enterprises marks out the members of the capitalist class. But shareholders are, typically, absentee owners, not engaged directly in business management. Their ownership of shares does not necessarily confer the power to control businesses, other than through causing share values to drop where a firm falls from favour with its shareholders. The broadening of the spread of share ownership that has occurred in the last couple of decades may therefore be seen as dissipating class power to some extent. This view has certainly gained traction in the popular press. A recent editorial, for example, suggested that widespread share ownership has made Australia 'a nation of capitalists', with ownership spreading from traditional elites to a broader demographic of 'ordinary investors' (*Sydney Morning Herald* 2006: 10). However, the available evidence suggests that, notwithstanding the growth of so-called mum and dad shareholders, the concentration of share ownership remains highly distinctive.

As the HILDA survey shows, the wealthier groups hold a much greater proportion of their wealth in equity investments and trusts, including shares, managed funds and property trusts. These assets replace bank deposits in importance as the wealth of households increases. While the least wealthy quintile of households in Australian society held an average of 27 per cent of their financial assets in bank deposits, this share declined to only 12 per cent for the wealthiest quintile. Conversely, while the least wealthy quintile held only 6 per cent of financial assets in equity investments and trusts, the wealthiest quintile held an average of 31 per cent of their financial assets in this form (Kohler *et al.* 2004: 3).

This concentration of share ownership reflects two factors, as shown in table 3.2. First, the number of households in each quintile holding these assets increases dramatically with wealth – from 9 per cent in the least wealthy quintile to 78 per cent in the wealthiest. Second, the median value of these assets held by each household also increases rapidly with wealth – from $3000 for the least wealthy group to $50 000 for the wealthiest (Kohler *et al.* 2004: 9). The Gini coefficient, measuring the degree of inequality in equity investments, is very high at 0.78. The wealthiest 10 per cent of Australian households own 61 per cent of the national total worth of these financial assets (Headey *et al.* 2005: 165).

Table 3.2 Wealth held in equity investments, 2002

Percentile of net worth	Percentage of households holding asset	Median value of holdings ($000)
Less than 20	9	3
20–39.9	27	6
40–59.9	40	6
60–79.9	54	13
80–100	78	50
All households	41	15

Source: Kohler *et al.* 2004.

Wealth in superannuation

Superannuation has commonly been considered to be an equalising element in the distribution of wealth. Federal government policies have made compulsory superannuation the norm for the Australian workforce over the last two decades, so most workers are now covered. However, the HILDA survey, from which the data in table 3.3 are extracted, shows that the resulting distribution of superannuation assets is highly unequal. While 76 per cent of households hold some assets in superannuation, the median value of these assets for households in the wealthiest quintile is forty times greater than for those households in the bottom quintile. The increase in value between each quintile is also telling, with a significant break between the bottom two quintiles, where the value increases over fourfold, then a slower increase in value throughout the middle quintiles and another break between the second highest and highest wealth quintiles, where the median value again takes a significant jump, this time almost tripling (Kohler *et al.* 2004: 9).

Such patterns indicate that the policy of making occupational superannuation a universal feature of working life in Australia has had a very uneven impact on different segments within the population. The wealthiest 10 per cent of households, according to the HILDA survey, own 40 per cent of the wealth held in superannuation (Headey *et al.* 2005: 165). The tax-favoured treatment of superannuation is very important in this context, especially following Federal Treasurer Peter Costello's 2006 decision to exempt the receipt of superannuation payments from income tax.

Table 3.3 Wealth held in superannuation, 2002

Percentile of net worth	Percentage of households holding asset	Median value of holdings ($000)
Less than 20	61	5
20–39.9	77	22
40–59.9	73	35
60–79.9	83	69
80–100	89	199
All households	76	35

Source: Kohler *et al.* 2004.

The effect is that inequality in superannuation asset holdings further intensifies economic inequalities over the lifecycle.

Property is wealth

Wealth inequality is also clearly apparent in the unequal ownership of real estate. The common image of Australia as a property owning democracy in which land and housing are widely distributed is not altogether without foundation. However, the evidence does indicate substantial disparities. Overall, about 68 per cent of Australian households own their own home (or are in the process of buying it with mortgage finance). But, as the HILDA survey reveals, only 5 per cent of households in the least wealthy quintile are homeowners, compared with 95 per cent of households in the wealthiest quintile. As with superannuation, there is also a significant jump between the lowest two wealth quintiles, with home ownership increasing elevenfold between these two groups.

These dramatic inequalities are illustrated in table 3.4, which also shows the marked disparities in the value of these owner-occupied real estate assets. The average value of the property is five times higher in the top quintile than in the bottom quintile of households. The lower quintiles are also largely unrepresented among those owning additional or investment properties, with only 2 per cent and 7 per cent respectively of the households in the bottom two groups owning such assets, compared to 42 per cent of

Table 3.4 Wealth held in housing, 2002

Percentile of net worth	Primary residence		Other residential property	
	Percentage of households holding asset	Median value of holdings ($000)	Percentage of households holding asset	Median value of holdings ($000)
Less than 20	5	80	2	120
20–39.9	56	120	7	98
40–59.9	89	200	13	125
60–79.9	94	300	20	160
80–100	95	400	42	300
All households	68	250	17	200

Source: Kohler *et al.* 2004.

the households in the wealthiest quintile (Kohler *et al.* 2004: 9). Overall, the wealthiest 10 per cent of households own 38 per cent of the wealth held in real estate (Headey *et al.* 2005: 165).

It is also pertinent to note how inflation in real estate values tends to compound wealth inequalities. This process is demonstrated by research undertaken at NATSEM, using data from the Australian Bureau of Statistics to determine the impacts of property price inflation on individual wealth. The NATSEM study found that, over the last decade, households in the wealthiest fifth of the population increased their wealth by $250 000 on average, with two-thirds of this increase resulting from gains in the property market. In contrast, the least wealthy fifth made only $3000 on average over the same period, with half of this increase resulting from superannuation (Button and Stevenson 2004). This bottom group was largely excluded from the wealth increases resulting from the boom in property prices, with up to 95 per cent of the households in this group renting their primary residence and 92 per cent owning no residential property at all (Kohler *et al.* 2004: 10).

Another study of the wealth impacts of the 2000–3 property boom, carried out by Merrill Lynch and Cap Gemini Ernst and Young (reported in the *Australian Financial Review* 13 June 2003: 5), noted that a rising property market, together with the relatively strong local stockmarket, had increased the number of millionaires in Australia by 5000 over the previous year. There were 105 000 people who were estimated to have wealth of over A$1.51

million (equivalent to US$1 million), up by 5 per cent over the preceding twelve months. The anarchist thinker Pierre Proudhon is famous for answering his own question 'What is property?' with the reply, 'Property is theft': whatever the more general basis for that remark there is little doubt that – narrowing the definition of property to modern Australian real estate – property is a major stepping stone to the accumulation of private wealth.

Inheriting wealth

Inequalities in property ownership have further implications for intergenerational disparities. For most people a house is the most substantial item they can ever expect to inherit, and those houses vary significantly in size and value. Whether such inheritances tend to equalise or polarise wealth disparities over time has been an ongoing debate. Analysts such as Peter Saunders, director of the Social Policy Research Centre at the University of New South Wales, have suggested that the sheer number of homeowners means that, in time, millions of Australians will inherit significant capital gains, resulting in a significant redistribution of wealth. Others, including urban geographer Blair Badcock, have argued that the existing concentration of housing wealth means that housing inheritance will tend to perpetuate economic inequalities (O'Dwyer 2001).

Judy Yates, a leading Australian housing economist, taking the latter view, argues that the wealth redistribution driven by the recent property boom has created 'a divide between owners and renters that could last for generations' (cited in Button and Stevenson 2004). She suggests that 'children of current home owners will be protected in part from the increase in house prices through inheritance (or through being helped into home ownership by parents)'. Others will do it tough, facing housing market conditions quite different from those faced by previous generations. In Sydney, for example, the median-priced house cost four times average annual wage earnings in 1986, but over twelve times average annual earnings by 2003 (Stilwell, 2003a), albeit slipping back somewhat since the housing bubble burst. Julian Disney, chair of the 2004 National Summit on Housing Affordability, has argued that this seachange in residential property prices can be expected to have a significant effect on inherited inequality (Button and Stevenson 2004). Unless they are aided by financial support from wealthy parents or inherit their property, new entrants to the housing market are disadvantaged in these circumstances.

A recent study of housing inheritance has provided some evidence that is relevant to this debate. The study, carried out by Lisel O'Dwyer from Flinders University in Adelaide, analysed the impact of wealth and housing inheritance on wealth inequality in South Australia during the 1990s. Examining the estates of home owners who died in 1990, her study found that around 80 per cent of wealth in those estates was held in housing and that, for most benefactors, house value was 'a valid predictor of wealth at death and thus inheritance' (O'Dwyer 2001: 88). O'Dwyer also found that the distributional impacts of inheritance were less than expected, since the older age groups (who were, typically, the benefactors) usually held less wealth, and less housing wealth in particular, than the middle-aged groups (who were usually the beneficiaries). The inheritances were also often split between a number of beneficiaries, with the total housing inheritance of $170 million translating into an average inheritance among beneficiaries of only around $38 000 each (O'Dwyer 2001: 89).

O'Dwyer's research found some evidence that the average inheritance of recipients tends to increase with 'occupational class'. Among the beneficiaries included in the study, managers, administrators and professionals received the largest inheritances, with a mean value of $47 291, while machine operators, drivers and labourers received the smallest average inheritances, averaging $32 181 (O'Dwyer 2001: 95). Of all beneficiaries of housing inheritances, 84 per cent already owned their own homes – a significantly higher proportion than the 68 per cent rate of home ownership for South Australia as a whole (O'Dwyer 2001: 91). Moreover, the inheritances received by owner-occupiers were, on average, worth 36 per cent more than those received by tenants (O'Dwyer 2001: 92). To the extent that occupational profile and home ownership are indicators of existing wealth, this suggests that inherited wealth was more likely 'to flow to persons who already [had] substantial wealth' (O'Dwyer 2001: 93).

O'Dwyer reserves judgement as to whether these trends support the thesis that housing inheritance tends to exacerbate wealth inequalities over time. She acknowledges that, despite the breadth of home ownership, housing inheritance remains 'class specific' and leads to 'intergenerational

continuities in housing wealth' (O'Dwyer 2001: 93), but infers that the absolute differences in inherited wealth among different occupational groups
were too small to indicate a trend towards wealth polarisation. Hence her
conclusion that, while inherited (housing) wealth 'may have significant
influences on the life-course of some individuals', it has 'little effect on
the distribution of wealth in society'. The more significant determinants of
wealth distribution are identified as labour market status and the relationship between income, access to housing and the accumulation of one's own
housing wealth (O'Dwyer 2001: 83, 97).

It is pertinent to note that O'Dwyer's study examined the distribution
of inheritances only among beneficiaries. This leaves open the question
of the effects of inheritance – and housing inheritance in particular – on
the distribution of wealth in the broader society. This is significant since,
according to Simon Kelly from the National Centre for Social and Economic
Modelling, only around 1–2 per cent of the Australian population inherit
in any given year (Kelly 2005: 24). Based on data from the second wave of
the HILDA survey, and averaging the figures across Australia, Kelly finds
stronger evidence than O'Dwyer of the unequal distribution of inherited
wealth. While the average inheritance among all Australians in 2002 was
just over $60 000, the distribution was significantly skewed, with 39 per
cent of recipients inheriting less than $10 000 and 17 per cent inheriting
over $100 000 (Kelly 2005: 23). In addition, Kelly echoes O'Dwyer's findings
that most beneficiaries of inheritances are middle aged by the time they
receive their inheritance. This undermines the redistributive potential of
inheritances since it is young people seeking to enter the housing market
who are usually most in need. Hence, Kelly argues, not only are 'your chances
of getting a really big inheritance . . . relatively low', but 'big inheritances
are [also] going to those who don't really need them' (quoted in Wade and
Cubby 2006: 33).

Moreover, despite O'Dwyer's caution regarding the distributional
impacts of inherited wealth, she notes that future patterns of inheritance
may cause a greater transfer of wealth than hitherto. A very high proportion
of baby boomers are homeowners, many of whom would have accumulated
significant housing wealth during the recent property boom. In addition,
the majority of their beneficiaries are in the current Generation X and are
less likely to own their own homes (O'Dwyer 2001). Chris Richardson from
Access Economics predicts that these trends will lead to a massive transfer

of inheritance over the coming decades, beginning in earnest in around ten years with a peak in around twenty to thirty years (Wade and Cubby 2006: 25). In addition, the baby boomers have, typically, had fewer children than did their parents' generation. Hence, as these baby boomers 'reach the end of their lifecycles in 20–30 years' time . . . the pie of wealth will not only be larger, but will be divided between fewer persons' (O'Dwyer 2001: 96). While the value of inheritances will be mediated by factors such as the baby boomers' consumption patterns, longevity and rates of divorce (O'Dwyer 2001; Kelly 2005), the concentration of housing wealth among that generation suggests that inheritance may play a much more significant role in wealth distribution than has previously been the case.

Debt: the dark side of wealth?

Along with increases in wealth over the last few decades has been a parallel rise in the incidence and extent of household debt. This is particularly focused on loans for the purchase of land and housing. The HILDA survey reveals that 50 per cent of home owners have outstanding loans on their primary residences, with the median value of these loans being $90 000 (Kohler *et al.* 2004: 6). Around 80 per cent of the total value of home loans is held in first mortgages, with 18 per cent in home equity loans or second mortgages and 2 per cent in loans from family and friends (Kohler *et al.* 2004: 6). In a recent *Sydney Morning Herald* report, Matt Wade notes that the total number of Australian households with a mortgage has reached 2.5 million. Using data from a Citibank survey on mortgage trends, he further notes that 44 per cent of these households expect to still be repaying their mortgages in retirement. This, he suggests, is an indication that 'the mortgage has been embraced as [a] lifelong financial tool', with the home mortgage 'fast becoming a debt for life' (Wade 2006: 3).

This increased reliance on mortgages has often been cited as a cause for social concern, with fears that many households may be caught in a debt trap if interest rates rise, as they did – three times – in 2006. The burden of this risk varies greatly according to wealth. While the median value of property loans generally increases with wealth, the gearing ratio for property debt declines rapidly: that is, the ratio of debt to asset values falls from an average of 98 per cent in the least wealthy quintile of households to an average of

12 per cent in the wealthiest (Kohler *et al.* 2004: 8). This indicates that the debt held by the wealthier households is more than offset by the greater value of their assets. Not surprisingly, it is the mortgage holders in the least wealthy quintiles who are in the most precarious position.

It is also pertinent to note that the proportion of households using loans to purchase investment properties increases significantly with wealth. For these households, the costs of financing their investments can be partially offset by claiming tax deductions for their interest expenses (as noted by Kohler *et al.* 2004). These negative gearing advantages are not available to households just seeking to put a roof over their own heads. So the taxation arrangements relating to housing debt accentuate the relative disadvantage of those with the lower levels of wealth.

According to the HILDA survey, housing debt as a proportion of total debt was highest for the second and third quintiles in the distribution of household wealth. For these households, home loans amounted on average to about three-quarters of their total debt. Below them, in the lowest quintile, were the households with the lowest average share of home loans in total household debt. Few of these can do more than dream of home ownership. For these poorest households, personal debt, including credit cards and personal loans, accounts for over half of their total debt (Kohler *et al.* 2004). Some of these households are undoubtedly in a debt trap, borrowing more to cope with previous debt accumulations and the interest payments thereon. This is indeed the dark side of the inequalities of wealth and debt.

Wealth: looking back to 1915

The first and only official survey of the wealth of all Australian households was conducted in 1915. This was the Commonwealth government's wartime census, taking stock of the nation's population and its assets (Knibbs 1916: see also Soltow 1972). The results still make interesting reading, giving a political economic snapshot of the time and an indication of how society has changed since then.

Of all people resident in Australia in 1915, 16 per cent had no wealth or had negative net wealth. A further 42 per cent had personal wealth of less than £100; 32 per cent had wealth between £100 and £1000. These three groups together comprised about 90 per cent of the population. The other

10 per cent had over £1000 per head. Of these, over half had between £1000 and £2500. At the top end of a very bottom-heavy distribution, 466 individuals, comprising 0.02 per cent of the population, declared personal wealth of over £100 000.

By current standards these all sound like paltry sums, but one has to take into account the massive inflation that has occurred in the intervening decades. Changes in the consumer price index, and the conversion of £ sterling to $, mean that the average household wealth of £558 in 1915 is roughly the equivalent of $35 000 today, less than 10 per cent of the $404 300 actual average household wealth in 2002, as estimated by the Reserve Bank of Australia. Although Australia in 1915 was a relatively wealthy nation by international standards, it was relatively poor by modern standards.

The wealth that did exist was markedly concentrated. The elite of Australian society had a dominating social and political influence in 1915, even though its wealth in purely economic terms was relatively modest. The wealth of the 466 richest people in 1915 was equivalent in value to $5612 million at the end of the twentieth century. In that latter year the 500 wealthiest people had total assets amounting to $57 090 million. So, in terms of broad aggregates, the wealth of the elite had multiplied about tenfold during the century. Even more startling is the observation that Australia's richest person today is wealthier than all 466 richest people combined in 1915, even allowing for the general inflation that has occurred in the interim.

Conclusion

Wealth inequalities are pervasive and multidimensional. The degree of wealth inequality exceeds that of income inequality. Because wealth is a stock and income is a flow, it is possible to be asset rich but income poor. As noted earlier, very wealthy people tend to hold more of their wealth in income-generating forms, such as shares and investment property, so it is hardly surprising that the high concentration of wealth is a major element in perpetuating and intensifying the inequality of income distribution. The result is the reproduction and accentuation of a deep divide between very wealthy households and the rest of Australian society.

The concentration of wealth in recent years has been accelerated by asset price inflation. The 1990s was a decade remarkably buoyant for share prices, with a further surge since 2003 pushing the ASX 200 index over 5000 points for the first time ever in March 2006 (Burrell and O'Sullivan 2006). The relentless growth in real estate values during the 1990s, accelerating further in the first three years of this decade, also widened the gulf between existing property owners and those aspiring to join this group. Inflation in land and housing values is sometimes said to have broadened the distribution of wealth, but existing home owners can only cash in their extra wealth if they are willing to move to smaller homes or to localities with lower real estate values. So an increase in their wealth is largely unrealisable. It is mainly those who own more than a single owner-occupied property who have been advantaged.[2] Indeed, the dominant effect of asset price inflation is invariably to intensify the advantaged position of those holding the greatest initial wealth. It is a classic example of the process whereby capital makes capital.

So, there is a mutual reinforcement between inequality in the distribution of incomes and the concentration of wealth. Increased disparities in income flows can be reliably expected to increase disparities between households in their wealth stocks over time. The phenomenal surge in payments to CEOs of large companies in recent years, for example, flows through into corresponding accumulations of wealth. An element of fluidity in class composition thereby exists, as some upwardly mobile people join a highly affluent elite. However, the economic gulf between this wealthy elite and the rest of the Australian population simultaneously widens.

[2] A recent Citibank report on mortgage trends found that, in order to fund their retirement, 21 per cent of older people plan to sell their existing homes and move into smaller ones. A further 17 per cent plan to sell investment property. However, the report warned that demographic trends may undermine their plans to free up their wealth: with the current baby-boomer generation approaching retirement age over the coming decades, there may be a flood of larger homes on the market. In addition, there is a growing trend towards smaller and single-person households. Hence, at the time when many baby boomers plan to cash in on their larger homes, an increased supply of bigger homes and increased demand for smaller ones may force many of them to accept a lower sale price or stay where they are (Wade 2006).

Chapter Four

THE RICH

Having surveyed the evidence on the overall distribution of wealth in Australia, it is interesting to look more closely at those at the top of the tree. We can do so by drawing on data from the *Business Review Weekly* (*BRW*) to provide insights into the economic situation of the nation's most wealthy people. The 'Rich 200' edition that the *BRW* publishes annually shows the wealth of the top 200 individuals and families. A study of the character and changing composition of this group can provide potentially useful insights into the economic situation of the very richest people in Australian society. Unlike some other data on income and wealth, the *BRW* information is published with no significant time lags, so it provides a very up-to-date picture of who owns what.

Before the *BRW* started publishing its annual 'Rich 200' list edition, spotlighting the wealthy was largely done by the publications of the political Left. In other countries, such as the UK and the USA, there had been a strong, popular, journalistic tradition of studying the wealthy (for example, Lundberg 1969; Davis 1982). In Australia, the Communist Party of Australia took the lead, running a series of portraits of the ruling class in its newspaper *Tribune* during the 1970s that were subsequently compiled into a booklet entitled *Who's Running Australia*. Pen portraits of Kerry Packer, Vincent Fairfax, Reg Ansett, Peter Abeles, Lang Hancock, Rod Carnegie, the Baillieus and other major property owners were included. Readers were invited to see the booklet as a contribution to the overthrow of the system represented by 'these well fed faces'. The introduction to that booklet said,

> The people in this pamphlet are a fair example of the class which owns and controls this country. They have their fingers in every pie – in mining and manufacturing, in finance, property and transport. They are, to use an unfashionable word, the bourgeoisie (Murphy 1979).

It is somewhat ironic that *BRW* has become the bearer of this tradition – but for the purpose of celebrating wealth rather than denouncing it.

This chapter is based on an analysis of the *BRW* data for each of the years 1994–2006. It considers how much personal wealth is necessary to feature in the list of the 200 wealthiest Australians, the total asset values of these people and how concentrated is the ownership of assets among them. It then proceeds to explore the principal sources of their wealth and some characteristics of the up-and-coming young and rich. Finally, consideration is given to the quality of the *BRW* data on which the analysis is based, some longer-term historical trends and the broader implications of the patterns and changes revealed in this analysis.

Entry to the rich list

How much wealth does it take to get listed in the *BRW* 'Rich 200'? Table 4.1 demonstrates the amount of wealth needed to be among the top 10, top 100 and top 200 richest Australians for each year from 1994 to 2006. The left-hand column shows the wealth necessary to just scrape into the list of the richest 200 individuals and families. In 1994 this was $37 million; by 2006 it was $196 million. The middle column shows that it took wealth of $75 million to be in the top 100 in 1994, but $381 million by 2006. The right-hand column shows that to get in the top 10 required $550 million in 1994, but $1800 million by 2004. So, in round terms, there was more than a threefold increase in the wealth needed to get into the top 10, and more than a fivefold increase to get into the top 100 or 200 over the period.

To put these changes in perspective, it is necessary to take account of inflation. But what measure of inflation? Using an asset price index would

Table 4.1 The wealth needed to be on the Australian rich list, 1994–2006

Year	To be in the top 200 (A$ million)	To be in the top 100 (A$ million)	To be in the top 10 (A$ million)
1994	37	75	550
1995	42	85	560
1996	50	95	560
1997	55	115	600
1998	60	130	700
1999	65	145	860
2000	95	215	950
2001	105	220	1200
2002	110	250	1300
2003	113	240	1000
2004	117	250	1140
2005	160	318	1420
2006	196	381	1800

Note: For years 1994, 1995, 1996, 1997 and 1998, the *BRW* published less than 200 names (including individuals and families): 184, 188, 186, 193 and 198 respectively. So the first column of this table relates to this number of wealth–holders in these years, that is, a little less than 200 in each case. All other years include the top 200 individuals and families listed.
Source: Analysis of *BRW* annual data.

show that inflation in the last decade and a half has been more rapid for assets than for consumer goods and services. However, the Consumer Price Index (CPI) is the appropriate deflator if it is the spending power of the wealthy that is at issue. The CPI rose by 38 per cent over the period 1994–2006.[1] That would mean that the $37 million needed to get onto the rich list in 1994 would have to have risen to about $51 million by 2006 just to keep pace with inflation. In fact, the entry qualification rose to $196 million. So we may infer that around 9 per cent ($14 million) of the $159 million increase in wealth needed to get onto the rich list involved the effect of inflation; the other 91 per cent ($145 million) represented real increases in the spending capacity of the wealthy.

[1] Calculations are drawn from ABS (2006c) *Consumer Price Index, Australia,* March 2006, 6401.0.

Table 4.2 Asset values of the super rich in Australia, 1994–2006

Year	Top 200 (A$ million)	Top 100 (A$ million)	Top 10 (A$ million)
1994	36 976	32 495	17 000
1995	37 389	32 325	15 200
1996	36 115	30 175	11 170
1997	40 673	33 528	12 370
1998	47 696	39 349	15 400
1999	56 963	47 028	19 150
2000	67 140	53 585	22 800
2001	67 973	54 079	22 910
2002	73 421	59 061	24 310
2003	72 747	57 939	23 760
2004	86 121	68 882	26 170
2005	97 999	76 766	28 720
2006	117 439	93 135	33 400

Note: The qualification indicated for table 4.1 applies again here.
Source: Analysis of *BRW* annual data.

The wealth of the wealthy

How much do these wealthy people own? Table 4.2 demonstrates the total wealth of the richest 10, 100 and 200 Australians for each year between 1994 and 2006. As for table 4.1, no distinction is made between individuals and families shown in the *BRW* lists.

The right hand column of table 4.2 shows that the wealth of the top 10 wealth holders increased from $17 billion to over $33 billion over the period 1994 to 2006, after slumping to only a little over $11 billion in the mid 1990s. The other two columns show that the wealth of the richest 100 and 200 increased proportionately rather more over the period. Over $117 billion is now held by the wealthiest 200 Australians. As with the data in table 4.1, the effect of inflation on these asset values needs to be taken into account, but these are prodigious volumes of wealth by any standards.

It should be emphasised that these figures on total wealth allow for comings and goings among the personnel. In other words, they show the wealth of whoever is in the top 10, 100 or 200 at any one time. But particular

Table 4.3 Concentration of assets among the Australian super rich, 1994–2006

Year	Share of the top 10 asset holders in the top 100 (%)	Share of the top 50 asset holders in the top 100 (%)
1994	52	85
1995	47	83
1996	37	78
1997	39	78
1998	39	78
1999	41	79
2000	43	77
2001	42	78
2002	41	77
2003	41	77
2004	38	76
2005	37	76
2006	36	76

Note: In the *BRW* list no distinction is made between individuals and families.
Source: Analysis of *BRW* annual data.

individuals have played a persistent role, sharply skewing the distribution at the top.

The most obvious example is the late Kerry Packer, whose estimated wealth put him at the top of the *BRW* rich list from 1996 until 2005. In 2006, Kerry's son, James, inherited his position as Australia's richest person, with an estimated personal wealth of $7.1 billion.

Also featuring prominently over many years are retail and property investor Frank Lowy and industrialist Richard Pratt. In 2006 these two men maintained their positions as Australia's second and third richest people, owning estimated wealth of $5.4 billion and $5.2 billion respectively (*BRW* 2006a).

The concentration of wealth

Is there growing concentration of wealth among the wealthy? Table 4.3 provides some information on the concentration of wealth holdings among the super rich themselves. As with the total value of wealth, there are evidently some fluctuations in these concentration ratios from year to year, but a clear overall trend is discernible. The shares of the top 10 and the top fifty among the top 100 asset holders both declined in the period 1994 to 2006. This contrasts with the preceding decade, when both the shares of the top 10 and the top fifty among the top 100 asset holders had risen, indicating an increased concentration of wealth among the super rich.

Looking back to earlier years suggests that the longer-term trend is to greater concentration. When the *BRW* list was introduced in 1983 the share of the top 10 asset holders in the wealth of the top 100 was only 25 per cent. In other words, the wealthiest ten people had one-quarter of the total wealth of the top 100. The sharp rise to over half of the total in the early 1990s showed the effect of the spectacular wealth concentration that had occurred in the 1980s. Although the general trend since the mid 1990s has been to a rather more even distribution of wealth among the top 100 wealth holders, the degree of concentration is still more than it had been in 1983.

The effect of particular individuals on the patterns of wealth concentration also needs to be taken into account. Media magnates Rupert Murdoch and the late Kerry Packer have been particularly significant in this respect. In the period 1983–94 Packer's estimated wealth had grown from $100 million to $5500 million, while the Murdoch family's wealth had climbed from a holding of $250 million in 1983 to match Packer's by 1994. In 1995 the Murdoch family's wealth increased to $6000 million; its subsequent delisting (because of Rupert's change from Australian to American nationality) explains the drop in asset concentration in 1996. Since then, the concentration of wealth among the top 100 wealth holders has been fairly consistent.

Young and rich

Who are the up-and-coming wealthy Australians? Some element of fluidity in the composition of the wealthy elite makes it interesting to consider who's who among younger Australians. Recently, *BRW* listed the wealthiest people under 40 years of age (*BRW* 2006b). Scrutiny of this list enables us to see how their characteristics and sources of wealth differ from those on the main, all-age rich 200.

One hundred people are identified, with an average age of 36, an average wealth of $48.6 million and a total wealth in 2006 of just under $4 billion. To get on the young and rich list requires assets of at least $12 million.

The wealthiest person, Edmund Groves, founder of childcare company ABC Learning Centres, had an estimated $260 million. Five others also received over $130 million, thereby qualifying for membership of the all-age rich 200 individuals in 2006.

There are some interesting features of these younger wealth holders. There were, for example, proportionately more females among them than on the main rich list – 17 per cent, compared with a mere 5.5 per cent among the all-age rich 200. However, the number of women on the young and rich list has been in decline for several years, falling to seventeen in 2006 from the previous year's twenty-one. The list's editor acknowledges that this is a 'disturbing trend' (Thomson 2006: 18).

What about the industries in which these younger Australians made their fortunes? Retail business ventures feature most prominently, accounting for 21 per cent of those on the list. Technology and services each accounted for 18 per cent, property 14 per cent, entertainment 9 per cent and sport 8 per cent. While residential property markets have slowed in recent years, a number of the young and rich have made their fortunes in commercial and retail property. Property developer Shaun Bonnet, for example, made his debut on the list in 2006 at number three, having accumulated wealth of $220 million through development of office blocks and shopping centres in Brisbane and Adelaide.

The fastest-growing fortune belongs to hedge-fund managers Angus and Richard Grinham, whose combined net worth in 2006 increased by 525 per cent since the previous year. Sport and technology were the routes to riches for the two youngest people on the list, tennis player Lleyton Hewitt and online retailer Michael Rosenbaum who, both at age 25, owned estimated wealth of $33 million and $15 million respectively. Entertainment was the route to riches for the richest woman – film star Nicole Kidman, whose estimated wealth of $200 million in 2006 made her the fourth wealthiest Australian under 40.

Sources of wealth

Where does the wealth come from? The question echoes a Wizard of Id cartoon that shows the king (of Id) being asked by journalists, 'What are you doing about the gap between the rich and the poor?' 'I'm encouraging the poor to close the gap', the king replies. 'How can they do that?' the journalist asks. 'Find out how the rich got rich', says the king! Beyond the humour lies a serious point, although the inference that the poor could thereby transform themselves into the rich is risible indeed. Analytically, the question is one that has to be confronted by all students of political economy – what is the source of wealth?

It is commonplace to point out that, in general, the economic wellbeing of a society derives ultimately from all the productive work – mental and manual – undertaken by labour. It is through productive effort – the creation of goods and services, technological innovation and investment of the fruits of that labour – that wealth is generated. The extent to which the wealth is then captured by particular groups or classes depends on their relative economic power. In the case of business interests this depends significantly on the sectors of the economy in which they operate. So the interesting question then becomes, 'From which sectors have the top businesspeople (and property owners) in Australia derived their concentrations of wealth?'

The individual commentaries on the wealthy individuals and families featured in the annual *BRW* listings provide some answers to this question. Table 4.4 on the next page shows the sources of the wealth of the top 10 super rich for the years 1994 and 2006, as an indication of the elements of continuity and of the changing patterns since the mid 1990s.

The sources of wealth among this elite are quite diverse. Property ownership and development features twice as a principal source of the fortunes of the top 10 wealth holders in 1994 and three times in 2006. Key vehicles for this aspect of wealth accumulation have been the changing land uses associated with building shopping centres and apartment blocks. Manufacturing and investment also feature conspicuously among the wealth sources of the top 10. Media, entertainment and investment are the principal sources of wealth for the richest Australian, James Packer, with investments in the gambling (or, rather more politely termed, 'gaming') industry accounting for an increasing share of his wealth.

There are also some puzzles in these patterns. The prominence of property in the sources of wealth of the top 10 is to be expected, with real estate development and investment having been such a buoyant component of capital accumulation over the last decade, as noted in the preceding chapter.

Table 4.4 Principal sources of wealth of top 10 wealth holders in Australia, 1994 and 2006

1994	2006
1 Media (Murdoch family)	Media / entertainment, gaming / investment (James Packer)
2 Media / investment (Kerry Packer)	Property – shopping centres, investment (Frank Lowy)
3 Manufacturing – paper, packaging, investment (Richard Pratt)	Manufacturing – paper, packaging, investment (Richard Pratt)
4 Investment (David Hains)	Energy (Shi Zhengrong)
5 Manufacturing – steel, plastics (Smorgon family)	Property (Harry Triguboff)
6 Retail – shopping centres, property (Frank Lowy)	Manufacturing – steel, investment (Smorgon family)
7 Property (John Gandel)	Investment (David Hains and family)
8 Investment (Jack Liberman)	Manufacturing – gaming machines (Len Ainsworth and family)
9 Retail, investment (Sidney Myer, Neilma Gantner, Marigold Southey)	Property – shopping centres, services – aged care (John Gandel)
10 Engineering, construction (Franco Belgiorno-Nettis and Carlo Salteri)	Resources – iron ore (Gina Rinehart)

Source: BRW, May 1994 and May 2006.

Manufacturing industry has not been so notable as a major growth sector in the Australian economy over the same period. However, generalisations are problematic in this regard, since finding niche areas within particular manufacturing industries – as in other sectors of primary and service industries – can evidently be a basis for the acquisition of enormous wealth. The foundation of third-place getter Richard Pratt's wealth, for example, has been in making paper and packaging, an industry that has been a highly profitable basis for capital accumulation. Len Ainsworth and his sons, eighth on the 2006 rich list, have specialised in manufacturing gaming machines.

The debut of Shi Zhengrong on the 2006 list is also interesting. As founder and CEO of a solar power company, his wealth reflects the economic potential of shifting from traditional to renewable sources of energy, in this case with substantial startup funding from the government of Wuxi in China (*BRW* 2006a).

It is also worth considering the significance of inherited wealth. *BRW*'s own editorials recurrently emphasise that individuals can achieve wealth from a poor background. Indeed, some do; however, according to researcher Michael Gilding (1999: 173), the *BRW* rich lists are biased 'toward self-publicizing individuals and spectacular success stories, and against old wealth and wealth distributed around old families'. The extent of that bias is difficult to discern but, taking the data at face value, we can identify some features of the social background of the wealthiest Australians.

Table 4.5 compares the top 10 wealth holders in 1994 and 2006 according to whether, for example, they were immigrants and whether they inherited substantial wealth. Inspection of this table reveals that five out of the ten richest Australians in 1994 and at least four out of ten in 2006 started their journey to riches with the aid of kinship networks and the inheritance of family businesses. While these inheritances represent only small fractions of the current wealth of the recipients in most cases, they do indicate the need for some scepticism about the popular notion of the rich list comprising self-made multimillionaires.

Also interesting to note is the relatively high incidence of wealthy immigrants and second-generation Australians, in both cases predominantly from Eastern European backgrounds. This feature is evident in the complete rich 200 lists, with a broader spread of origins. However, being an immigrant is not synonymous with having a poor background: inheritance and family connection may apply equally strongly among immigrants as they do among the Australian-born.

How reliable is the evidence?

The propensity of the rich to conceal wealth in family trusts, diverse company transactions and other financial legerdemain is notorious, although having a contrary relationship with their propensity to flaunt it in conspicuous consumption. Because there is no general wealth tax in Australia, there are no

Table 4.5 Selected background characteristics and wealth sources of the top 10 wealth holders in Australia, 1994 and 2006

1994	2006
1 Inheritance (Murdoch family)	Inheritance (James Packer)
2 Inheritance (Kerry Packer)	Migrant; started own business (Frank Lowy)
3 Inheritance, second-generation Australian (Richard Pratt)	Inheritance, second-generation Australian (Richard Pratt)
4 Unknown (David Hains)	Migrant; started own business (Shi Zhengrong)
5 Migrants (Norman and Victor Smorgon); inheritance and started own business; second and third generations (Smorgon family)	Migrant; started own business (Harry Triguboff)
6 Migrant; started own business (Frank Lowy)	Migrants (Norman and Victor Smorgon); inheritance and started own business; second and third generations (Smorgon family)
7 Inheritance; second-generation Australian (John Gandel)	Unknown (David Hains and family)
8 Migrant, started own business (Jack Liberman)	Unknown (Len Ainsworth and family)
9 Inheritance; second-generation Australians (Sidney Myer, Neilma Gantner, Marigold Southey)	Inheritance, second-generation Australian (John Gandel)
10 Migrants, started own business (Franco Belgiorno-Nettis and Carlo Salteri)	Inheritance; first female Australian billionaire, first woman in top 10 (Gina Rinehart)

Source: BRW, May 1994 and May 2006.

official government statistics on personal wealth against which one could test the *BRW* estimates, so it is important to maintain a cautious stance. Attempts to compile estimates of personal wealth necessarily face the difficulty of extracting and aggregating information on different types of assets, ranging from land and residential property to business assets, bank deposits and shareholdings. For all these reasons, the reliability of the *BRW* data is uncertain.

A careful analysis of earlier *BRW* rich 200 data by Michael Gilding (1999) indicates two major methodological problems. First, individuals are taken as the main component of investigation – since they are 'irreducible and marketable' – but *BRW* cannot sustain this consistently in practice, having frequent recourse to a more ambiguous unit of analysis, the family. The separate list of wealthy families shows fortunes disseminated through kinship networks, predominantly through inheritance.

The second problem is that of calculating the value of the private fortunes. According to Gilding (1999: 171), *BRW* collects the data from 'public records and business intelligence; drawing upon public company records and property listings, obtaining value estimates on known assets, and questioning reliable and key industry contacts'. Gilding notes that 'concealed or inconspicuous forms of wealth' are likely to be overlooked in these calculations. In recent years, there has been more of an attempt to gain information from the listees themselves.

When *BRW* began publishing its estimates, one critic speculated that the list missed 'many widows who passively enjoy their estates and thus are not flagged in documentation or city gossip', as well as 'quite large enterprises occupying minor market niches or based outside central business districts', thereby escaping scrutiny; and 'old families who make a point of staying inconspicuous' (Ries, cited in Gilding 1999: 171). The outcome is that the wealth held by the more reserved old families tends not to be given equivalent attention. In Gilding's words:

> The combined effect of methodological dilemmas in defining a unit of analysis and reliability of data is to overstate the wealth vested in individuals, at the expense of kinship and business networks. More specifically, the lists are tilted towards new wealth accumulated by individuals on the cusp of a speculative wave, and against old wealth spread around kinship networks in a variety of investment activities, sheltered in private companies, trusts and nominee holdings (1999: 172).

In an effort to create what he considered to be a more accurate rich list, Stephen Mayne of the Australian website *Crikey* published the 'Crikey Revised Wealth' (CRW) list in 2005, calling on readers (especially accountants) to anonymously dob in a low-profile multimillionaire (Mayne 2005). The list highlighted dozens of wealthy individuals who *Crikey* believed should have made it onto the *BRW* rich list but didn't. In 2006, nine of these individuals, owning wealth ranging from $135 to $515 million, debuted on the *BRW* list (*Crikey* 2006).

Despite the methodological difficulties in gathering rich-list figures, what gives some degree of confidence in the *BRW* data is that there is no obvious reason why the tendency to overlook concealed wealth should vary dramatically from year to year. So there is no cause to expect systematic bias in the sort of time-series analysis of wealth concentration presented in this chapter.

One may reasonably presume that more than two decades of experience in researching this issue, since *BRW* published the first rich list in 1983, has produced some valuable cumulative expertise. Moreover, it seems that most people on the recent *BRW* lists are cooperative with the magazine's investigators, many of them posing for photographs and agreeing to be interviewed. This may indicate that the rich are not particularly concerned to conceal their wealth (or less so than their incomes), which should occasion little surprise, since the general absence of wealth taxes in Australia means that there is less need to have regard to the taxation consequences of having one's wealth publicised. A marked increase in wealth can arise from inflation in the values of existing assets as well as from having income substantially in excess of expenditure. So the public display of wealth does not necessarily attract the attention of the Australian Taxation Office.

The all-time richest Australians

How does Australia's current wealthy elite compare to that of the past? A study by William Rubinstein (2004), utilising probate records and other valuations of individual wealth along with the more recent *BRW* rich 200 data, indicates some answers. Rubinstein lists Australia's 'richest-ever' 233 people. The wealth of each individual is expressed as a percentage of Australia's GDP at the time of valuation. This enables a comparison of different individuals' wealth over time, adjusted for changes in the overall size of the economy.

Table 4.6 All-time richest Australians in 2004, selected entries

Rank	Name	Year of death or birth	2004 Value (A$ billion)	% of GDP
1	Samuel Terry	(d. 1838)	24.37	3.395
2	Rowland Hassal	(d. 1820)	14.35	1.991
3	Robert Jenkins	(d. 1822)	13.54	1.886
4	William John Turner Clarke	(d. 1874)	10.74	1.496
5	James Tyson	(d. 1898)	9.42	1.313
6	Rupert Murdoch	(b. 1931)	9.12	1.271
17	Kerry Packer	(b. 1938)	6.5	0.918
35	Richard Pratt	(b. 1934)	4.2	0.593
36	Frank Lowy	(b. 1930)	4.2	0.593
92	Smorgon Family		2.37	0.334
119	Harry Triguboff	(b. 1933)	2.0	0.282
142	David Hains and family	(b. 1930)	1.8	0.254
188	John Gandel	(b. 1935)	1.4	0.197

Note: Rubinstein's analysis terminates with the *BRW* rich 200 data of 2004.
The 2006 data are used in the other tables in this chapter.
Source: Rubinstein 2004.

The study suggests that, in general, members of the wealthy elites of Australia's distant past owned more of the country's wealth, in comparative terms, than do most of the current multimillionaires. Right at the top of the list are individuals from the first two or three generations of Australians of British origin, who built or expanded their fortunes through agriculture and trade. The richest Australian of all time was Samuel Terry, an ex-convict who amassed wealth of £200 000, largely through mortgage ownership. By 1820, Terry apparently owned over one-fifth of the value of all mortgages in the area covered by present-day New South Wales, Queensland and Victoria. Although small by today's standards, his wealth equalled nearly 3.4 per cent of Australia's GDP at that time, which would be equivalent to a massive $24.4 billion today.

Although individual fortunes have grown significantly in dollar terms, Rubinstein's study suggests that, over time, they have declined as a proportion of Australia's GDP. Indeed, all but nine of the 233 all-time richest

Australians (according to this definition) were born before 1900. The trend to declining relative size of individual wealth was greatest from 1940 to 1970, when a combination of higher taxes and restrictions on capital flows placed greater limits on capital accumulation. However, since the 1980s there has been some evident reversal of this trend.

Table 4.6 demonstrates that many of those listed at the very top of the 2004 *BRW* 'Rich 200' list were, in that year, in the same league as the richest Australians of all time. Rupert Murdoch came in at number six on the all-time rich list, with Kerry Packer at number seventeen and property developer John Gandel the last of the 2004 *BRW* rich list to gain entry on the all-time rich list at number 188.

Conclusion

Analysis of the *BRW* 'Rich 200' publications reveals the prodigious wealth concentrated in the hands of a small number of Australian individuals and families. The data have limitations as a measure of economic inequality and as a means of understanding processes of wealth accumulation. However, it is clear that the most wealthy Australians have become much richer since the *BRW* began publishing its lists. Even allowing for inflation, there has been a substantial hike in the price of the entry ticket to the rich list, more than tripling since 1994. The volume of wealth held by the wealthy elite is also continuing to increase in both absolute and relative terms.

As the all-time rich list demonstrates, there has never been a golden age of Australian egalitarianism since the European invasion and settlement of the continent: the ownership of wealth was always strongly concentrated. One would hardly expect otherwise in a capitalist society. Yet therein lies a characteristic Australian tension – between highly concentrated wealth and a widespread belief in the absence of class-based inequality. The striking concentration of wealth is important because economic assets are a lever which can be used for other social and political purposes, as emphasised by contributors to another recent book on the ruling class in Australia (Hollier 2004). So the *BRW* data on wealth holding can be regarded as indicative of class power.

Chapter Five

THE POOR

At the other extreme from the wealthy are the poor within Australian society. There is some sense in the traditionally pessimistic remark that 'the poor are always with us'. Indeed, economic misfortune can affect individuals and families for all sorts of reasons, some of which are difficult to anticipate and avoid. But a hallmark of a good society is that poverty not be pervasive and systemic. There is a world of difference between individual poverty that is exceptional and societal poverty that is regularly reproduced.

How does Australia rate in regard to the extent of poverty? Not very well, considering its overall level of affluence. The *United Nations Human Development Report 2006* ranked Australia fourteenth among eighteen OECD countries according to a human poverty index. This puts Australia ahead only of the UK, the USA, Ireland and Italy in terms of its success in eliminating poverty (UN 2006: 295). The extent of poverty in Australia has been variously estimated at between 8 and 17 per cent of the population, according to the level of income for which the poverty line is set for different household types (King 1998). Lloyd *et al.* (2004a), for example, note that, if the poverty line is set at half of the median income of different types of Australian households, about 11 per cent of households fall below it. Such a measure requires critical evaluation, as will be argued in this chapter (see also Saunders and Bradbury 2006), but it draws immediate attention to the inherent connection between economic inequality and poverty.

Much conventional economic thinking has rested on the optimistic expectation that continued economic growth would eventually eradicate poverty, but if the fruits of economic growth are unevenly distributed, as shown in previous chapters, the persistence of poverty is patently predicable. Indeed, if poverty is interpreted relative to the prevailing socioeconomic standards, an increasingly unequal society is one in which poverty is inevitable. This chapter explores the principal dimensions of this problem, beginning with a discussion of alternative concepts of poverty, before turning to the evidence on whether its incidence is shrinking or growing. Then comes an examination of particular groups that are most vulnerable to poverty – the elderly, children, the unemployed, sole parents, Indigenous peoples, immigrants, refugees and people with disabilities. In this way we build up an analysis of the structural elements in this persistent and pervasive socioeconomic problem.

Poverty: absolute or relative?

Poverty may be considered in absolute terms – simply not having enough food to eat, clothing to wear, or basic housing to inhabit – and malnutrition, destitution and homelessness are its most obvious manifestations. By international standards, particularly in comparison to the less affluent nations of Africa, Asia and South America, these problems are of relatively modest significance in Australia. Yet they are not altogether absent, indicating that there are serious impediments to the trickle down of incomes and wealth from the more affluent strata of the economy and society. The material circumstances of Indigenous Australians, particularly those living in remote communities, are an obvious case in point. Their health and living conditions are often similar to those prevailing among poor people in developing countries.

Among non-Indigenous people there are also significant pockets of absolute poverty, of which homelessness is one indicator. One ABS study estimated the number of homeless people in Australia to be around 100 000 nationally (ABS 2003b: 2), although it is important to acknowledge that definitions of homelessness can vary significantly (Flatau et al. 2006). Hostels catering for the otherwise homeless in the major metropolitan areas regularly report that they cannot cope with the demand for places. Over the last couple of decades, homelessness has become a problem for a much broader demographic, with the ABS reporting that 46 per cent of homeless Australians are now under the age of 25 and 42 per cent are female (ABS 2003b: 4). As poverty touches a broader cross-section of society the stereotype of 'older alcoholic men living in dormitory style night shelters' (Burke 1998: 293) no longer fits.

What of those people whose material living conditions are above this standard but who are still unable to afford the things that most Australians regard as necessary for a decent standard of living? Peter Saunders of the Social Policy Research Centre argues that, in addition to measures of absolute poverty, poverty must be determined in relation to the prevailing social standards. Relative poverty exists where people 'lack those necessities that are rendered important by the culture of that space' and where various forms of hardship are experienced relative to the cultural norm (Saunders 2002: 147).

In examining the incidence of this relative poverty, a key question is where to set the poverty line. What amount of income is regarded as sufficient for evading poverty? Which 'functionings', to use the terminology coined by the Nobel Prize-winning economist Amartya Sen (cited in Saunders 2002: 146), are deemed critical enough that their non-existence is indicative of poverty?

One interesting study, by Clive Hamilton, executive director of The Australia Institute, shows the difficulty of dealing with this issue if people's own assessment of their circumstances is taken as a primary indication of hardship. Hamilton's study divides Australian households into income quintiles and shows how people assess the adequacy of their incomes relative to their (socially conditioned) needs (Hamilton 2003a). Not surprisingly, most – 84 per cent – of households in the lowest-income quintile reported that they could not afford to cover all of their needs. An earlier ABS survey had found that only 20 per cent of households in this lowest-income quintile said they were unable to afford 'special meals, new clothes and leisure activities', while 56 per cent said they could afford 'a week's holiday away from home each year' (Hamilton 2003a: 49). The implication is that their more general self-identification of being in need referred to other forms of relative deprivation. Meanwhile, at the other end of the scale, Hamilton's survey also found that 46 per cent of households in the richest income quintile said they could not afford all the necessities, but the ABS data showed that only 7 per cent said they could not afford a week's holiday away from home each year, and only 4 per cent said they 'could not afford a night out' (Hamilton 2003a: 49). Hamilton concludes that

> a majority of high-income households believe that they cannot afford every-
> thing they really need and a large proportion believes they spend nearly all
> their income on the basic necessities of life. By contrast, significant minori-
> ties in the lowest income group say that they can afford everything they need
> (Hamilton 2003a: abstract).

As Hamilton notes, these findings do not trivialise the experience of poverty in Australia or suggest that poverty is voluntary. Rather, they suggest that there is a significant difference between 'real and imagined hardship' in Australia (Hamilton 2003a: 51). Evidently, when people's own perceptions of what constitutes material hardship are considered, poverty becomes a very elusive concept. Some attempts have been made to develop multidimen-sional measures that incorporate people's subjective experiences or cultural understandings of poverty. However, most official studies have narrowed the concept to a more concrete variable, adopting income-adequacy measures of relative poverty, such as defining a household as poor if its income is less than half the national average.

Setting the poverty line at half the median national income is the basis on which the Economic Policy Institute in the USA, using consistent interna-tional comparative data from the 2004 *Luxembourg Income Study*, compares poverty rates. According to this measure, Australia has the second-highest incidence of poverty among the OECD nations, ranking only behind the USA (Mishel *et al.* 2005). This international league-table is reproduced in table 5.1, together with related data on the incidence of poverty among chil-dren and the elderly. The evidence shows that Australia also rates poorly in respect of child poverty, third behind the USA and Italy. It rates even worse in respect of poverty among the elderly, topping the international league-table in this respect.

Poverty estimates tend to be conservative to the extent that they ignore housing costs. Poverty manifest in the form of homelessness is the most obvious expression of income inadequacy relative to the cost of obtain-ing affordable housing. In Australian cities, where housing costs have risen

Table 5.1 Poverty rates in OECD countries

Country	Percentage of people in poverty		
	Total	Children	Elderly
USA	17.0	21.9	24.7
Australia	14.3	15.8	29.4
Italy	12.7	16.6	13.7
UK	12.5	15.4	20.9
Ireland	12.3	14.4	24.3
Canada	11.4	14.9	5.9
Spain	10.1	12.2	11.3
Switzerland	9.3	10.0	8.4
Denmark	9.2	8.7	6.6
Germany	8.3	6.8	11.6
Austria	8.0	10.2	10.5
Belgium	8.0	7.7	11.7
France	8.0	7.9	9.8
Netherlands	7.3	9.8	2.4
Sweden	6.5	4.2	7.7
Norway	6.4	3.4	11.9
Finland	5.4	2.8	8.5

Note 1: Japan, New Zealand and Portugal are excluded from the list of OECD nations because comparable data for these countries were not generated by the *Luxembourg Income Study*.
Note 2: The poverty line is set at 50% of the median income in each country.
Source: Mishel *et al.* 2005: 408.

very rapidly in recent decades, this problem tends to be particularly acute. But for low-income households who already own their own homes or who occupy subsidised public housing, housing costs are a less significant problem. Indeed, these households are less likely to be classified as poor if the definition of the poverty line takes housing costs into account. So, the dilemma for researchers is whether to measure poverty before or after housing costs are considered. This has a major bearing on calculations about the relative incidence of poverty in city and country and among young and old, as well as on calculations about whether poverty is increasing or falling over time.

Multidimensional poverty and social exclusion

Debates about poverty are often plagued by conflict over how it is defined. In Australia, such debates have become so intense that they have been dubbed the 'poverty wars' (Saunders 2005). As noted in this chapter, one aspect of the debate is whether to measure relative or absolute poverty. Another is where to set the poverty line. More recently, discussions about underprivilege have highlighted the importance of multidimensional perspectives on poverty, with concepts such as social exclusion and deprivation being used to describe the interaction of income poverty with other forms of disadvantage.

A focus on multidimensional poverty recognises that non-economic measures are equally as important as economic ones. As economic researcher Boyd Hunter notes, 'The command over resources is undeniably a major factor determining whether a person is poor', but such measures need to be understood in the context of non-monetary poverty, such as 'social welfare indicators, including health, housing and security' (Hunter 1999: v–vii). Hunter suggests that these indicators are not discrete: each impacts upon the others, so that analysis of any factor in isolation will give an incomplete picture of a person's social and economic situation. Similarly, Peter Saunders of the Social Policy Research Centre has argued that, while measuring income poverty is valuable in identifying elements of the population most in need, informing income support policies and allowing longitudinal and international comparisons, it is only 'the first stage in a long journey of understanding that involves a deeper level of appreciation of the many other factors at play' (Saunders 2005: 50).

Recent research has attempted to link measures of income poverty to people's actual experiences and living conditions. This has involved a move away from a narrow concept of poverty to a broader consideration of deprivation and social exclusion. Deprivation, for example, may include a lack of access to services such as adequate public transport. As Saunders notes, while some forms of deprivation may be countered by increasing income, 'more money for bus fares will not combat transport deprivation if there is no local bus service' (Saunders 2005: 64–5). Social exclusion draws on the notion of multidimensional poverty and the inter-action of various factors over time. It can apply to individuals and areas, and it includes 'causes' (such as unemployment and low incomes) and 'outcomes' (such as poor health, high crime and family breakdown) that may 'become apparent . . . as an accumulated response' over time (Saunders 2005: 74). One NATSEM study that developed measures of social exclusion to assess the wellbeing of Australian children reveals significant variability between Australian regions and finds the spatial patterns to be rather different from those based only on a household-income measure of poverty (Daly, McNamara, Tanton, Harding and Yap 2006).

This more multidimensional conception of poverty may also be useful in understanding some of the local community breakdowns and inter-ethnic conflicts that have occurred in Australia in recent years. The ten-sions generated in the outer western Sydney suburb of Macquarie Fields in 2005 are a case in point: here was an area in which people experienc-ing a concentration of problems of social exclusion erupted into sporadic violence on the streets. Running battles between Aboriginal youths and police in the inner Sydney suburb of Redfern in 2004 illustrated the point yet more dramatically. While both episodes were sparked by fatal-ities of young men after reportedly being chased by police, the violence that ensued was indicative of much longer-term problems of social and economic marginalisation.

The concepts of social exclusion and deprivation illuminate the com-plex realities of people's lived experiences and the interplay of various forms of disadvantage. Of course, what constitutes disadvantage may always be disputed. Cross-national comparisons of the incidence of depri-vation and exclusion may be particularly hazardous: after undertaking one such comparison (of Australia and the UK) the authors conclude that 'direct national indicators of deprivation and exclusion cannot be as readily compared cross-nationally as indirect, income based measures' (Saunders and Adelman 2005: 19). Acknowledging and working within those differences is required if researchers are to contribute positively to the lives of Australia's most underprivileged people.

Is poverty declining or growing?

Judgements about long-term trends in the incidence of poverty in Australia are possible because of the classic study undertaken thirty years ago by the distinguished social scientist Professor Ronald Henderson, often referred to as the *Henderson Report* (Henderson 1975). Henderson's main focus was identifying the extent of poverty in terms of inadequate income relative to need. The emphasis given to income in his report was justified on the grounds of 'practicality and significance' in that it is both quantifiable and fundamental to living standards (Saunders 1998: 56). Henderson's study defined the poverty line as a percentage of average Australian earnings, adjusted for household size. For a 'standard family' (that is, a family comprising a man in paid work, a woman not in paid work and two dependent children), the poverty line was set at 56.5 per cent of average earnings (Henderson 1975: 13–14). This has since become known as the 'Henderson poverty line'. According to Henderson's measure, 8.2 per cent of the population were in poverty in 1972–3, accounting for almost 1 million individuals. When housing costs were taken into account, the overall poverty rate was estimated to be 6.4 per cent[1] (King 1998: 83). This reflected the relatively low costs of housing for a number of the poor, particularly the elderly.

Henderson's 1975 study also examined the incidence of poverty in various social groups. Poverty before housing costs was most prevalent among single people aged over 65 and sole parent families headed by women. This latter group was also most likely to experience poverty after housing costs, along with 'the unemployed, the sick and invalid and recent (non-British) migrants' (Saunders 1998: 60). The study also found a very high incidence of poverty among Indigenous Australians and independent young people[2] between the ages of 15 and 20. Assessed according to housing type, the rate of poverty after taking housing costs into account was highest among private renters, who comprised around 40 per cent of the 'after-housing

[1] The Henderson poverty line enables the incidence of poverty to be assessed before and after housing costs are taken into account. As Saunders notes, 'After-housing costs are derived by deducting actual housing costs from income and comparing the remaining income with a poverty line that excludes the housing cost component' (Saunders 1998: 59–60).

[2] The *Henderson Report* categorised children and young adults aged 15–20 as dependent if they were undertaking full-time secondary education. Others in this age group were classed as independent in that they had 'a right to an independent income of their own' and were treated as separate units in measures of poverty (Saunders 1998: 57–8).

poor' (Saunders 1998: 60). This pointed to the importance of the relationship between affordable housing and income-related poverty.

The *Henderson Report* also examined the relationship between poverty
and social security benefits. It found that, while the rate of pension for
married couples was close to the poverty line, the rate for single people
was 20 per cent below the poverty line. For couples with children and for
single parents, the gap between social security benefits and the poverty line
increased with the number of children (Saunders 1998: 61). Because poverty
was most prevalent among the elderly and families with dependent children,
the report argued that job creation would not solve poverty and that social
security benefits needed to be raised.

Henderson's analysis of the causes of poverty warrants revisiting. In addition to inadequate social welfare payments, his report identified the level of
rents for private rental housing, the lack of employment opportunities, geo-
graphic location, Aboriginality and recent arrival in Australia (especially
from non-English-speaking countries) as factors contributing to poverty.
Reflecting this wide range of causes, the anti-poverty measures he recom-
mended were broad-based, including housing policies and specific policies
to address the needs of the most disadvantaged groups.

How does the current situation compare to that identified in Henderson's
report? Has there been progress in reducing the incidence of poverty in
Australia? A simple definitive answer is difficult because there are so many
dimensions to poverty; also, there are conceptual and practical issues to
be considered in determining the appropriate adjustments to be made to
the poverty line over time (Johnson 1996). However, a number of research
studies have shed some light on what has changed in the three decades since
the *Henderson Report*. One such study, conducted by Anthony King in the
mid 1990s, used the Henderson poverty line to establish what had happened
to poverty in Australia over the preceding two decades. It found that 14.4
per cent of Australians (over 1.4 million people) were in 'before-housing'
poverty in 1996, an increase of over 6 per cent since 1975 (King 1998: 83).

More recently, NATSEM has used the ABS *2000–01 Survey of Income and
Housing Costs* to determine the level of poverty (Lloyd *et al.* 2004a). Like the
Henderson Report, the NATSEM study assesses poverty according to income,
in this case setting the poverty line at half the median income, equivalised for
household size. This is a widely used measure of poverty and puts the 2001
poverty line at $408 per week after tax for a standard family (comprising a

couple with two children) and $194 per week for a single person (Lloyd *et al*. 2004a). The NATSEM study found that the 'before housing' poverty rate among all Australians was 11 per cent in 2001, meaning that over 2 million people (almost one in every nine Australians) were living in poverty (Lloyd *et al*. 2004a: 4).

Direct comparisons of this NATSEM study with the Henderson study are problematic. The two utilise different equivalence scales to take account of household size, so comparisons of the data sets should be done with some caution, although this difference in scales has only a marginal impact on results (see Appendix B at the end of this book). Of more fundamental significance are the different definitions of the poverty line. Setting the poverty line for a standard family at half the median income, as the *NATSEM Report* does, is a more austere measure of poverty than the 56.5 per cent of average earnings used in the *Henderson Report*. The *NATSEM Report* therefore presents a more conservative estimate of the number of Australians living in poverty than would be the case if the Henderson methodology were applied. So, comparing the 8.2 per cent of people in before housing poverty in 1972–3 with the 11 per cent in poverty in 2001 probably tends to underestimate the increase in relative poverty over the three decades. Supporting this inference, a recent review of the evidence on poverty presented to the 2004 Senate Inquiry into Poverty and Financial Hardship found that, on the lowest estimate, poverty in Australia had 'hardly changed' since the mid 1970s, and on most estimates had increased (Saunders 2005: 2).

Why, despite the rising national income in Australia over the last three decades, has poverty proved so persistent, even increased? The most obvious answer is that, if poverty is defined in relative terms, it must persist unless economic growth is accompanied by a more even distribution of income. Indeed, increased economic inequality necessarily produces more relative poverty. That is a matter of simple arithmetic. More subtly, another explanation is that, because particular social groups are structurally disadvantaged, they persistently miss out in terms of their capacity to share in the wealth of an increasingly affluent society. Why that is so, then, becomes a matter for detailed social analysis, looking at how poverty affects relatively marginalised groups – the aged, the unemployed, sole parents, Indigenous Australians, recent immigrants and people with disabilities.[3]

[3] Note that both the NATSEM (2004) and Henderson (1975) poverty studies exclude people who are permanently institutionalised. The NATSEM study also excludes those in

Poverty and age

Which groups in society are most vulnerable to poverty? Traditionally, one would have said, first and foremost, the elderly. This was certainly the case at the time of Henderson's study, when single people aged 65 and over were particularly highly represented among the poor. Of single males and single females over 65, 36.6 per cent and 31 per cent respectively then had incomes below the poverty line (Henderson 1975: 18). However, over the past thirty years, the aged have fared relatively better than the young, although people commonly still experience their maximum incomes in the middle years of life and lower incomes at the earlier and later stages.

The NATSEM study found that 9.9 per cent of Australians aged 65 and over were living in poverty in 2004,[4] a rate somewhat below the national average household poverty rate of 11 per cent (Lloyd et al. 2004a: 7). Although, as noted earlier, the findings of the NATSEM study and the *Henderson Report* are not directly comparable in terms of the absolute numbers of people identified as being in poverty, this lower rate is indicative of significant shifts in the incidence of poverty among the different age groups. Nevertheless, the earlier OECD comparison, although calculated on a different statistical basis, suggests that Australia lags behind other countries' performance in dealing with the vulnerability to poverty of aged people. Australian pensions policies have put much less emphasis on maintaining incomes close to pre-retirement levels than have European and North American nations.

A further comparison of poverty rates across age groups is provided in figure 5.1, which shows the highest average poverty rate in 2001 to be among people aged 15–24 years, with 17.4 per cent of this group having incomes below the poverty line (here measured as half the median income, equivalised for household size) (Lloyd et al. 2004a: 7). The incidence of poverty among these young people varied significantly according to whether they were still living in the family home or living away from home. Those living at home and dependent on the family income had a poverty rate of 6.8 per cent, well below the national average. Those living at home but financially independent had the highest rate of poverty, at 30.4 per cent. Those living away from home

'non-private dwellings', such as temporary accommodation (for example, boarding houses). The following discussion also largely excludes these groups from analysis.

[4] Unless otherwise stated, this and all subsequent references to poverty rates refer to 'before housing' poverty.

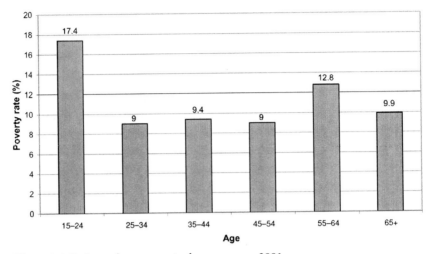

Figure 5.1 Estimated poverty rates by age group, 2001
Note: Indicates 'before housing' poverty, estimated for people aged 15 years and over.
Source: Lloyd *et al.* 2004a: 7.

had an intermediate poverty rate, at 18.8 per cent (Lloyd *et al.* 2004a: 8). There are a number of reasons for these quite high rates of youth poverty. People in this age bracket are more likely than those aged 25–64 to have insecure, low-paid jobs. They are also more likely to be engaged in further education, which has significant effects on the incidence of poverty since the maximum rate of social security benefits paid to students or unemployed people of this age has been below the poverty line – by an estimated $49 per week in 2001, according to the NATSEM study (Lloyd *et al.* 2004a: 7).

Another age group vulnerable to poverty is that of people aged 55–64. The NATSEM analysis shows 12.8 per cent of this group as having incomes below the poverty line in 2001 (Lloyd *et al.* 2004a: 7). This above-average incidence of poverty sits at odds with a popular perception of 55–64 year olds 'enjoying the good life' (as noted by Lloyd *et al.* 2004a: 8). Early retirement is evidently a factor here. A different study carried out by NATSEM (in conjunction with the financial institution AMP) found the average age at which Australians are retiring to be 41 for women and 58 for men (Kelly *et al.* 2004, cited in Lloyd *et al.* 2004a: 8). Since the majority of people cannot receive the aged pension until they are 65, those retiring younger are usually living off other sources of income, such as their personal savings or superannuation (which is normally paid at a reduced rate to early retirees). The NATSEM-AMP study found that, of those who retired between the ages of 50 and 54, most were living on incomes below $10 000 a year (in Lloyd *et al.* 2004a: 8). In addition, of those aged 55–64 and continuing to work, the number employed part-time increased with age (Lloyd *et al.* 2004a: 8). The rate of poverty in this 55–64 age group may also be affected by the increasing tendency of children to continue living in the family home well into their twenties, placing demands on their parents' financial resources for longer periods of time (Lloyd *et al.* 2004a: 7–8; Harding *et al.* 2003: 2).

What about the incidence of poverty among children? Henderson's earlier study had identified about a quarter of a million dependent children living in families that were in poverty (Henderson 1975: 1). Labor Prime Minister Bob Hawke famously claimed in the 1980s that his government's policies would ensure that no child need live in poverty. A recent Senate committee set up to investigate poverty and financial hardship in Australia – hereafter called the Senate inquiry into poverty – found that the incidence of child poverty did decline between 1982 and 1997–8, but it then rose in the last two years of the 1990s (Senate Community Affairs References Committee Secretariat 2004). Using the half median poverty line indicates a smaller percentage of children in poverty than using either the updated Henderson poverty line or setting the poverty line as half the average income. But, while the magnitude of such changes differs significantly according to the particular poverty line used, the general direction of the shifts remains the same.

Based on the more conservative measure of half median income, poverty among dependent children fell from 13.1 per cent in 1982 to 8.8 per cent in 1997–8, rising to 9.6 per cent in 2000. This would mean that 479 000 children were in poverty in that latter year (Senate Community Affairs References Committee Secretariat 2004: 242). About another 145 000 young people aged 15–24 are also estimated to be living in poverty, half of whom live at home (Mission Australia 2004). Child poverty evidently persists as a major social problem (see also Bradbury 2003). Journalist Adele Horin notes that the most striking rise in child poverty in the 1990s was among children of the 'working poor'. She argues that this reflects the program of 'welfare reform', which moved 'social-security recipients into low-paid or casual jobs', but which did 'not necessarily lift families out of poverty' (Horin 2000: 2). In 2000 child poverty rates were considerably higher after their carers' housing costs were taken into account, at 17.0 per cent. This is the opposite of poverty among the aged, perhaps reflecting the higher than average housing costs of couples with children and the increased number of working poor families who have relatively high housing costs as a result of trying to purchase a home (Senate Community Affairs References Committee Secretariat 2004: 242–3).

Out of work: in poverty

The unemployed have always been particularly vulnerable to poverty. This is not surprising, but the tendency has become accentuated. According to social policy researcher Anthony King, over the last quarter century 'Australian poverty has shifted from a problem for the aged to a problem for the unemployed' (King 1998: 85). Of course, before then – going back to the interwar years of the Great Depression in particular – the nexus between unemployment and poverty had been the dominant political economic concern. Unemployment has never hit these catastrophic levels since, but its connection with poverty remains very strong. In the early 1970s the poverty rate among the unemployed was around 17 per cent, but King's study indicates that it had increased to a staggering 74 per cent by 1996. Over the same period unemployment had grown from 1.8 per cent to 8.5 per cent of the labour force (after peaking even higher at around 11 per cent in 1991), so the total number of unemployed people in poverty had grown even more than the fourfold increase in the poverty rate suggests.

The slow but fairly steady decline in official unemployment rates since the 1991 peak has evidently not eradicated the problem of unemployment-related poverty. The recent NATSEM study found that the poverty rate among the unemployed was higher than in any other group defined in the study (see figure 5.2). At 41.1 per cent, the poverty rate for this group was almost four times the national average poverty rate of 11 per cent (Lloyd et al. 2004a: 14), apparently rather lower than in the mid 1990s but still disturbingly high.[5] The NATSEM Report also noted that the maximum rate

[5] The NATSEM findings are based on a more conservative measure of poverty than King's 1998 study, setting the poverty line at half the median income rather than using the Henderson

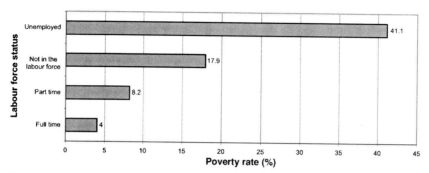

Figure 5.2 Estimated poverty rates by workforce
Note: Indicates 'before housing' poverty, estimated for people aged 15 years and over.
Source: Lloyd *et al.* 2004a: 15.

of unemployment benefits in 2001 was $19 per week below the poverty line (Lloyd *et al.* 2004a: 14). A recent report by the Melbourne Institute of Applied Economic and Social Research (2006), using an updated Henderson poverty line, suggests that this situation has deteriorated even further since then. Single adults receiving unemployment benefits fare worst, having weekly incomes $77 below the poverty line; for unemployed couples the combined weekly benefit is $28–34 below the poverty line.[6]

The 2001 NATSEM study found that, when viewed according to labour force status, 58 per cent of all Australians living in poverty were deemed to be 'not in the workforce'. This includes people out of work but not seeking employment, such as those on disability and carers' pensions, and long-term unemployed people who have given up looking for work and are therefore no longer receiving unemployment benefits. Of these people, 17.9 per cent had incomes below the poverty line (Lloyd *et al.* 2004a: 15).

Although waged employment is the principal antidote to poverty, it does not necessarily eradicate it. Low-paid jobs, especially when less than full time, can leave employed people with disposable income below the poverty line (Eardley 2000). According to the NATSEM study, the poverty rates

poverty line. While the *NATSEM Report* tends therefore to relatively understate the incidence of poverty, the large discrepancy between the two figures is likely to be at least in part attributable to a decline in poverty among the unemployed since the mid 1990s.
[6] These calculations include Family Tax Benefits Part A and Part B and rent assistance. They do not include non-cash benefits such as concessions for health care, transport and other services.

for people in part-time and full-time work in 2001 were 8.2 and 4 per cent respectively. Combined, full-time and part-time workers made up 27 per cent of all Australians living in poverty, when analysed according to workforce status (Lloyd *et al.* 2004a: 15). A comparison with the Henderson poverty study suggests that the incidence of working poverty has grown over the last thirty years, employment in the early 1970s having previously been regarded as 'a virtual guarantee against poverty' (King, in Watson and Buchanan 2001: 208). It is not so now, as journalist Elizabeth Wynhausen's documentation of her personal experiences among Australia's working poor graphically illustrate (Wynhausen 2005: see also Rooney 2006).

Perhaps the most striking feature of the last two decades is the emergence of the growing divide between households with two income earners and those with none (Watson and Buchanan 2001). The NATSEM study found that poverty rate among households with no one in paid employment in 2001 was 26.2 per cent, well above the national average of 11 per cent and over ten times greater than for households with two full-time earners, among whom the poverty rate was only 2.4 per cent. Households with no income earners accounted for 62.9 per cent of all people in poverty (Lloyd *et al.* 2004a: 16). The NATSEM study also showed households with one part-time earner to be almost three times as likely to be living in poverty as households with one full-time earner: the poverty rates for these two groups were 17.8 and 6.2 per cent respectively (Lloyd *et al.* 2004a: 16).

Rather different figures on the poverty rates of unemployed individuals, according to whether they live in households with other people who are employed or unemployed, derive from data in the HILDA survey (Scutella and Wooden 2004). These show a poverty rate of 56.2 per cent for people who are unemployed and living in households where no one else has a job either, six times higher than the poverty rate for unemployed people who live in a household where someone else has a job. In the latter case the poverty rate is 9.4 per cent, which is only a couple of percentage points below the overall poverty rate for employed people.

Being out of work for an extended duration predictably creates a particular propensity to poverty. Unemployment is officially considered to be long-term when the duration of unemployment is more than one year. During the 1980s about one-quarter of the unemployed were, according to this definition, long-term but this proportion rose to around one-third for most of the 1990s. The ABS estimates on workforce participation showed 518 400 people as unemployed in August 2006, representing 4.8 per cent of the work-force. Of these, 18.1 per cent were classified as long-term unemployed (ABS 2006d: 5). The average length of unemployment was 39.7 weeks, or around nine months (ABS 2006d: 48), which compares to an average duration of unemployment of only ten weeks in 1973 when the last golden age of full employment was drawing to a close (Watson and Buchanan 2001: 196). This increased average length of unemployment is problematic since, as noted previously, the maximum rate of unemployment benefits for couples and single adults remains below the poverty line.

Solo poverty

Although less numerous than the unemployed poor, single people and sole parents are dramatically overrepresented among those classified in the NATSEM study as living in poverty. These are overlapping categories. Assessed according to income unit type, 45 per cent of those in poverty are single and a further 14 per cent are sole parent households. Together, these groups account for almost six out every ten people in poverty (Lloyd *et al.* 2004a: 10). Among single people, poverty rates decrease with age, from 29.6 per cent among single 15–24 years olds to 15.6 per cent among single people aged over 64. In all age groups, poverty rates among single people are higher than the national average of 11 per cent (Lloyd *et al.* 2004a: 11).

Poverty rates for sole parents have also been well above the national aver-age, at 18.2 per cent, or nearly one in five (Lloyd *et al.* 2004a: 11). According to King's earlier study, 23.6 per cent of female sole parents and 20.2 per cent of male sole parents were living in poverty in 1996. This indicated a decrease in poverty among female sole parents and an increase in poverty for male sole parents since 1975, when the rates were 36.5 and 13.1 per cent respec-tively (King 1998: 88). As was the case in these earlier periods, single parent families still experience a higher rate of poverty than any other family type. Not surprisingly, the risk is greater in single parent families with more than one child (Senate Community Affairs References Committee Secretariat

2004: 224). Expenses in these families are higher, and the additional time needed for childrearing means that possibilities of taking paid employment are more limited. Other more general causes of the high incidence of poverty among sole parents may include disadvantages in the labour market, such as discrimination against sole parents in employment, the difficulties of combining parenting with paid work and the resultant increased reliance on paid childcare, which is usually expensive. The unequal financial positions of custodial and non-custodial parents, the higher costs of separated families and the inadequacy of income support payments are further factors contributing to poverty among this group (Senate Community Affairs References Committee Secretariat 2004: 226–7).

Indigenous peoples' poverty

Indigenous Australians have particularly high poverty rates, which interact with their experience of the long-standing problems of discrimination and exclusion. This was recognised in the 1975 Henderson study and has been a recurrent theme in subsequent poverty studies. The recent Senate inquiry into poverty, for example, commented that Indigenous Australians are still 'the most disadvantaged and marginalised group in Australia' (Senate Community Affairs References Committee Secretariat 2004: 301). The nature and extent of Indigenous disadvantage has led Boyd Hunter from the Centre for Aboriginal Economic Policy Research at the ANU to argue that Australia is divided into three distinct nations: 'the rich, the poor non-indigenous Australians, and indigenous Australians' (Hunter 1999: v).

On all socioeconomic indicators – income, employment, housing, education and health – Indigenous Australians fare worst. They experience a lower life expectancy, higher rates of infant mortality, higher unemployment rates, lower general standards of health and housing and higher rates of homelessness, arrest and imprisonment (Lamb 2005; see also Altman and Hunter 1998). The average life expectancy of Indigenous Australians is almost twenty years below that of other Australians: while the average life expectancy at birth for all Australians is 76.6 years for males and 82.0 years for females, the corresponding figures for Indigenous Australians are only 59.4 years and 64.8 years respectively[7] (ABS 2005e). Increased health risks and higher mortality rates for Indigenous peoples perpetuate the cycle of poverty and disadvantage, limiting employment opportunities and increasing the burden of care.

Although this evidence on social and economic disadvantages is incontrovertible, reliable comparative data on Indigenous poverty are difficult to obtain. Most statistics on income inequality, from which poverty rates are derived, exclude people living in remote communities, which includes significant numbers of Indigenous Australians. Nevertheless, some calculations of the extent of Indigenous income poverty have been attempted. One estimate is that around 30 per cent of Indigenous households have incomes inadequate to avoid poverty (Senate Community Affairs References Committee Secretariat 2004: 302).

Boyd Hunter (1999) has argued that measures of poverty are culturally specific and that a focus on a lack of income is inadequate in representing the Indigenous experience. He suggests that poor health and negative encounters with the criminal justice system, for example, are disproportionately experienced by even the relatively wealthier Indigenous households. Similarly, the Senate inquiry into poverty noted that 'non-material poverty, in terms of dispossession from the land, and absolute material deprivation suffered by Aboriginal people suggest a different order of poverty from that experienced by the rest of the population' (Senate Community Affairs References Committee Secretariat 2004: 301–2).

Rates of absolute poverty as well as relative poverty are also much higher among the Indigenous population. The lack of infrastructure and services in many remote Indigenous communities indicates a qualitatively different nature of poverty as compared to more populous areas. It shows up in the high prevalence among Indigenous Australians of malnutrition and diseases that have been largely eradicated in the rest of the population (Senate Community Affairs References Committee Secretariat 2004: 303). Such evidence ranks Australian Indigenous

[7] The figures for Indigenous life expectancy are the latest available at the time of writing and refer to the period 1996–2001. The life expectancies for all Australians refer to the period 1998–2000. It should be noted that, due to limitations of the data, the ABS categorises the Indigenous life expectancy figures as 'experimental'.

poverty alongside countries as poor as Bangladesh. It also illustrates the importance of recognising that poverty is multidimensional, with poor health often undermining income-earning potentials.

The interplay of multiple dimensions of poverty was highlighted recently when the Northern Territory community of Wadeye was thrust into the national spotlight following claims of community breakdown and 'civil war' there. While the violence in Wadeye and other remote communities has had its roots in the dispossession and ill treatment of Indigenous Australians and cannot be reduced to a purely economic cause, it has no doubt been exacerbated by the lack of adequate local services and employment. As Thamarrurr Council's Dale Seaniger reported on Wadeye, the fundamental problem is 'the basics, the housing, the health, the education' (ABC Online 2006). On all accounts, and by any measure, Indigenous poverty remains 'deeply entrenched and persistent' and should be an area of serious national concern (Senate Community Affairs References Committee Secretariat 2004: 322).

Immigrants and refugees in poverty

Recently arrived immigrants also remain overrepresented among the poor, as they were when Henderson's original poverty study was conducted in 1975. According to the *NATSEM Report* (2004), 16.5 per cent of Australian residents born in non-English-speaking countries were living in poverty in 2001. This compares to 10.1 per cent of people born in Australia and 7.2 per cent of people born in English-speaking countries other than Australia (Lloyd *et al.* 2004a: 9).

There are a number of factors contributing to these differential poverty rates, of which participation in the labour market is perhaps the most important. The recent Senate inquiry into poverty found that, excluding those on business visas, recently arrived immigrants tend to experience unemployment rates above the national average (Senate Community Affairs References Committee Secretariat 2004: 352). Difficulties in finding employment often arise from problems with English proficiency and from the lack of recognition of qualifications gained in overseas countries on the part of the Australian government. The report of the Senate inquiry into poverty identifies immigrants as facing increased risk of long-term unemployment and underemployment, noting that their need to quickly find work to support their families can create a poverty trap, with many immigrants finding themselves 'in jobs that not only have poor pay but [may] also be less secure than other jobs' (Senate Community Affairs References Committee Secretariat 2004: 358). This vulnerability is of particular concern since most immigrants arriving in the 'skilled' and 'family' streams face a two-year waiting period before they can access unemployment benefits. According to evidence presented by the Canterbury–Bankstown Migrant Resource Centre to the Senate inquiry (Senate Community Affairs References Committee Secretariat 2004: 357), immigrants affected by this two-year waiting period often experience an increase in mental illness, poor nutrition, inadequate housing, homelessness and exposure to workplace exploitation.

A Department of Immigration and Multicultural Affairs (DIMA) report found that, in 2004–5, of the total Australian workforce 24.9 per cent were overseas-born. Of these, 14.5 per cent were from non-English-speaking countries (NESC) and 10.4 per cent from the main English-speaking countries (MESC) (DIMA 2006). While unemployment rates have improved for both of these groups over the last decade, they have remained significantly higher among NESC immigrants. Recent figures indicate an unemployment rate of 6.2 per cent for this group, compared to a rate of 4.7 per cent for the Australian-born and only 4.1 per cent for MESC immigrants. The DIMA report also noted that, for people from non-English-speaking countries, unemployment is 'more strongly affected by changes in economic conditions' (DIMA 2006: 83).

The problems are partly transitional. For immigrants from both English-speaking and non-English-speaking countries, average unemployment rates decrease and median weekly incomes increase with the passage of time after arrival in Australia. Moreover, the proportion of immigrants employed in skilled occupations increases with the length of residence (Department of Immigration and Multicultural Affairs 2005: 85). Many first- and second-generation immigrants in Australia have created their own job opportunities through self-employment as small-scale entrepreneurs (Collins *et al.* 1995). Some have gone on to develop large businesses and reap considerable economic rewards, including a number of wealthy people on the *BRW*'s 'Rich 200' list discussed in chapter 4. Not surprisingly, immigrants who enter Australia under the 'business' and 'skilled' categories have commonly found work in technical and professional occupations (Collins *et al.* 1995).

Ivan Light (2005) has argued that the tendency of immigrants to move into self-employment or employment in family businesses is often a response to disadvantage and the inability to find alternative work, particularly for immigrants from non-English-speaking backgrounds. While some find success, many others become trapped in low-productivity, low-income work, often in the informal sector. Light draws from the American experience; for immigrants with poor English-language skills and without recognised qualifications, similar patterns are likely to be present in Australia. We do know that there are clear differences in economic outcomes for immigrants in different streams of immigration programs: while incomes for both skilled and family immigrants increase with length of stay, those of family immigrants remain significantly lower. For immigrants arriving between September 1999 and August 2000, for example, the median weekly incomes of those with skilled migrant visas had reached $600 eighteen months after arrival. In contrast, the median income for those with family visas was still only $200 per week (Department of Immigration and Multicultural Affairs 2005: 85). Overall, there is a positive long-term economic outcome for most immigrants and their families; however, this does not negate the obvious difficulties faced by some groups of immigrants, nor should it obscure questions regarding the adequacy of support services available to them.

Concerns about adequate services are nowhere more apparent than in relation to refugees. Official government data show that people accepted into the country on humanitarian grounds experience consistently higher unemployment rates than other immigrants. For those arriving between September 1999 and August 2000, the unemployment rate for humanitarian visa holders six months after arrival was over 70 per cent compared to around 20 per cent for those with family visas and just over 10 per cent for skilled immigrants. Eighteen months after arrival, the unemployment rates for the latter two groups were around 10 and 5 per cent respectively, while around 40 per cent of humanitarian visa holders were still unemployed (Department of Immigration and Multicultural Affairs 2005: 86).

Restricting the support services available to humanitarian visa holders is an issue of particular concern. Some refugees are granted Permanent Protection Visas (PPVs), but the federal government invented the special category of Temporary Protection Visas (TPVs) in 1999 to limit the rights of other refugees to stay in the country and to deny them access to a range of services and benefits while they are here (Mares 2002). For example, TPV holders have been ineligible for government-assisted language programs and intensive job-seeking assistance, which limits their capacity to escape poverty while they are in Australia. TPV holders are also entitled to only 80 per cent of the standard unemployment benefit (Senate Community Affairs References Committee Secretariat 2004). The restriction on benefits increases the risk of poverty among those unable to get work, particularly because even the full rate of unemployment benefit is below the poverty line. In practice many of the refugees holding TPVs have sought jobs, sometimes by going to country towns – such as Young (NSW), Murray Bridge (SA) and Albany (WA) – to work in abattoirs (Stilwell 2003b).

Poverty among people with disabilities

The presence of personal disability correlates strongly with the incidence of poverty. The landmark Henderson study found a poverty rate of 21.4 per cent among households in which the household head had experienced sickness or handicap for more than eight weeks in the year, more than twice the incidence of poverty in the total population at that time (Henderson 1975: 283). King later study found that, by 1996, this figure had increased to 26.7 per cent, although it was much lower – only 6.2 per cent – after housing costs were taken into account (King 1998: 88). The more recent Senate inquiry into poverty also noted the persistence of poverty among people with disabilities, with poverty described as isability close companion(Queensland Government, in Senate Community Affairs References Committee Secretariat 2004: 363).

A number of factors contribute to this close connection between disability and poverty. They include problems of workforce participation, the extra costs of living and inadequate official assistance. On average, people with a disability have lower workforce participation rates and higher unemployment rates than most other groups in society. Combined with the higher costs of living associated with having a disability – such as the costs of medication, special equipment and appropriate housing – this leads to an increased risk of poverty. Peter Saunders estimates that the costs of disability verage about 29 per cent of (equivalised) household income, rising to between 40 and 49 per cent of income for those with a severe or profound restriction Taking account of these costs, the estimated incidence of poverty among people with a disability rises to about six times higher than for people without a disability (Saunders 2006: 22).

Inadequate government assistance in a number of policy areas exacerbates the situation. Several reports to the Senate inquiry into poverty argued that income support for people with disabilities is insufficient and does not cover the increased costs brought about by having a disability. The inquiry also identified significant deficiencies in government service provision, with an estimated 12,500 people needing accommodation and respite services and 5400 people with disabilities needing access to employment services (Senate Community Affairs References Committee Secretariat 2004).

Social researcher Peter Gibilisco (2003) argues that, fundamentally, the disadvantage experienced by people with disabilities is due to discrimination and exclusion. The dominant representation of disability as a purely medical phenomenon shifts the focus away from the responsibility of society to accommodate people with a disability, labelling the impairment, rather than society response to it, as the problem. This reasoning emphasises that what constitutes a disability is, to an extent, subjectively defined. Argyrous and Neale (2003) note the impact of this ambiguity in policy relating to social security payments, arguing that changing criteria for establishing disability have enabled governments to shift income support recipients between unemployment benefits and disability pensions. Hence, decreases in the official unemployment rate have coincided with rapid increases in the number of people of working age receiving disability support pensions. This may be clever politics, but it makes it more difficult to assess the changes in the proportions of people vulnerable to poverty because of disability and unemployment.

Conclusion

Deprivation continues to exist in Australian society despite substantial increases in overall material living standards. Indeed, the poor are still with us. Of course, there will always be different conceptions of what constitutes poverty, how to measure it and how to tackle it, but it is clear that, as a society, we cannot get rid of relative poverty (defined by having incomes below a certain proportion, such as 50 per cent of the overall median or mean incomes) while substantial economic inequality exists. It is a point that can be made with various political inferences. On the one hand, those on the political Right tacitly accept the persistence of poverty, in relative terms, as a necessary condition for the 'incentivation' processes that neoliberal policies promote.[8] On the other hand, those on the political Left emphasise the need to tackle the broader structures of economic inequality from which the particular problems of poverty derive. An echo of the Marxian concept of the reserve army of labour sounds in both of these chains of reasoning. In the former case, the emphasis is, in effect, on reproducing poverty in order to keep the rest of the workforce on its toes. In the latter case, the emphasis is on changing the economic system to one that does not require major inequalities as a condition for its normal functioning.

Another inference to be drawn from the detailed evidence reviewed in this chapter has a more social democratic – or even small 'l' liberal – character. It is that, because particular social groups are vulnerable to poverty, their needs must be explicitly considered if the overall problem of poverty is ever to be resolved. This suggests the need for a more tailored approach to the eradication of poverty and recognises the diverse character of the problems of economic and social marginalisation. It is a conclusion that sits uncomfortably with the current trend towards mainstreaming in social and welfare services. By the same token, it is also important to recognise that the uneven incidence of poverty also has a spatial dimension – varying systematically between different cities and regions.

[8] Others on the political Right are in denial. The report prepared by NATSEM for the Smith Family (Harding, Lloyd & Greenwell 2001) was a particular target for critics from the Centre for Independent Studies, the pro-market neoliberal 'think' tank (Saunders [CIS] & Tsumori 2002). Deep-seated philosophical and moral differences over the meaning of poverty and what to do about it, as well as some technical issues of poverty measurement, were revealed in the subsequent public debate. According to Peter Saunders from the SPRC (not the Peter Saunders from CIS), the CIS intervention was intended 'to shift the focus of debate away from the growing numbers in poverty . . . onto an obsession with the failure of the poor themselves and of the welfare state programs to assist them' (Saunders 2006: 7).

Chapter Six

DIVIDED SPACES

Where do the rich and poor live? Not surprisingly, there are distinctive geographical patterns. Social differences based on class, age, gender, sexuality, religion, culture and health are etched into city structures. The same is true of the broader regional landscapes, where social and economic conditions vary significantly between the metropolitan and non-metropolitian areas. Economic inequalities, based on industry and occupation, employment and unemployment, produce a complex mosaic of relative wealth and disadvantage.

The spatial dimension to economic inequality exists in all countries. This reflects its systemic character. Space acts as a medium through which those with the most wealth and income express their preferences – for business locations, housing, recreation and transport, among others – while those with less economic resources take what is left. As the geographer David Harvey put it, 'Low income populations, usually lacking the means to overcome and hence command space, find themselves for the most part trapped in space' (Harvey 1989: 265). Space then becomes more than a medium through which inequalities are expressed: it becomes a mechanism by which those inequalities are reproduced and reinforced. The spatial dimension of inequality is particularly striking in Australia because a highly urbanised pattern of population coexists with vast tracts of what has come to be known as 'regional and rural Australia'.

The socioeconomic significance of location is reflected in the common process of seeking to pigeonhole a new acquaintance by asking 'Where do you live?' instead of the more traditional 'What do you do?' or 'What is your job?' In academic research the equivalent tendency is to prioritise study of the spatial aspect of inequality as if it were the primary causal factor of socioeconomic inequality in general. Somewhere between that spatial fetishism and the opposite extreme of spatial blindness – still characteristic of much orthodox economic thinking – lies an important avenue of enquiry and analysis. In other words, we need to recognise that, while socioeconomic inequalities may have deeper roots – as noted in preceding chapters – they are manifest in distinctive spatial patterns. In seeking to explore these issues, this chapter describes the relationship between economic inequality and location in Australian cities, discusses the broader problems of regional inequality and reflects on why spatial inequalities matter.

Urban inequality

Penny Wong, Labor Senator for South Australia, stated in her maiden speech to the Australian Parliament in 2002 that 'We are a nation in which where you live determines your likelihood of success' (Wong 2002). Her statement echoed former Labor Prime Minister Gough Whitlam's famous remark about inequality.

> Increasingly, a citizen's real standard of living, the health of himself and his family, his children's opportunities for education and self-improvement, his access to employment opportunities, his ability to enjoy the nation's resources for recreation and culture, his ability to participate in the decisions and actions of the community are determined not by his income, not by the hours he works, but by where he lives (1972 Policy Speech, cited in Badcock 1984: 50).

Indeed, this spatial dimension of inequality has long been of concern for progressive reforming politicians – and for good reasons. Spatial inequalities can be a major obstacle to achieving the goal of social justice. Their roots are complex, including the operations of housing and labour markets and differences in the quality and availability of schools, transport and local services.

Housing costs are a particularly significant driver of urban socioeconomic differentiation. Affluent suburbs and poorer areas are effectively defined by the different property values that prevail in each. The residential property market acts, in effect, as a sorting mechanism. It produces complex socio-economic patterns rather than a simple polarisation between rich and poor suburbs, because even silvertail suburbs often have some poorer housing and *vice versa*. Moreover, the patterns can change significantly over time, as they have done in inner-city suburbs experiencing gentrification over recent decades. That said, the broad patterns of intra-urban inequality in all Australian cities are of long standing and widely recognised. There is also evidence that housing costs – which fundamentally reflect land values – are tending to increase these inequalities.

The impact of the housing market on urban spatial inequality has been particularly apparent in recent years, ratcheted up by urban real estate booms such as that of 2000–3. The higher costs of land and housing have outstripped increases in average incomes, causing a crisis of housing affordability in many Australian cities. This increased ratio of housing costs to earnings has created a scissors effect for many low- and middle-income households, requiring higher proportions of income to be allocated for housing expenditure. Relatively low interest rates – in comparison to those prevailing in the late 1980s and early 1990s – masked the problem to some extent up to 2006, by enabling new owner-occupiers to take on larger debts. Now, home owners and tenants are having to cope with acute stresses, which current and future interest rate rises predictably intensify.

A household is officially defined as being in housing stress when it pays 30 per cent or more of its net income for housing (Hawtrey 2002). By 2003, low- and middle-income earners in Australian cities were usually paying between one-third and one-half of their income for housing, which includes rent, mortgage repayments and interest on housing loans. For first home buyers, the average proportion of income going to mortgage repayments was 47 per cent (Wade 2004). These aspiring home owners have been the most obvious losers in this situation of declining housing affordability, but those on low and middle incomes in the private rental sector have also felt the squeeze, as increases in rents have tended to follow increases in housing prices.

The distributional consequences of the fall in housing affordability have also been geographically diverse, partly because the severity of the crisis has not been spatially uniform. Property price inflation has been most pronounced in the state and territory capitals, including Perth, as well as those on the eastern seaboard, but even within those cities the impacts have been uneven. Those areas that are more attractive to live in (due to their environmental features and residential amenity) have generally experienced the highest housing prices, with the gentrifying suburbs featuring particularly rapid inflation. This has created distinctive local patterns of housing stress (Randolph and Holloway 2002). It has also locked lower- and middle-income earners out of the most desirable areas. Hence, one general effect of the decline in housing affordability has been to accentuate locational differentiation between income groups.[1]

The labour market also affects spatial inequality. Higher-income earners tend to be concentrated in particular geographical locations within cities, while those at the other extreme, without regular jobs, form different distinctive clusters. Within Sydney, for example, the official unemployment rate in the southwestern suburbs centred on Fairfield and Liverpool was 9.9 per cent in 2001, twice the average for the rest of the city at that time (ABS 2001: 5). Looking more closely at individual suburbs, the disparities are even more striking. Eight of the suburbs within the Fairfield–Liverpool area had unemployment rates of over 17 per cent. In Cabramatta, 21 per cent of residents were out of work (Senate Community Affairs References Committee 2003). Meanwhile, affluent areas on Sydney's north shore were experiencing unemployment rates as low as 2 per cent. A similar picture is evident in other Australian cities. In northwestern Melbourne 7.7 per cent of the local population were out of work in 2001, compared to 5.9 per cent for the rest of the city (ABS 2002a: 4). Not surprisingly, areas with higher rates of unemployment also tend to be the least well off in terms of a range of socioeconomic indicators and thus constitute significant pockets of urban disadvantage (Vinson 1999; Macklin 2002; Senate Community Affairs References Committee 2003).

Some interesting recent research by NATSEM has sought to map these patterns of disadvantage for small areas in Victoria, Queensland and the ACT (Chin, Harding and Tanton 2006). Using microsimulation techniques, and

---

[1] See Harding *et al.* (2002) for details of the spatial dimension of income inequality within each of Australia's states and territories.

defining households as poor if their equivalised disposable income in 2001 was below $205.20, an average of 10.1 per cent of households were estimated to be in poverty. However, many localities had an estimated incidence of poverty around twice that average, or even higher. Prominent examples in urban areas are Braddon (ACT) with 27 per cent, Inala (Brisbane) with 23 per cent, and parts of Melbourne (Preston, Essendon, Maribyrnong and central Melbourne: remainder) that also have above average scores. Striking concentrations of poor households are also indicated for non-metropolitan areas such as Mount Morgan, the Darling Downs and the Wide Bay–Burnett region in Queensland and the Latrobe Valley and Gippsland, Loddon and the central goldfields areas in Victoria.

There is also some evidence of particular localities being more vulnerable to cyclical factors affecting the demand for labour. Between August 2005 and 2006, for example, the unemployment rate in the Fairfield–Liverpool region of southwestern Sydney suddenly jumped from 5 per cent to 10 per cent. This compared with a national rate that was fairly steady at 4.9 per cent and a New South Wales state average of 5.7 per cent (Wade 2006). Simultaneously, the workforce participation rate in Fairfield–Liverpool dropped by about 6 per cent to 57 per cent, well below the national rate of 65 per cent. So the economic progress made in those working-class suburbs in the years since 2001 was very quickly being reversed. A downturn in manufacturing activity and new building starts, particularly following interest rate rises in 2006, were contributory factors, but the intensity of the impact suggests particular locational vulnerability.

The nature of urban labour markets makes the link between employment, unemployment and spatial inequality quite complex in practice. The availability of different types of work in different localities reflects decisions by businesspeople about where to locate their firms, as well as decisions by local governments about which commercial and industrial land uses to permit. The high unemployment rates in particular areas are not necessarily due to a lack of local employment opportunities though. They are just as likely to reflect the spatial concentration of more disadvantaged social groups. The persistently high rate of unemployment in the Fairfield–Liverpool area, for example, is due to the high proportion of immigrants from non-English-speaking (NESB) backgrounds among the local population (ABS 2004a), as well as the supply and demand conditions in the local labour market. As discussed in the previous chapter, immigrants who do not speak English as their first language tend to experience above average rates of unemployment and poverty, wherever they are located. So, even if there were more job opportunities in the local labour market, the local NESB immigrants would not necessarily get them and the unemployment rate would likely remain problematic. Spatial inequality results not just from intrinsic locational features, but also from social and economic processes that intersect in space.

Education is another factor compounding urban spatial inequalities. Access to high-quality educational facilities is often an important influence on choice of residential area. As real estate agents know, the proximity of a property to good schools can be an effective selling point for housing in areas of high socioeconomic status. That can elevate property values. Thus, in effect, access to higher-quality local schools is auctioned off through the residential property market to the households with the greater economic resources. This process tends to reproduce existing inequalities intergenerationally. Households with a higher level of educational attainment, and therefore higher incomes, are more likely to be able to afford to live in areas where the educational facilities are more highly regarded. Graduates of these schools then tend to have higher rates of employment and higher incomes than their counterparts in the less wealthy suburbs. Spatial variations in educational quality thereby compound inequalities originating in spatially differentiated urban labour and housing markets.

Spatial inequalities also reflect differential access to transport and other local services. This problem of access to services is of long standing in the outer metropolitan suburbs, where the provision of public infrastructure has often lagged behind housing development (as Bryson and Thompson noted in their pioneering 1972 study of an outer Melbourne suburb). The problems persist in more recently developed fringe areas. Meanwhile, difficulties of a different type now exist in many middle-ring suburbs that are experiencing infrastructure stress. Typically, these are the suburbs developed between about 1930 and 1970, representing the 'first wave of large-scale low density urban expansion of Australian cities' (Randoph 2004: 1). According to a range of socioeconomic indicators, they are becoming the most disadvantaged parts of the metropolitan areas. They often have ageing physical infrastructure and lack the local tax base of the more affluent and gentrifying areas. The ability of local governments to provide adequate services in these suburbs is often under severe stress. Where redevelopment has occurred, including partial conversion to higher-density housing, it has often been *ad hoc* and not accompanied by the improvements to the physical infrastructure that are necessary to cope with the increased demand. Hence, as urban researcher Bill Randolph argues, 'In many cases, redevelopment is simply building in more disadvantage for the future' (2004: 2).

All these factors shaping spatial inequality within cities – housing, employment, education and infrastructure – interact through processes of circular and cumulative causation. Vicious and virtuous cycles, rather than the equilibrating mechanisms posited by orthodox economists, shape the outcomes. Local government finance is one arena in which those processes operate. Differential land and housing values in the different suburbs, and the associated clustering of similar income groups, create significant variations in local governments' tax bases. Revenue-raising potential is most restricted in areas where property prices are low and the residents have generally low incomes. So the capacity to provide adequate services in those areas is circumscribed. This in turn reduces the attractiveness of such areas to businesspeople and professionals.

Scott Baum, from the Centre for Research into Sustainable Urban and Regional Futures at the University of Queensland, has analysed key socioeconomic variables associated with these 'distinct clusters of advantage and disadvantage', showing a number of interlinked and reinforcing processes (Baum 2003: 16). The most advantaged areas have typically been those with substantial employment in the so-called new economy (characterised by information technology and service industries), and with high levels of workforce participation. They have also tended to have high levels of residential turnover, possibly associated with processes of gentrification. Not surprisingly, these areas are also closely characterised by high levels of postsecondary education, above average incomes and low unemployment rates among their inhabitants (Baum 2003: 18). At the other end of the socioeconomic spectrum, the clusters of more disadvantaged localities are characterised by their focus on old economy industries and vulnerable occupations (such as manufacturing) and by high levels of unemployment, low workforce participation and lower levels of residential turnover. These clusters also have above average proportions of residents with low incomes and only basic education and who are experiencing housing stress or living in public rental accommodation (Baum 2003: 21–2; see also Baum 2004a, 2004b: 170–2).

The concentration of socioeconomic problems in particular suburbs and fringe metropolitan areas in Australia has been well documented in other studies. Historian Mark Peel's study of Elizabeth, north of Adelaide, was a particularly memorable depiction of a locality – with a distinctive British migrant presence – coping with the loss of jobs in the vehicle manufacturing industry (Peel 1995). Sociological research by Bob Birrell and Byung-Soo Seol (1998) foreshadowed the developing presence of an urban underclass with disproportionate representation of lower-skilled immigrants from non-English-speaking backgrounds in other suburbs, such as those in southwest Sydney. Economist Bob Gregory had previously done research on Census data in the 1990s to show the nationwide dimensions of increasing urban economic inequalities (Gregory and Hunter 1995). Other data compiled by NATSEM, estimating poverty rates in postcode areas across Australia, revealed distinctive spatial concentrations – with poverty rates ranging from 0.7 per cent in the affluent north Sydney suburb of Spit Junction to 29.8 per cent in Adelaide's Ferryden Park and over 35 per cent for children in that suburb (Lloyd *et al.* 2001).

Clearly, where people live in the different parts of Australian cities has a significant bearing on their opportunities. As sociologist Adam Jamrozik emphasises, spatial clustering reinforces other inequalities, 'creating cumulative and compound power differentials in the command over resources through time' (cited in Baum 2003: 4).

Spatial inequalities: education, income and housing

Education is crucial in the transmission of inequality and its spatial patterns, interacting with employment opportunities and housing affordability. For individuals it offers the prospect of success according to personal merit – and provides opportunities for social mobility – but its effect in practice is to concurrently reproduce existing socioeconomic inequalities. This is because access to good-quality education (measured according to quantifiable outcomes such as university entrance rates from particular schools and the incomes and employment status of graduates) is geographically differentiated.

Lower socioeconomic status areas typically experience poorer educational performance. This then shapes the income patterns of their inhabitants. Not surprisingly, median weekly incomes are highest among those with tertiary educational qualifications. According to Census data, people with tertiary qualifications are also concentrated in residential areas with high property values. The reverse is also true: people with fewer educational qualifications tend to have lower incomes and reside in areas with lower residential property values. The economic inequalities in Australian society are thereby perpetuated through the interaction between the housing market, the labour market and the educational institutions.

Looking at the 2001 *Social Atlas of Sydney*, for example, shows a consistently high proportion of people with tertiary qualifications in the suburbs north of the harbour, where they constitute up to 38.5 per cent of the population. This is in sharp contrast to Sydney's outer western and southwestern suburbs, where the percentage of tertiary qualified residents falls to below 11 per cent in particular localities (Rodrigo 2003: 42–3). These patterns reflect the locational choices of graduates. They also reflect, and compound, rates of university admissions from schools in the different areas. The proportion of students from schools in the western and southwestern suburbs who enter university ranges from 20 to 34 per cent, compared with up to 99 per cent in some schools in Sydney's northern suburbs (Rodrigo 2003). Shortages of experienced staff are also concentrated in the west and southwest regions of Sydney. The 2002 Inquiry into Public Education in New South Wales found that, while 28 per cent of experienced teachers in that state worked in schools in Sydney's southwest and western regions, only 10 per cent wished to remain there during their next posting (Vinson, Esson and Johnston 2002: 237). Schools in Sydney's west and southwest have also had a history of greater numbers of students leaving school before the age of 15 (Glover *et al.* 1999), and continue to have relatively high proportions of school leavers who have not completed Year 12. These are the young people most vulnerable to high rates of unemployment (Rodrigo 2003: 48–9).

In principle, schools can be a circuit breaker for this sort of vicious cycle. The provision of public education in Australia is the responsibility of state, rather than local, government, so spatial variations in the quality of schooling need not reflect the socioeconomic character of the residential population in each locality. However, to the extent that it does so in practice, the lower standards of education in poorer areas lead to increased problems of unemployment, below average incomes and associated problems of poverty and crime (Vinson 2004). The circuit of disadvantage continues. Meanwhile, areas with higher property values tend to attract people with higher incomes, generating more revenues for local government and contributing to an upwards spiral of better amenities and increased property prices. If, as is typically the case, the schools in these wealthier suburbs produce superior educational outcomes, these circuits of advantage exacerbate the urban spatial inequalities. It is not surprising that, in terms of incomes, wealth and access to adequate services, the major cities are becoming increasingly divided.

To turn this situation around would require policies to support public education in general, and public schools in disadvantaged areas in particular. State and territory governments have pursued these goals to some extent, but with great difficulty in the context of a federal government educational funding policy that has given more subsidies to private schools and encouraged their growth relative to public schools. The prospect of public education creating a more level playing field is challenging, to put it mildly. Meanwhile, the circular and cumulative causation tendencies that normally operate in social–spatial processes become yet more accentuated.

Regional inequality

Looking at the broader patterns of regional development nationwide, spatial inequalities are equally apparent. Of course, the metropolitan areas are themselves regions within a national economy. They coexist with other regions that have much lower population densities and much higher dependence on a limited range of economic activities, characteristically agricultural but sometimes based on mining. Therein lies the long-standing tension within Australian society – the city versus the bush. Non-metropolitan areas experience distinctive social and economic problems, particularly in inland rather than coastal regions. Not all are economically stagnant by any means, but the dominant picture is of a significant dualism between their prosperity and that of the metropolitan areas. As geographers Phil McManus and Bill Pritchard note, 'Study after study has shown that, in general, rural and regional Australia is disadvantaged when compared with the capital cities' (2000: 2). A report by prominent social researcher Tony Vinson (2004) found that almost 80 per cent of the most disadvantaged areas, defined according to postcodes in New South Wales and Victoria, are in non-urban regions. Similar patterns exist in other Australian states and territories.

As in cities, average incomes vary significantly between regions. A NATSEM study into regional inequality found that, in 2001, the average household income in Australia's capital cities was $56 975, significantly higher than average household incomes across the rest of the country. As table 6.1 shows, the average incomes of households in regional and rural towns were particularly low, at $42 503 and $38 769 respectively. The figure for rural towns was almost 50 per cent below the average household income in the major capital cities (Lloyd et al. 2004b: 3).[2]

Capital cities have also experienced the greatest increase in average household income, while the regional towns have fared worst. The relevant data for the period 1996–2001 are shown in figure 6.1, adjusted to take account of differences in housing costs in the different types of area. This adjustment is important because average housing costs are higher in capital cities and an unadjusted income inequality measure would therefore exaggerate the difference in average living standards between cities and regional areas. Figure 6.1 shows that, after making adjustment for these housing cost differences, the growth in incomes was still the lowest in regional towns, but rural

---

[2] 'Capital cities' refers here to state and territory capitals and surrounding areas. Examples include Sydney and the Blue Mountains (NSW), Perth and Fremantle (WA) and Brisbane and Ipswich (Qld).

'Major urban areas' are major non-capital cities with populations over 99 999, such as Geelong (Vic), Wollongong (NSW) and the Gold Coast (Qld).

'Regional towns' are towns and cities with populations of 1000–99 999, such as Bourke (NSW), Bunbury (WA) and Longford (Tas). 'Rural towns' are towns with populations of 200–999, such as Cue (WA), Tambo (Qld) and Warooka (SA).

'Rural areas' are other rural areas with more dispersed populations (Lloyd et al. 2004b).

Table 6.1 Estimated average household incomes by
region, 2001

Region	Average household income($)
Capital cities	56 975
Major urban areas	46 093
Regional towns	42 503
Rural towns	38 769
Rural areas	45 890
Australia: total	52 125

Source: Lloyd *et al.* 2004b, p. 3.

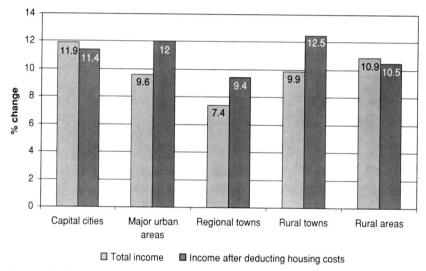

Figure 6.1 Estimated increase in average household income by region, before and
after adjusting for housing costs, 1996–2001
Source: Lloyd *et al.* 2004b: p. 5.

towns and major urban areas showed the greatest increase. While these latter
areas did not experience the same growth in gross incomes that occurred
in the capital cities, they had much slower increases in housing costs (Lloyd
et al. 2004b: 5). More recent trends have accentuated this difference.
According to evidence compiled by the Productivity Commission (2004),
the land and housing property boom of 2000–3 was much more dramatic

Table 6.2 Estimated average household income by state and region, as a percentage of average Sydney household income, 2001

	Capital cities %	Major urban areas %	Regional towns %	Rural towns %	Rural areas %	All regions %
New South Wales	100	75	65	61	73	88
Victoria	90	70	66	58	77	84
Queensland	84	72	70	61	70	76
South Australia	74		62	60	74	72
Western Australia	82		77	67	69	80
Tasmania	71		60	57	66	65
Northern Territory	97		99	79	72	94
ACT	109				94	109

Note: According to NATSEM's classification of regions, 'major urban areas' are absent in South Australia, Western Australia, Tasmania, the Northern Territory and the ACT. The ACT encompasses only its capital city – Canberra – and rural areas.
Source: Lloyd *et al.* 2004b: p. 07.

in the capital cities and some of the larger regional centres (including New-castle in New South Wales and Alice Springs in the Northern Territory) than in smaller regional areas.

There are also significant variations in incomes between the states and territories. Table 6.2 compares the average household incomes of differ-ent regions across the country at the time of the last national Census by taking Sydney as a benchmark (that is, having a score of 100). This illustrates the income gap between the capital cities, as well as between each capital city and other parts of each state and territory. Households in Canberra enjoyed the highest average incomes in the nation, followed by those in Sydney and Darwin. Among capital cities, Hobart experienced the lowest average incomes, while regional and rural areas in Tasmania had the lowest average incomes of all. On a state-by-state basis, 'South Australia vies with Tasmania as the least affluent region in Australia' (Travers 2005: 55). Research conducted by regional economist Christine Smith (2004) shows that these Australian regional inequalities have been fairly consistent over a long period. The average income inequalities between the states and territories increased a little between 1976 and 1986, declined a little between 1986 and 1991, and remained stable between 1991 and 2001. Within some of the states and territories particular statistical divisions have been diverging a little from the overall national income average: upwards in the case of Sydney, downwards in the cases of Eyre and the northern regions of South Australia, Mersey–Lyell and the southern region of Tasmania and the Illawarra region of New South Wales (Smith 2004: 209). These are small changes though. The general picture is of consistent and persistent inequalities, notwithstanding periodic flurries of governmental interest (and then disinterest) in formulating policies to promote more balanced regional development across the nation.

The relative prosperity of Sydney and Melbourne has been the subject of particular interest because of the long-standing rivalry between these two metropolitan regions and the impact of global restructuring (Fagan and Webber 1994: 71). The average value of household assets is higher for Sydney, largely reflecting higher residential housing prices (and therefore only realisable for those willing to leave town). However, one recent empirical study, based on indices developed by Commsec and the *Sydney Morning Herald*, suggests that Melbourne may have recently pulled ahead in terms of general material wellbeing. The indices combine measures of economic growth, employment, interest rates and consumer spending with prices of common expenditure items, including housing, cars and petrol prices (Burrell 2006a). According to this study, the prosperity of the average Sydneysider has been undermined by a more rapid decline in housing affordability than that experienced by their Melbourne counterparts, as well as slower economic growth and consumer spending in New South Wales. During the decade since 1996, the material prosperity of property and share owners in Melbourne increased by 46.9 per cent, compared to 44.6 per cent for their Sydney counterparts. The differences between Melburnians and Sydneysiders who lack these assets are even more pronounced, with estimated average increases in prosperity of 15.9 per cent and 12.1 per cent respectively over the same period (Burrell 2006b: 4). The data, although not conclusive, illustrate the complex processes affecting regional economic advantage and disadvantage. Spatial inequalities in wealth and income are shaped – and reshaped – by the dynamics of contemporary political economic change.

Regional dynamics

Urban and regional inequalities, such as those discussed in this chapter, reflect particular features of the geography of Australian capitalism. Capital investment is the most important driver of change: where it occurs shapes the spatial patterns of employment opportunities. The considerable distances between cities and major urban areas and the remoteness of smaller towns inhibit travel to find work. Thus, the tyranny of distance causes broad regional labour markets to be more self-contained than intra-metropolitan labour markets. To a large extent, then, the industrial structure of different regions determines the type and number of jobs available to local residents. In a period of rapid industrial restructuring and technological change the regional imbalances are accentuated. One study of the regional distribution of growth notes that, while incomes, output and expenditures have risen nationally, 'fewer places have participated in that outcome' and that 'the differences between the clusters of high income jobs with diverse consumption experiences and those with high unemployment and social security dependence have probably widened over the last decade' (O'Connor, Stimson and Baum 2001: 61).

This greater regional inequality is further illustrated by a NATSEM study that looks at regional changes in employment in a range of industries between 1996 and 2001. While the proportion of people employed by firms in the mining industry, for example, declined across Australia as a whole, the fall in regional towns was more than three times the national average. Rural towns were hardest hit by declining employment in manufacturing industries, followed closely by capital cities, while employment in financial, property and business services grew five times faster in capital cities than in other regions (Lloyd *et al.* 2004b: 15).

Regional variations in rates of unemployment also reflect these differences in economic and industry structure. As shown in figure 6.2, based on data from the NATSEM study, the 2001 unemployment rates were, at 6.3 per cent, lowest in rural areas. This correlates with the very high proportion (close to 30 per cent) of rural residents employed in agriculture. At the other extreme, unemployment was greatest in major urban areas, which had been hard hit in the preceding five years by declining employment in mining, manufacturing and communications industries (Lloyd

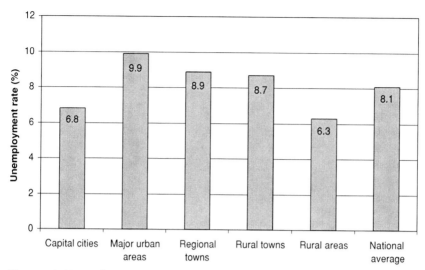

Figure 6.2 Unemployment rate by region, 2001
Source: Lloyd *et al.* 2004b: p. 12.

et al. 2004b). Not surprisingly, unemployment rates were lower in capital cities than in smaller cities and towns.

Unemployment rates also vary significantly across the states and territories, notwithstanding the relatively minor differences in overall living standards that are evident at that level of spatial aggregation. Table 6.3 shows that Tasmania and New South Wales had the highest proportions of people who were registered as unemployed in 2001, at 10.2 per cent and 8.7 per cent respectively. This compares to a rate of only 5.2 per cent in the ACT. The highest regional unemployment rate was experienced in Tasmania's regional towns, at 11.3 per cent (Lloyd *et al.* 2004b). Although official unemployment rates have trended downward a little since then, the regional differences persist.

Regional inequality in Australia is also a story of unequal access to services. Recent years have seen, for example, a concentration of financial services in the major cities and a corresponding reduction in services directly located in rural areas. Between 1993 and 2002, the number of bank branches fell by 33 per cent Australia-wide, with most of the closures occurring in non-metropolitan areas (Connolly and Hajaj 2002; see also Gray and Lawrence 2001: 106). The banks claim that banking services can still be accessed with

Table 6.3 Unemployment rates by state and territory, and by region, 2001

	Capital cities %	Major urban areas %	Regional towns %	Rural towns %	Rural areas %	All regions %
New South Wales	6.1	10.0	9.8	10.3	7.1	8.7
Victoria	6.6	9.3	8.3	8.2	5.2	7.5
Queensland	7.8	9.9	8.6	8.6	6.9	8.4
South Australia	7.9		8.3	6.8	4.7	6.9
Western Australia	7.6		8.2	7.2	4.6	6.9
Tasmania	9.3		11.3	10.7	9.7	10.2
Northern Territory	6.7		4.6	8.0	4.9	6.1
Australian Capital Territory	5.2				5.2	5.2
Australia	6.8	9.9	8.9	8.7	6.3	8.1

Note: According to NATSEM's classification of regions, 'major urban areas' are absent in South Australia, Western Australia, Tasmania, the Northern Territory and the ACT. The ACT encompasses only its capital city – Canberra – and rural areas.
Source: Lloyd *et al.* 2004b: p. 13.

modern technology – online banking – but the social and economic impact of bank closures in many country towns has been acute. Bank closures commonly precipitate the closure or departure of other local businesses, thereby accelerating the processes of circular and cumulative causation, which then accentuate regional inequality. In addition, where services are limited, queuing for long periods may further undermine the quality of service enjoyed. What Kempen (1997), in the American context, called 'regional poverty pockets' have come to be characterised by limited services where 'queuing, waiting in vain and harsh and rush treatment are often the norm'.

Access to educational facilities is also uneven in regional Australia. This is particularly apparent in the limited opportunities for tertiary education in non-metropolitan regional areas. Universities are disproportionately concentrated in the major cities; even the (valuable) opportunity to live away from home while attending them, or to study at regional campuses (such as UNE, CSU, JCU, CQU or USQ), does not eradicate the spatial bias. NATSEM 2004 study into regional inequality found that almost 42 per cent of adults in capital cities had undertaken tertiary education in 2001, compared to only 24 and 27 per cent in rural and regional towns respectively. While the number of residents with tertiary qualifications increased in all regions in the five years to 2001, this increase was considerably larger in capital cities, at 4.9 per cent, compared to 3.7 per cent in major urban areas and only 2 per cent in rural towns (Lloyd *et al.* 2004b: 16). This is consistent with other studies indicating a growing divide in educational qualifications between the richest and poorest regions of the country (Harding, Yap and Lloyd 2004). Analysis by the Bureau of Transport and Regional Economics (cited in Harding, Yap and Lloyd 2004) confirms that there is a positive correlation between higher numbers of tertiary-educated residents and higher regional incomes, so the educational inequalities reinforce the regional economic disparities.

The combination of inferior educational and employment opportunities, together with poor and declining access to services, has led to outmigration from many of the rural and regional areas. This process has been particularly apparent among younger people, drawn to urban areas in pursuit of higher education or improved prospects for work. Many of the people going to the cities for university study do not return, thereby depleting the regions of some of their brightest and best.

The results of the rural–urban immigration also show up in regional trends in population change. One analysis found that, while the number of people of working age (15 and over) in capital cities increased by almost half a million people over the period between 1996 and 2001, 'rural areas, regional towns and major urban areas together lost almost 200 000 people' in this same age group (Lloyd *et al.* 2004b: 14). Not all the movement was to the capital cities: rural towns experienced a modest increase of around 15 500 people (Lloyd *et al.* 2004b: 14). This reflects the sponge effect, whereby the larger regional centres draw away population from smaller towns and villages in rural areas. These are complex processes, involving intra-regional redistribution as well as inter-regional shifts.

The overall effect of rural population decline in inland areas is to compound the problems of regional inequality, contributing to a loss of skills and human capital as well as business closures and the further withdrawal of

Table 6.4 Proportion of households in given income groups, by region, 2001

Income group	Capital cities %	Major urban areas %	Regional towns %	Rural towns %	Rural areas %	All regions %
Low (under $15 600)	12.5	15.8	17.4	18.1	13.8	13.9
Lower middle ($15 600–$52 000)	43.7	51.4	53.9	58.0	54.7	47.4
Upper middle ($52 000–$104 000)	32.3	26.8	24.2	20.8	25.4	29.5
High (over $104 000)	11.5	6.0	4.5	3.1	6.1	9.2

Source: Lloyd *et al.* 2004b: p. 11.

local services. These trends have also generated regional concentrations of poverty. As shown in table 6.4, while capital cities had the highest proportion of high-income households and the lowest proportion of low-income households in 2001, almost one-fifth of all households in rural and regional towns had incomes of under $15 600 per year (Lloyd *et al.* 2004b: 11). This is less than one-third of the average household income for the country as a whole. Some of these low-income people may have been attracted to the region by lower costs of living: anecdotal evidence suggests that this applies to particular cases of single mothers and other welfare recipients joining the seachange and treechange movements from the major cities. Regional variations in costs of living also need to be considered before drawing strong inferences from the sort of regional income data shown in table 6.4. Housing costs are almost invariably lower in rural towns and rural areas, for example, although transport and communications costs are often higher because of the greater distances involved. As with other cost differentials between metropolitan and non-metropolitan Australia (documented previously by Stilwell and Johnson 1991), the net effect may go either way, depending on the needs and activities of different households.

So, are place-specific policies necessary? The spatially distinctive features of socioeconomic inequality may be taken as providing a case for urban and regional policies that target suburbs or regions experiencing particular disadvantages. Former ALP leader, Mark Latham, emphasised the importance of this spatial dimension in public policy more than any other political leader in recent times (see particularly Latham 2003: 109–22). In his book *Civilising Global Capital* he argued that

> the economic strategies of government require a strong spatial focus. The Australian economy should not be regarded as a homogenous entity; it needs to be treated as a series of highly differentiated regional economies and neighbourhood labour markets . . . If the public sector does not fund the extra costs of distance in service delivery, basic infrastructure and employment opportunities, it is unlikely that the free market will (Latham 1998, pp. 113–15).

Latham's demise as a prominent political figure does not mean that such concerns disappear. The advocacy of urban and regional policies as a means of achieving social equity is one of long standing (for example, Troy 1981, 1999, 2000), and some of the best modern writing on Australian cities (for example, Gleeson and Low 2000; Gleeson 2006) emphasises the nexus between urban form and equity. People prosperity and place prosperity can be quite different focal points for public policy, but only the latter directly addresses the processes of circular and cumulative causation that cause divided spaces. The evidence reviewed in this chapter indicates that, without a sustained urban and regional policy commitment, spatial inequalities tend to intensify.

Why spatial inequality matters

Whether the spatial inequality described in this chapter is a problem requiring redress is not self-evident. Indeed, it is inconceivable that, in a huge continent such as Australia with such diversity of regional and urban settlement patterns, all citizens would enjoy equal physical access to all opportunities and facilities. Moreover, some would say that spatial differentiation allows people to find places to live and work that suit their personal skills, tastes and incomes. From this perspective, spatial inequality is relatively benign. The existence of large variations in land values and housing prices in different suburbs and regions means that most people can find some place they can afford. As the old adage states, people cut their cloth to suit their pocket. If we view spatial inequalities in this way – that is, as a consequence of multiple choices and accommodations to different economic circumstances – policy interventions are unwarranted.

Benign neglect may not be the best stance though. Such a passive policy posture ignores some rather more problematic features of spatial inequality. Segmentation of the population can create ghettos, divided cities and deprived regions that inhibit socioeconomic mobility. The evidence provided in this chapter has shown that, while people may initially be spatially divided according to accidents of birthplace or according to the locations in which they can afford to live, processes of circular and cumulative causation then accentuate the inequalities between them over time. These processes are driven by the interacting effects of the labour market, the housing market, educational provision and local services. Divergences in the local tax bases then cause local government finance to reinforce those inequalities. In the larger cities the outcome is a deeper disparity between the inhabitants of upper-income suburbs and the more economically and socially deprived localities. At the regional level, the disparities associated with uneven economic development become yet more deeply entrenched.

Most fundamentally, these spatial inequalities are a matter of concern because they sit at odds with widely held values of equality of opportunity and a 'fair go'. As such, concern with spatial inequality is on a par with concerns about sexism and racism. If we hold that equality of opportunity should not be violated by discrimination according to gender and ethnicity, then nor should it be systematically violated according to location.

Conclusion

There is an important spatial, as well as class, dimension to the distribution of income and wealth in Australian society. Divided cities and regions reflect the dynamics of the economic changes that are affecting patterns of investment and employment. They also reflect problems of social fragmentation and exclusion. These spatial inequalities impact on the life chances of local residents and undermine the possibilities for greater equity in Australian society.

Considerations of space and place need to be central to public policy, just as they need to be central to economic and social analysis. Of course, federal and state government policies targeted at disadvantaged localities may fail to turn the tide, as regional policy sceptics have often pointed out, and some regional DIY may be appropriate (see, for example, Sorensen 1994, 2001; Rogers and Jones 2006). However, public policies aimed at creating greater spatial equity need not create problems of economic inefficiency. If localised unemployment is reduced by targeted job creation, for example, both spatial equity and economic efficiency are enhanced.

Getting the balance right is the challenge. It is important to ensure that policies to redress spatial inequality do not substitute for attention to the broader societal forces, such as class relationships, that shape economic and social inequalities. So place management and regional policies need to be integrated with policies for redistribution of income and wealth. By similar reasoning, measures to redress inequality also need to take account of how it is structured, not only by class and space, but also by gender.

Chapter Seven

A GENDER AGENDA

Gender inequality is a dimension of economic inequality in Australia that warrants special attention. Despite changing social attitudes and public policies over the last four decades, economic inequality between women and men remains a significant concern. At the highest levels in business and within the most prestigious professions, men continue to dominate. A report showing the highest-paid executive officers in the top 150 Australian corporations, for example, with 'power salaries' ranging between $200 000 and $28.6 million per year, had just three women on the list, the highest paid of whom earned an annual $1.5 million (*Sydney Morning Herald* 2003). While women make up 44.8 per cent of the workforce, they make up only 3 per cent of CEOs and 8.7 per cent of the directors of Australia's top 200 listed companies (EOWA 2006: 5). Of the 200 wealthiest Australians in 2006, only 11 (or 5.5 per cent) were women (*Business Review Weekly* 2006a).

A similar pattern recurs outside the corporate world, although less striking. In Federal Parliament only 64 of the 226 members are women (Commonwealth of Australia 2006). Similarly, although many women enter prestigious and highly paid professions such as medicine and law, they tend to occupy the lower ranks within them. There are, for example, only six women among the forty-six judges serving on the Federal Court of Australia: male judges in this court still outnumber female judges by a ratio of over seven to one (Federal Court of Australia 2006). Only two women have ever served on the High Court of Australia, the highest court in Australia's judicial system. In medicine, most women doctors are in general practice, while the upper echelons of specialists and surgeons remain male-dominated. In 2002 women made up 31 per cent of the total medical workforce, accounting for 36 per cent of general practitioners, but only 20 per cent of specialists and 6 per cent of surgeons (Australian Institute of Health and Welfare 2002: 4). In higher education women are better represented in lower levels of university teaching and research, but comprise only 21 per cent of the vice-chancellors at Australian universities (EOWA 2006: 5).

Gender disparities are also clearly evident in the wages gap between men and women. The average weekly pay for all female employees is just 65.5 per cent of that received by males. When casual workers are excluded and only full-time workers are compared, women, on average, are still paid only 80.7 per cent of the wages paid to male employees (ABS 2006e: table 3). These statistics are indicative of broader gender differentials in access to positions of economic and political power and a systematic inequality in the distribution of economic rewards.

Certainly, moves have been made to redress these inequalities in recent decades. In the 1960s women were routinely paid less than men for doing the same job or work of equal value. Decisions made by the Commonwealth Arbitration Commission in 1969 and 1972 made this practice unlawful, establishing the principles of 'equal pay for equal work' and 'equal pay for work of equal value' (NSW Office of Industrial Relations 2004). The *Maternity Leave Act 1973* (Cwlth) enabled federal public servants to return to the same job after taking time off for childbirth. The *Sex Discrimination Act 1984* (Cwlth) made it illegal to give jobs to men rather than women simply because of their gender (Pritchard Hughes 1997: 13). The *Affirmative Action Act 1986* (Cwlth) went beyond anti discrimination legislation, requiring employers of large numbers of employees to take positive action to remove barriers faced by women in employment, including their own management practices (Probert 1997). Policies towards childcare and education have also sought to enable women to enter the paid workforce and pursue careers in fields previously reserved for men.

Attitudes have changed, too: while many men (and some women) were strongly opposed to women entering the paid workforce in the 1960s and 1970s, today it is commonly expected that women will pursue a career in paid employment, with most families relying on women working to bring in a necessary first or second income (Gilding 1997). The political rhetoric is being modified accordingly: in a recent address to the National Press Club, Federal Treasurer Peter Costello championed the government's commitment to making Australia 'the most female-friendly environment in the world' (cited in Horin 2006).

An observer of these changes could be forgiven for thinking that gender inequality in Australia is a thing of the past, but the progress made during the 1970s and 1980s seems to have stalled. The gender wages gap has ceased closing. The pipeline argument – that equal representation of women in the most influential positions would occur over time – has apparently been discredited. As labour researchers Alison Preston and John Burgess (2003: 514) concluded, after carefully reviewing the evidence on women at work during the last two decades, 'The Australian labour market remains highly gendered while the gender equity agenda has stalled and, in some quarters, disappeared from view'. Moreover, aggregate statistics ignore the differences between women, glossing over the experiences of those women who are worst off, most notably Indigenous women and women from non-English-speaking backgrounds (Pritchard Hughes 1997). The experience of many Australian women remains that of economic and social marginalisation.

This chapter sets out the evidence of economic inequality between women and men in contemporary Australia and seeks to explain these trends. Why is it that women are still paid, on average, less than men? Why is it that women remain underrepresented in positions of power and influence? Educational differences are explored, along with differences in occupations, industries and average working hours. Questions about the dual responsibilities of women as workers and childbearers and the effects of government policies on tax and childcare are also raised. So, too, are fundamental issues about patriarchy and the prospects for gender equality in the absence of more substantive political economic change.

Unequal pay

More Australian women are in paid jobs today than ever before, representing a huge cultural and social shift over the last four decades. However, the

Table 7.1 Male and female average weekly earnings, February 2006

	Full-time adult ordinary time earnings	Full-time adult total earnings[1]	All employees total earnings[2]
Males	$1099	$1165	$983
Females	$925	$939	$644
Relativity (F/M)	84.2%	80.7%	65.5%

[1] Includes overtime.
[2] Includes part-time employees and employees under the age of 21.
Source: ABS, 2006e: table 3.

latest official data, presented in table 7.1, clearly show that, even accounting for differences in the number of hours in paid work, women earn substantially less than men. There are significant variations between industries and occupations. In 2006 the gender wages gap was smallest among workers in accommodation, cafes and restaurants (at 94 per cent), only a little lower in the communications sector (at 92 per cent) but extraordinarily wide in the finance and insurance industry where women averaged only 62 per cent of male earnings (Irvine 2005).

Changes in the gender wages gap over the last two decades are shown in table 7.2. There has evidently been a slight increase in women's full-time wages relative to men's over the period, with women's average full-time ordinary time earnings rising from 82.2 per cent of men's in 1985 to 84.2 per cent in 2006. Overall, the 1970s saw a rapid increase in women's wages relative to men's, following the introduction of equal pay legislation (Daly *et al.* 2006). Further increases were slow but steady through the 1980s, but the increase has since petered out. A similar pattern is apparent when overtime hours are taken into account, with the gender wages gap closing less than 3 per cent since 1985. In the year to February 2005, for full-time workers, average male earnings rose by 6.5 per cent, but women's earnings rose by only 5.7 per cent (Irvine 2005). When all employees – full-time and part-time – are considered, there has been virtually no change in the gender wages gap over the last two decades, with women's total earnings hovering at around 66 per cent of men's, as shown in the right hand column of table 7.2 (ABS 2006e).

Table 7.2 Female earnings as a percentage of male earnings, 1985–2006

Year	Full-time adult ordinary time earnings (%)	Full-time adult total earnings[1] (%)	All employees, total earnings[2] (%)
1985	82.2	78.3	66.2
1990	83.2	79.2	65.6
1995	83.5	79.1	66.2
2000	83.9	80.5	65.9
2005	85.2	81.0	66.4
2006	84.2	80.7	65.5

[1] Includes overtime.
[2] Includes part-time employees and employees under the age of 21.
Figures were recorded for February of each year.
Source: ABS 2006e.

What explains these persistent inequalities? Gillian Whitehouse cautions against a narrow interpretation that ignores changes in the overall distribution of wages – and the possibility that women are 'swimming upstream' in circumstances where wage differentials are generally widening (Whitehouse 2003: 119). The failure to achieve further closure in the gender wages gap in recent years, despite women's educational attainments, is particularly troublesome though. Conventional economists seek to account for pay differentials by positing that, in a capitalist economy, employees are paid according to their economic contribution. Human capital theory adds that the economic contribution of individual employees is influenced by their level of education and training. On that basis one would certainly expect steady closure of the gender gap as women's educational attainments come to equal, even exceed, men's. One of the products of the women's movement over the last four decades is that women are now entering universities in much greater numbers. In 2004, 57 per cent of students enrolled in bachelor degrees at university were women (DEST 2005: section 3.1, table 3), so human capital theory evidently cannot explain the persistent gender wages gap.

More insight can be gained in looking at what fields of study female university students choose. In 2004, female bachelor degree students were most highly concentrated in courses in education (where they made up

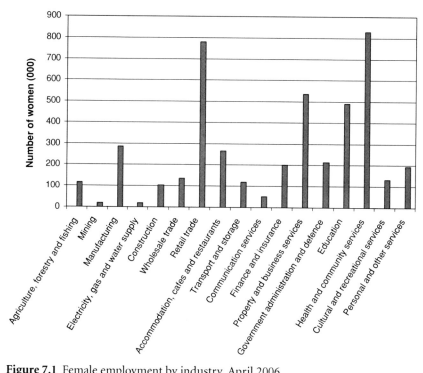

Figure 7.1 Female employment by industry, April 2006
Source: ABS, 2006f: table 2.2.

75 per cent of total enrolments), health (also 75 per cent), society and culture (67 per cent) and creative arts (65 per cent). They also outnumbered men in natural and physical sciences (55 per cent), management and commerce (53 per cent) and agriculture and environmental studies (51 per cent). Women were least likely to be enrolled in engineering and related technologies, where they made up 14 per cent of enrolments in bachelor degrees (ABS 2002b: 57).

These educational differences have long-term impacts on women's careers, with similar patterns of gender segregation evident in occupational differences between women and men. ABS data, presented in figure 7.1, show that women working in health and community services, retail, property and business services and education make up over half of all female employment (ABS 2006f: table 2.2). Even within these industries, women tend to specialise in particular areas. While women vastly outnumber men as teachers in primary schools, for example, men continue to dominate in tertiary education. In 2004, women accounted for 80 per cent, or four out of every five, primary school teachers in Australia, while in the same year they made up only 40 per cent of academic staff within Australian universities (ABS 2005d: 87). Whatever explains these imbalances, they have significant consequences for economic inequality because primary school teaching is generally the lowest-paid educational field, while tertiary education has the highest pay and prestige. In the education sector, too, while women outnumber men among teaching staff in primary schools, men are much more likely to be school principals. According to Mary Bluett, Victorian president of the Australian Education Union, this gender imbalance is so pervasive that if you are a male primary school teacher 'over 35 and not a principal, there are questions about you' (quoted in Dunn 2003).

The same pattern is evident elsewhere. By and large, the industries in which women are clustered are those with lower rates of pay. As American social scientist Paula England notes, 'Even controlling for the human capital of the incumbents and for occupational skill demands', industries with a predominance of women 'pay less than those containing more men' (England 2005a: 276). Taking Australian university graduates as an example, female bachelor degree graduates received only 86 per cent of the pay received by their male counterparts in 2001. Among postgraduates the pay ratio was even lower, with females earning only 76 per cent of male postgraduate wages, with a large part of this difference attributed to differences in fields of study and, consequently, employment (ABS 2002b: 83).

Even within the industries in which women are clustered, they are often in the lower echelons. The single largest employer of women is the health and community services industry, employing 18.5 per cent of all women in the Australian workforce. In this industry, women outnumber men by almost four to one (ABS 2006f: table 2.2). However, a 2003 study found that the men employed in this industry are twice as likely as women to be managers or administrators and, while 47 per cent of women in health and community services are at intermediate level or below, the equivalent figure for men is only 30 per cent (ABS 2003c: 49). The second-largest employer of women is the retail trade. Here, the picture looks even worse for women, who are over twice as likely as men to be in elementary sales jobs, whereas men are three times as likely as women to be managers. Indeed, almost 60 per cent of women in the retail industry are in entry level positions, compared to

26 per cent of men (ABS 2003c: 49). In other sectors, such as information technology, the relative occupational positions of men and women are much less clear cut, although there is evidence of working-time commitments leading to women in IT being more concentrated in programming and technical support jobs rather than in high-paid consultancy roles (Whitehouse and Diamond 2006: 88).

Considering all industries, men are over twice as likely as women to be in management or administration positions (ABS 2006f: table 2.4). This suggests that a glass ceiling for women is still intact.[1] Moreover, even within the same occupations, women tend to earn less than men. An ABS study of recent university graduates, for example, found that while those working as managers and administrators had the highest salaries, the average pay for male managers was $1230 per week, compared to an average of only $987 for female managers (ABS 2002b: 82).

Part of this inequality may be explained by the longer average hours worked by men. Indeed, re-examination of the data in table 7.1 illustrates that a large part of the pay differential between men and women results from the concentration of women in part-time work. It has already been noted that the 66 per cent relativity between women's and men's average earnings narrows to 81 per cent when only full-time workers are considered. When overtime pay is excluded from consideration, the differential closes further – to a relativity of just over 84 per cent (ABS 2006e: table 3). This is because men, on average, work more overtime. Taking part-time, full-time and overtime work into account, men work an average of 40 hours per week, compared to an average of 29.2 hours for women. Even among those at the top of their organisations, women are much less likely to do overtime. Among managers and administrators, women work an average of 37.3 hours per week, while men work an average of 47 hours (ABS 2006f: table 2.6). Assuming that at least some of these additional hours are paid,

---

[1] Janeen Baxter and Erik Olin Wright (2000) have made a conceptual distinction between a 'gender gap in authority', evidenced by a disproportionate number of men in senior management positions, and a 'glass ceiling', in which the barriers to promotion for women get stronger as they progress up the management chain. Based on a preliminary empirical study, they suggest that, while a gender gap in authority is clearly evident in Australia, the barriers for promotion for women appear strongest at the middle levels of management, a result inconsistent with their definition of a 'glass ceiling'.

Table 7.3 Workforce status of males and females, May 2006

Workforce status	Males (000)	Females (000)	Male and female (000)	Females as % of total
Full-time	4742.2	2464.7	7206.9	34.2
Part-time	823.9	2111.4	2935.3	71.9
Total	5566.2	4576.1	10142.2	45.1

Source: ABS, 2006g: table 3.

this helps to explain the differentials in earnings between male and female managers. It also points to some deeper considerations, such as how shorter average working hours reflect women's childbearing role and their tendency to undertake the majority of unpaid domestic work.

The differences between men and women in employment patterns, wage rates and working hours during their careers then cause major differences in their retirement incomes. Successive Australian governments have pursued a policy of extending compulsory occupational superannuation. This has both advantages and disadvantages – as noted by various contributors to a special issue of the *Journal of Australian Political Economy* on this topic (Coates, Vidler and Stilwell 2004) – but one problem that women in general face is accumulating adequate independent retirement income. Jefferson and Preston (2005: 80) point out that, among baby boomers, women will tend to spend an average of 35 per cent less time in paid employment than men. So 'since superannuation accumulation is directly dependent on time spent in paid employment, a 35 per cent gap in the latter will translate to a gender superannuation accumulation gap of at least 35 per cent'.

Unequal work

Despite a general trend towards the casualisation of the workforce over the last two decades, women are still much more likely than men to work in casual or part-time jobs. As table 7.3 shows, while women make up 45 per cent of the total workforce, they constitute 72 per cent of those working part time (ABS 2006g: table 3).

Table 7.4 further shows that, while the absolute number of women working part time has grown over the last two and a half decades, the proportion

Table 7.4 Female participation in the workforce and workforce status, June 1980–June 2006, selected years

Year	Number of women employed (000s)	% of total employees who are female	% of part-time employees who are female
1980	2285.6	36.5	79.5
1985	2561.0	38.5	78.7
1990	3289.8	41.6	78.0
1995	3600.0	43.4	74.9
2000	3967.3	44.1	73.1
2005	4497.2	44.9	71.5
2006	4596.5	45.1	70.9

Source: Calculated from ABS 2006h.

Table 7.5 Workforce status of males and females, June 1980–June 2006, selected years

Year	% of female employees who work part time	% of male employees who work part time	% of all employees who work part time
1980	34.8	5.1	16.0
1985	37.3	6.3	18.2
1990	40.5	8.1	21.6
1995	43.2	11.1	25.0
2000	44.2	12.9	26.7
2005	46.2	15.0	29.0
2006	45.9	15.4	29.2

Source: Calculated from ABS 2006h.

of part-time employees who are female has slowly declined, from a high of just under 80 per cent in 1980. Indeed, table 7.5 illustrates that, while the proportion of female employees who work part time has increased from 35 per cent to almost 46 per cent since 1980, the proportion of male employees who work part time has increased rather more, tripling from a low base of 5 per cent in 1980 to just over 15 per cent in 2006.

The strong representation of women in part-time work is related to the role of women in childbearing and to the cultural norms and economic pressures that see them still take the bulk of responsibility for childrearing and domestic work. Indeed, part-time (and casual) work are often seen as rational choices for women seeking flexibility in working hours to fit family responsibilities into the day. In this regard, recent debates about the concentration of women in part-time work have parallelled those about the gendered division of labour across industries. Sociologist Catherine Hakim (2002), in particular, has argued that the over-representation of women in part-time work is a result of lifestyle preferences and 'genuine choice'.

This inference has been widely contested. In a longitudinal study of young Australian women aged 18–23, for example, Deidre Wicks and her colleagues (2001) found that the majority of women aspired to full-time work when they were 35, a result that remained relatively stable over the four-year study. In a study of British women, labour researcher Sally Walters (2005) found that a significant number of part-time workers were dissatisfied with their jobs and had strong career aspirations, but felt constrained by their family obligations. Similarly, research by Janet Walsh (1999) found that a 'significant minority' of Australian women working part time would prefer to work full time. Evidently, the predominance of women in part-time work cannot be fully explained by lifestyle choice. The socialisation of gender roles probably plays an important part, as does the concentration of women in particular industries traditionally associated with childrearing and home making.

Whatever the reasons for women entering part-time work, it often comes at a significant economic cost. Not only do part-time jobs provide less income, but they are often less secure than full-time jobs, offer fewer opportunities for training and career advancement and fewer benefits in terms of sick leave, holiday pay and superannuation. In addition, flexibility in working hours may be to the disadvantage of employees who lack influence in determining rosters and shifts.[2] As Australian social researcher Barbara Pocock (2003: 182) notes:

> Many part-time workers are happy to work less than full-time in order to meet other obligations and desires: they are glad to be part-time. But, given the option, many would prefer to have part-time work without degraded

---

[2] For perspectives on job quality and part-time work, see Burgess (2005); Chalmers, Campbell and Charlesworth (2005); Watson (2005) and Wooden and Warren (2004).

conditions of insecurity and marginality – and to have better transition arrangements into and out of part-time/full-time work over the life-cycle.

The current failure to create this ideal means that women in part-time work are often economically marginalised at the lower end of the pay scale and excluded from senior positions. Moreover, while many women may expect to take time out of full-time work to have children, and then return to pursuing a career, this interruption to their career advancement can have long-term effects, with men advancing more rapidly, developing stronger workplace connections and occupying the most senior positions. The resultant tendency of men to continue to occupy the most senior positions and to earn higher incomes then perpetuates the cycle: if women expect to earn less than their male partners, it is more likely to seem a rational choice for them to work part time and do most of the domestic labour.

Socialisation or rational choice?

While gender segregation in industries, occupations and educational fields has declined in recent decades, the broad differences remain. Opinions vary as to why this may be the case. Is the predominance of women in lower-paid fields a genuine choice, or does it reflect processes of socialisation and the cultural value attached to different types of work?

Human capital theory suggests that women's educational and career paths are based on objective choices, albeit influenced by their expectations of more interrupted working lives. Orthodox economists taking this viewpoint argue that if women 'anticipate shorter and more discontinuous work lives' than men because of their predominance in childrearing roles, they have less incentive to invest in training or education designed for long-term employment in a particular occupation or enterprise (noted in Blau and Kahn 2000: 80). Women may avoid occupations that require significant work experience or on-the-job training. Moreover, to the extent that jobs requiring on-the-job training have lower starting wages but a faster pay rise trajectory, women avoiding these jobs tend to exclude themselves from the highest-paying occupations.

A contrary view is put by Paula England (2005a), who argues that gender segregation across occupational fields is formed well before women consider becoming mothers. She notes the early formation of occupational aspirations, with young girls expressing a preference for work that involves creative expression or helping others. She argues that, while this may have some basis in historical 'ideals of women as mothers, there is little evidence that these fields appeal to girls because they think they will be easier to combine with their own future roles as mothers' (England 2005a: 270). She also cites evidence that women are actually more likely than men to participate in on-the-job training and that, rather than choosing jobs with higher starting wages but slower wage trajectories, women are clustered in occupations that have lower wages from the outset. According to England's reasoning, the more important factor in determining women's educational and occupational choices is socialisation.

Kate Pritchard Hughes also emphasises the effect of socialisation, pointing out that female students concentrate in fields of study that are seen as socially acceptable and appropriate for women to undertake. She argues that

> Women, rather than men, are thought well-equipped to teach small children which is why women undertake education degrees at university and then become primary teachers and men don't. In much the same way, women are seen as less able engineers than men, less well-equipped to understand mathematical formulae and science and consequently stay away from studying them and the careers which involve these skills. The crucial fact is that although there are no longer any concrete barriers to their involvement, they choose not to get involved, by and large, and opt for the 'helping' professions (Pritchard Hughes 1997: 9).

Social scientists Raewyn Connell and James Messerschmidt (2005) take the view that this sex role theory is too simplistic. While accepting the role of social processes and dominant gender norms in influencing behaviour, they note that there are multiple expressions of masculinity and femininity and that both men and women have agency in challenging cultural norms. Moreover, as sociologist Jerry Jacobs (cited in England 2005a) has argued, socialisation on its own cannot explain the gendered division of occupations, since people's job choices often change over time, although such occupational shifts are more typically incremental than fundamental.

Whatever the reason for women tending to concentrate in certain fields, there is some evidence that once a field becomes dominated by women it incurs a wage penalty. This supports the 'devaluation thesis' – that 'cultural ideas deprecate women and thus, by association, devalue work typically done by women' (England 2005b: 382). Paula England, Michelle Budig and Nancy Folbre (2002) give the example of care work (a field typically associated with women), which is undervalued and underpaid in part because the skills required are seen as natural skills of mothers and properly provided out of altruistic rather than pecuniary motivations.

It is difficult to untangle these complex processes of socialisation, cultural value, personal preference and career choice that lead to women's predominance in fields with lower average pay. While the evidence points to a significant role for socialisation and cultural norms, rational choices can also play a part. However, the choices are made within the prevailing cultural climate, and within labour markets where continuing discrimination on the demand side may also constrain the available supply side options.

Meanwhile, back at the house

Clearly, the tendency of women to take on responsibility for the majority of unpaid domestic work – whether by consent, coercion or necessity – is a significant factor in their poorer economic position (Folbre and Nelson 2000). This is often referred to as women's double burden. The movement for women's liberation has been successful in facilitating the widespread entry of women into the workforce, but many women now question whether this has made them free. As Gilding argues, while women have increasingly moved into the paid workforce, this move has not been matched by 'a corresponding shift of men into unpaid work in the home . . . Since the mid-1970s, a substantial body of research has addressed this issue, and the findings are unambiguous. Women still do most unpaid work' (Gilding 1997: 199). Indeed, surveys show that this is the case even when both partners are in paid full-time employment (Bittman *et al.* 2003). Table 7.6, based on the HILDA survey for 2001, shows that, in households with an adult couple, both of

Table 7.6 Average hours per week of unpaid domestic work in couple households, 2001

	Woman employed full time		Woman employed part time		Woman unemployed	
	Men	Women	Men	Women	Men	Women
Man employed full time	6.0	14.3	5.2	20.1	5.5	20.5
Man employed part time	6.7	14.3	5.7	18.7	5.6	23.4
Man unemployed	10.6	16.0	9.5	16.1	8.9	14.7

Note: The number of households in the study in which women were unemployed and men employed part time, and in which both partners were unemployed, was 5 and 15 respectively. Results for these two household types should be interpreted with some caution.
Source: HREOC 2005: 28.

whom are in full-time paid work, women do an average of 14.3 hours per week of unpaid housework, compared to an average of only 6 hours done by men. The same survey shows that women in full-time paid work do more unpaid work at home than men, even if their partners work part time or are unemployed (HREOC 2005: 28).

The definition of housework in the HILDA survey is limited to indoor tasks, including 'preparing meals, washing dishes, cleaning the house, washing clothes, ironing and sewing' (HREOC 2005: 28). Earlier time-use surveys conducted by the ABS found that, while women's work within the home vastly outstripped men's, men were more likely than women to participate in home maintenance activities or outdoor tasks. However, even when these traditionally male activities were taken into account, women, on average, spent almost twice as long each day as men doing unpaid work around the home (HREOC 2005: 26).

The economic value of this domestic work is far from trivial. Estimates have consistently shown that, 'in terms of input, value added and output' unpaid domestic labour rivals 'not only the major sectors . . . but the whole market economy itself' (Ironmonger, in Gilding 1997: 192). One survey, based on of over 3000 Australian women, found that, in 2002, the value of unpaid labour carried out by women was the equivalent of between $151 and $251 billion – around one-fifth to one-third of Australia's GDP (Doughney *et al.* 2004: 6). The same survey calculated that, if actual earnings were averaged over the total hours of paid and unpaid work performed, the ratio of women's to men's hourly incomes would be only 47 per cent (Doughney *et al.* 2004: 6).

Certainly, there are some households in which men do the majority of domestic work. Some observers have represented these households as the 'vanguard of social change' (Harper, in Gilding 1997: 202), but they remain the exception. As Gilding suggests, while men commonly profess egalitarian values regarding the sharing of household labour, it is not backed up by the reality of who does the bulk of the domestic work. Indeed, he argues that the apparently egalitarian values may actually hide the lack of real change and, as such, be both a 'symbolic concession and a means of resistance by men' (Gilding 1997: 205). Similarly, Australian sociologist Janeen Baxter presents the argument that the unequal division of household labour 'is more than just an unequal distribution of tasks between men and women': it also involves 'the reproduction and maintenance of gender itself' (1997: 220). Feminist accounts of these processes emphasise the continued inequality in power relations. In summary, while women were 'once exploited as housewives, they are now exploited through the double shift' (Gilding 1997: 209).

Concerns about the adequacy and cost of childcare are another important part of the story. Many women are unable to find adequate childcare support: costs have risen rapidly in recent years and there have been chronic shortages of accessible places (Peatling 2005; Harvey 2006; Osborne 2006). Inadequate maternity leave provisions are another constraint in some cases. The result is that the choice between waged work and domestic labour is highly constrained for women with children. Political economists Ray Broomhill and Rhonda Sharp (2005) note that these difficulties have disproportionately affected women from lower socioeconomic households. In wealthier households that can afford childcare and elder care, and where women have accessed core positions within the labour market, women have gained increased bargaining power and established a more equal gender order within the home. However, in many poorer households, where women have been restricted to lower-paid jobs on the periphery of the labour market, they have continued to carry the weight of social reproduction, and traditional male-dominated power structures within the home have persisted.

Some of these jobs on the periphery include domestic work in other people's houses. This may be interpreted as the growth of a new servant class, employed to take on the domestic labour of wealthier households. Some of these women in paid housework find that their jobs are a dead end, trapping them in low-waged, low-skilled work. To a significant extent, though, this experience is moderated by age and ethnicity: it is most often older, migrant women from non-English-speaking backgrounds who 'find themselves unable to move into better paid, higher-skilled jobs' (Meagher 2003: 96). However, while the latest ABS data suggest that there is some growth in the outsourcing of domestic work, the bigger change involves buying products (such as preprepared and takeaway meals) rather than hiring housekeepers or cleaners (ABS 2005e: table 2). To this extent, Australia has not (yet) seen the 'flourishing of a low-waged, low-skilled market for . . . waged domestic labour' that has been evident in the United States (Meagher 2003: 96).

International comparison

How does gender inequality in Australia compare with that in other nations? One basis on which it is possible to make international comparisons is by comparing statistics on wage differentials between women and men. Table 7.7 shows the ratio of average estimated female to male incomes in selected countries. According to this measure, Australia ranks equal fifth on the list, well behind Sweden and a little behind Norway, Denmark and Finland. At the lower end of the scale is a mix of developed and developing countries, including India, South Africa, Japan and Germany. However, wage differentials alone do not provide an adequate representation of gender inequality, particularly for developing countries where the vast majority of women's work is unpaid. For this reason, the table also includes estimated ratios of female to male work times, taking into account unpaid work.

Table 7.7 International comparison of gender inequalities in income and burden of work

Country	Female income as % of male	Female work time as % of male	Gender Empowerment Measure Ranking
Sweden	81	–	2
Norway	75	108	1
Denmark	73	98	4
Finland	71	105	6
Australia	70	104	8
New Zealand	70	101	13
UK	65	100	16
France	64	108	–
Canada	63	98	11
USA	62	106	12
Germany	58	100	9
South Africa	45	122	–
Japan	44	108	42
India	31	117	–

– Figures not available.

Note: Estimates of work time are based on time-use surveys.

Source: United Nations 2006: tables 25 and 28.

The United Nations uses these and other statistics (including the number of women in parliament and senior management positions) to develop its Gender Empowerment Measure (GEM). According to this measure, Australia ranks eighth in the world. These figures provide an interesting comparison across countries. They indicate that, while gender inequality remains a serious concern in Australia, our response to it may have been more effective than in many other parts of the world, with the obvious exceptions of the Scandinavian nations.

That said, these United Nations statistics also need some qualification. The ratio of female to male earnings in Australia that is reported by the UN is quite different to the most recent ABS calculation, provided earlier in this chapter. One reason for the discrepancy is that the United Nations figure is based on an earlier year, consistent with the UN statisticians' use of the most recent year for which comparable data were available between 1991 and 2004. Moreover, while the ABS figure is based on a survey of average weekly earnings, the UN figure is an estimate derived from a comparison of non-agricultural wage rates, 'the female and male shares of the economically active population, the total female and male population and GDP per capita' (UN 2006: 366). Presumably, the UN creates these estimates in order to produce data that are directly comparable across countries. While the result is likely to be a relatively accurate international ranking, the ABS figures are more accurate for examining recent trends in wage relativity in Australia.

In addition, while the GEM attempts to amalgamate various elements of gender equality, it does not represent the sum total of women's experiences or opportunities. Being a composite measure, it also obscures the performance of different countries on particular variables. Australia's eighth ranking on the GEM, for example, belies the fact that Australia performs poorly in an international comparison of women in corporate leadership. As noted earlier, the proportion of board directors of the top 200 Australian companies who are women is 8.7 per cent. This compares to 14.7 per cent in the USA, 12 per cent in Canada and 10.5 per cent in the UK. Australia also rates poorly in terms of women in politics. It is twenty-ninth on the league-table published by the Inter-Parliamentary Union to show the proportion of women MPs in lower houses of parliament. New Zealand is in fifteenth place, the position Australia occupied in 1999 (Horin 2006).

The middle column of table 7.7 should also be read with some caution. The ratio of female to male work time is indicative of the almost universal tendency for women to carry a larger share of the total workload. However, as noted by Marilyn Waring, even time-use surveys that are explicitly designed to include unpaid work may exclude some forms of work done by women. Under these circumstances, statistics on women's working hours are likely to be underestimates (Waring 1996: 62).

Capitalism and patriarchy

Earlier chapters of this book have referred to economic inequalities that reflect differences of class, ethnicity, age and geographical location. Gender inequality adds yet another dimension. Within much of the early feminist literature, particularly that of the 1970s, this was explored through the notion of patriarchy. Although there is dispute about what this term means, it can be broadly defined as a system of gender domination, in which men (as a group) hold more social, economic and political power than women (as a group). If contemporary society is characterised by such systematic gender domination and if, as political economists argue, capitalism is a system of class domination of capital over labour, then the two systems of inequality must necessarily overlap.

Whether one of these two power structures takes precedence over the other has been a theme in academic debates. Some political economists see class relations as the primary cause of socioeconomic inequalities and suggest that women's oppression is a secondary concern (Bloodworth 2005). Because capitalism requires a division of labour and a reserve army of labour in order to function, it has exploited the historical subordination of women for those purposes. This perpetuates women's economic disadvantage. From this perspective, it is the class position of women and the contrasting experience of women from different socioeconomic groups that matter.

Others argue that patriarchy is paramount: that social and economic inequalities between men and women exist primarily because of men's disproportional power and their desire to retain it (a position that is outlined by Pritchard Hughes 1997: 5). Such arguments stress that patriarchy predates capitalism and imply that gender inequalities under capitalism are merely its most recent manifestation. So, patriarchy is not simply a sideline to the real issues of class. While some groups of women may be better off than others, it is the relative disadvantage of women as a whole that is regarded as important.

Both of these views on the sources of gender inequality suggest that the effects of capitalism and patriarchy are mutually reinforcing. Earlier generations of feminists saw their positions as housewives as a form of both capitalist and patriarchal exploitation, providing unpaid domestic labour that was fundamental to the functioning of the economy, while keeping them out of the paid workforce and thereby rendering them economically disempowered and dependent on men. Meanwhile, men could divorce themselves from household work and engage in activities that gave them social, economic and political power (Pritchard Hughes 1997). Today, while many women work outside of the home, the problem of economic and political marginalisation persists. The dramatic underrepresentation of women among senior corporate executives is illustrative of their class position: as a whole, women lack the capital required to control the commanding heights of the economy.

While the notion of patriarchy is still prevalent, the complexity of gender identities and power relations has led some modern feminists to question whether it remains a useful conceptual tool. As Ann Curthoys notes, some argue that patriarchy is a circular proposition: it presupposes gender domination rather than examining its causes, thus 'asserting what it seeks to explain' (Curthoys 2000: 23). Others, echoing earlier debates about the intersection of gender and class, have pointed to the interaction of multiple identities, such as gender, ethnicity, and sexuality. Social scientist Jeanette Hägerström (2003), for example, argues that these complex identities cannot be understood as discrete categories that add on top of one another. Rather, they are experienced differently by different individuals, being contingent on the social context and the multiple experiences and identities of each person. This suggests that the experience of gender 'is produced in a series of competing discourses, rather than by a single patriarchal ideology', and that there is significant room for female agency whereby gender relations involve both 'strategies and counter-strategies of power' (Curthoys 2000: 22–3).

These more subtle interpretations deepen our understanding of women's political economic positions. However, as the evidence presented in this chapter shows, despite myriad differences between them, women as a whole still face significant economic disadvantage. In particular, the double burden commonly experienced by women raises questions about their genuine choices for equal participation in paid employment. Catherine Hakim implies that it is acceptable that men have retained 'their dominance in the labor market, politics, and other competitive activities' since many women 'choose' to prioritise family responsibilities over full-time work (2002: 437). But such choices are made in the context of cultural norms that limit women's employment opportunities and aspirations, and undervalue domestic work. To see this as a legitimate basis for women's continued disadvantage, rather than a reason for a more fundamental reorientation of political and economic arrangements, is evidence of a patriarchal ideology still at work.

Conclusion

Although it has remained firmly on the agenda of social science research, gender inequality often does not come to the attention of the public. One reason may be that it appears less extreme than other dimensions of inequality. The wages gap between men and women seems modest in comparison with the huge income inequalities between corporate executives and workers on average weekly earnings, or the different economic conditions of remote Indigenous communities and the residents of affluent suburbs in the major cities. Moreover, women and men are everywhere, so gender inequalities are less evident when comparing living standards in different households or regions.

Nonetheless, gender inequality is important for two fundamental reasons. First, it intersects with other dimensions of economic inequality, such as class and ethnicity. Women from lower class positions, Indigenous communities, disadvantaged ethnic communities and marginalised social groups, such as single parents, are often doubly disadvantaged, faring worse than men in similar social positions and ranking at the bottom of the economic scale. Second, gender inequality is significant precisely because it is so pervasive. Women make up over 50 per cent of the Australian population, and yet consistently show up as less well off on a range of indicators, including income, employment and political representation. There are significant gender biases in public policy too – an issue we take up in the next chapter.

In a society in which equality of opportunity is commonly espoused, the persistence of gender inequality is a continual reminder of the gulf between principle and practice, whose roots are in a complex interaction of factors such as education, occupation, working hours and the social construction of gender roles. These are among the broader array of forces that drive economic, social and political disparities in Australian society.

Chapter Eight

DRIVING THE DISPARITIES

What determines who gets what? What causes the dramatic inequalities in the distribution of income and wealth described in the preceding chapters? Probing these questions requires a shift from a description of patterns to an analysis of causation. Complex political economic judgements are required. The inequalities in the distribution of income and wealth, for example, may be regarded as embedded in the normal working of capitalist economy. Such a view leads those on the political Right and Left to draw markedly different inferences – either accepting economic inequality as a natural phenomenon or advocating radical challenge to the system that produces it. On the other hand, if the inequalities are traceable to more contingent factors – particular features of labour markets or welfare state provisions, for example – more piecemeal reforms may be worthy of consideration. A more social democratic response then beckons.

Evidently, understanding the causes of economic inequality is a precondition for making some sense of debates about appropriate responses. This chapter seeks to identify the principal causal clusters. These include, first, structural factors, such as the nature of the capital–labour relationship, the use of economic power and changes associated with corporate globalisation and financialisation. Second, there are the more directly political influences of government, particularly the effects of neoliberalism on public policy. Third, there are labour market conditions and the effects of industrial relations policy changes. A fourth factor is discrimination according to gender and ethnicity. Finally, consideration is given to land and housing markets, the effects of urban form and the inheritance of wealth. These influences on economic inequality are interconnected in various ways, so what follows can be regarded as building up a layered explanation of a complex phenomenon. The inference is that a correspondingly multidimensional strategic policy response is warranted.

Inequality as business as usual

A basic, bold proposition to begin: the normal functioning of a capitalist economy generates economic inequality. It is a proposition that draws immediate attention to the systemic elements underpinning distributional outcomes. Of course, organising economic activity on capitalist principles has its pros and cons – as do all types of political economic organisation. In the case of capitalism, its great strength is also its Achilles heel. That is the quest for profit – the essential dynamic of the capitalist system that drives the process of capital accumulation. The resulting process of wealth generation depends on firms continually seeking to minimise their production costs, which puts downward pressure on the incomes of those who do not own and control the means of production – the working class. The periodic regeneration of a pool of unemployed people within this class – the reserve army of labour – simultaneously facilitates capital accumulation while further polarising the income distribution. These features of capitalist production and distribution, somewhat baldly stated here, have been characteristic of the system since its inception and have been a central concern of studies in political economy for over two centuries.

The fundamental tendency towards economic inequality under capitalism arises because capital makes capital and poverty breeds poverty. Owning capital opens up possibilities for generating income without personally undertaking wage labour; the more income is received as profit, rent or interest payments, the more capital can be reinvested. Capital accumulation thereby operates in a cumulative manner. Meanwhile, those without any capital are trapped into social and economic processes geared to the simple reproduction of labour and of life itself. So, as liberal American economist Lester Thurow puts it, 'Capitalistic economies are essentially like Alice in

Wonderland where one must run very fast to stand still – just stopping inequality from growing requires constant effort' (Thurow 1996: 245).

Indeed, what really needs to be explained is why capitalist societies such as Australia are not even *more* unequal than they are. That is where trade unions and reformist governments enter the story. Historically, trade unions have fought for higher wages and the defence of workers' rights – and they are still doing so. However, their coverage of the workforce has fallen: only around 23 per cent of Australian workers are now members of unions (ABS 2006i; Peetz 2006: 54). Concurrently, reformist governments have sought to redistribute incomes through the development of progressive taxation and the welfare state. But this commitment has been muted, if not reversed, as a result of the ascendancy of neoliberalism as an influence on public policy in the last two decades. So, both of the principal institutional impediments to growing economic inequality are now less effective. The outcome has been a shift in the relative power of capital and labour.

The capital–labour relationship is a class relationship. Employment of one class (those people dependent on the sale of their labour) by another (those owning and controlling the means of production) involves a structural imbalance of economic power that has its roots in distinctive property rights. The owners of capital hire labour, not *vice versa*. The imbalance of class power is further accentuated by the integration of the capital's senior managers: interlocking directorates involve many of them sitting on the boards of directors of two or more companies (Murray 2001; Pietsch 2005: 26). It is further accentuated where the businesses have exceptional market power because they operate under conditions of oligopoly or monopoly. This concentration and centralisation of capital enhances their capacity to control the business environment. It gives the managers of the corporations greater power to administer prices and wages, and thus greater power over consumers and employees – even over government policies, albeit more indirectly. Such features of corporate power have been particularly evident in Australia in the past decade, as mergers and takeovers have swept through many sectors of the economy, including mining, key manufacturing industries, retailing, financial services, media ownership and even the funeral business (see Pritchard 1994; Cottle and Keys 2004; Jones 2005).

Corporate globalisation generalises the tendency towards the centralisation and concentration of capital, leading to yet greater income disparities. It has facilitated a more cohesive integration of the capitalist class worldwide (Sklair 2001; Tabb 2004). This has not necessarily undermined state capacity, but it has generally led national governments towards an embrace of the competitiveness agenda and the restructuring of state regulations in order to satisfy the demands of transnational capital (Bryan and Rafferty 1999; Holton 1998: 80–107). The increased power of transnational corporations and financial institutions has created strong pressures to reduce costs of production, especially labour costs. For a nation such as Australia, whose neighbours include low-wage nations such as China, Indonesia and the Philippines, seeking international competitiveness through wage reductions is particularly problematic. Such a solution cannot stem the loss of jobs in industry sectors such as textiles, clothing and footwear, but it has become an integral part of the redistribution of the national income from labour to capital.

As noted in chapter 2, the relative shares of wages and profits have shifted substantially in the last two decades in favour of those deriving their income from the ownership of capital. This constitutes a major redistribution of income between social classes. One might have expected the broader spread of share ownership to be an offsetting factor. The proportion of households owning shares in businesses has certainly risen dramatically – up from about 14 per cent in 1991 to over 50 per cent in recent years (White et al. 2004: 100). The privatisation of government-owned business enterprises has encouraged many workers to buy tiny individual parts of what they had previously owned collectively. Other households with some savings have been enticed into share ownership by the surge in share values, especially in the 1990s. However, in practice, the pattern of share ownership has remained very lopsided, as noted in chapter 3. A NATSEM study found that about 90 per cent of the value of shares is owned by the wealthiest 20 per cent of households (Kelly 2002: 5). According to the ASX data, only about 5 per cent of shareholders have sufficient shares to generate an income that exceeds 25 per cent of the average adult income (Anderson 2002). So, contrary to claims about 'people's capitalism', the spread of share ownership still leaves the distribution of income from capital markedly concentrated.

More households than in the past now derive some income from capital but the bulk of income from capital still remains in the hands of an already affluent elite.

How wisely has that capital been used? This is a moot point because, while the profit motive can generally be expected to lead to a continual search for the highest rates of return on capital, it does not necessarily lead to the most productive outcomes for the society as a whole. In the Australian case, the last two decades have seen some particularly problematic tendencies in corporate activities that have tended to compound inequality in the distribution of wealth while doing little to contribute to the production of total wealth. Many of the mergers and takeovers mentioned above, motivated primarily by the financial gains associated with reorganisation of the structure of asset holdings, have added little to overall productive capacity. Rather, they have tended to deflect resources away from improvements to infrastructure and from the expansion and modernisation of productive industry. Gross fixed capital formation, as a proportion of GDP, has remained disappointingly low. Capital has not been used with social responsibility, nor even, in some cases, with commercial success. It may be business as usual for Australian capitalism, but the economic inequalities have had dubious payoff in terms of their aggregate economic and social effects.

As Australian political analyst Boris Frankel argues, there is a further systemic element here – the process of 'financialisation' that is reshaping the political economy of redistribution. Financialisation refers not only to the increasing influence of financial markets in corporate activities, but also to 'the growing infusion of financial calculation and criteria into a wide range of spheres of economic and political life' (Frankel 2002: 78). The financial markets exercise a distinctive discipline on investment behaviour, prioritising a short-term focus on maximising shareholder value. As political economist Geoff Dow notes, this 'finance-led capitalism disadvantages firms that need long-run rather than short-run criteria in the provision of finance (that is, most manufacturing operations), but also the economy as a whole, by increasing the volatility of "hot money" flows and investment generally' (Dow 2002: 67). Another effect of financialisation is to constrain government initiatives, favouring those consistent with a short-term market-oriented agenda over other policies with more long-term developmental nation-building and egalitarian intentions. The international credit-rating agencies are effectively working off a neoliberal scorecard in determining what risk premium will be added to the interest rate applicable to federal and state government borrowings.

Neoliberalism

Governments are directly involved in the politics of distribution. Historically, their policies have recurrently raised the possibility of progressive redistribution but frequently delivered the opposite outcome. As neoliberalism has become the dominant influence, the policies of successive Australian governments in the last two decades have clearly exhibited this characteristic. Neoliberalism, as a set of political ideologies and practices, prioritises the economic over the social and the market over planning. It builds on the 'economic rationalism' that emerged as the ascendant economic orthodoxy in the 1980s (Pusey 1991; Stilwell 2000: chapter 4). It rests on a simplification of neoclassical economics. The more sophisticated versions of that economic theory acknowledge that market forces operate efficiently only in very special circumstances that seldom prevail in the real world. Indeed, pure neoclassical theory makes no general claim that markets produce equitable distribution: its dominant concern is with allocative efficiency, not distributional equity. However, a vulgarised version of the theory, and the corresponding set of social values about the primacy of market forces, has proved to be very influential. Therein lies the political economic significance of neoliberalism as a means of legitimising regressive redistribution.

The federal Labor government, in the period 1983–96, paved the way for the embrace of neoliberalism by pursuing policies of financial deregulation, trade liberalisation and privatisation of government enterprises (Quiggin 2002: 163). However, these policies were partly constrained by the government's commitment, under its Accord agreement with the unions, to increase the social wage so that at least some of the fruits of economic growth would flow through to workers and welfare recipients. The Coalition government, since 1996, has implemented a much sharper version of neoliberalism. Its policies are also constrained, but differently now because they are designed to cater for the interests of its business supporters through an array of trade, tax and industry policies.

Neoliberalism strongly favours trade liberalisation as an article of faith. In the 1980s, the federal Labor government put strong emphasis on the reduction of tariff protection for industries such as vehicle manufacturing, textiles, clothing and footwear, but accompanied that policy thrust with some specific industry plans. The tariff cutting has been continued by the Coalition, albeit without consistent application in practice and with a contradictory relationship to the more recent enthusiasm for bilateral trade agreements (Dieter 2006). Job losses for workers in industries more exposed to international competition have been commonplace. Many of these workers (such as migrant women) have had difficulty getting other paid work, sometimes because of their geographical location, sometimes because they lack the necessary skills required by the other industries that are expanding. It was the difficulties faced by the casualties of policy-induced structural economic change that had led the Crawford Committee to recommend in the 1970s that tariffs not be reduced whenever the unemployment rate exceeds about 5 per cent. It is advice that has since been ignored. It seems that the neoliberal faith in trade liberalisation, although capable of accommodating the shift from a more principled multilateralism to a pragmatic bilateralism, remains largely blind to the distributional effects and their distinctive sectoral, spatial and social dimensions.

A regressive distributional tendency has been a yet more consistent theme in budgetary policies. The federal budget of May 2005, for example, significantly reduced welfare payments to some of the most disadvantaged groups in society. New applicants for the disability pension who were deemed capable of working part time, as well as sole parents with children of school age, were put on unemployment benefits rather than the disability or sole parent pensions. This was estimated to reduce the payments to affected disabled persons and sole parents by $40 and $22 a week respectively, while increasing their effective marginal tax rate by 20 cents in the dollar for any additional income they earned. Simultaneously, the budget reduced the marginal tax rates for the highest-income earners and gave the greatest tax concessions on superannuation to the most wealthy (Gittins 2005b).

An analysis of the 2005 and 2006 federal government budgets taken together shows how regressive were the tax changes that were introduced. The richest 1 per cent of individual taxpayers received 9 per cent of the tax cuts, the richest 5 per cent received 26 per cent of the cuts and the richest 10 per cent received 43 per cent of the cuts. The poorest 50 per cent of taxpayers received just 19 per cent of the cuts. Looked at in terms of households the distribution was somewhat less skewed towards the rich, the poorest 50 per cent of households receiving 27 per cent of the tax cuts while the upper 50 per cent received 73 per cent (Leigh 2006: 57). Tax policies such as these directly affect people's living standards, their capacity to save and therefore accumulate wealth. This is neoliberalism in action as inegalitarian social policy.

The unequalising effects of government policy have been further compounded by cuts in company tax rates, dividend imputation and reduction of the effective rate of capital gains tax. The halving of the effective rate of capital gains tax in 1999 was perhaps the most dramatic of the changes made in the last decade of neoliberal policies. One journalist has commented that it created a situation in which 'it is now far more tax effective to buy and sell assets than earn a salary' (Garnaut 2005b). Analysis of the official tax statistics shows that the annual revenue collected from that tax fell from $5.3 billion to $3.3 billion over the three years immediately following the capital gains tax cuts. In the very first year some 68 000 taxpayers earning over $100 000 – less than 1 per cent of all taxpayers – received half of all the capital gains received by individuals during that year. So the benefits resulting from the capital gains tax cuts were remarkably concentrated among the richest Australians, amounting to an average tax cut of $220 per week for those top 68 000 income recipients (ABC 2004). The dividend imputation credit system has had a yet more long-standing effect on income distribution. Ostensibly designed to alleviate double taxation of dividends, this imputation system allows tax paid by companies to be refunded to shareholders receiving franked tax-free dividends. The effect has been a massive redistribution of income to corporate shareholders.

Tax concessions such as these also undermine the government's – any government's – fiscal capacity. Its ability to spend on public goods, social services and social security provisions is constrained. So the generosity to the owners of capital is matched by a corresponding austerity in respect of social infrastructure spending and payments to welfare recipients. Not surprisingly, this has given rise to increased selectivity or targeting in the social security system and the corresponding demise of the principle of universality. The long-run tendency is to undermine the legitimacy and financial viability of a healthy public sector providing for the collective needs of society.

Employment and industrial relations

Labour market conditions have also changed. The global reorganisation of production by transnational corporations, coupled with changes in technology, has markedly affected the volume and variety of employment opportunities available. As ANU economist Bob Gregory noted in the early 1990s, there has been some polarisation in the distribution of jobs – between the well-paid and the low-paid (Gregory 1993). The changing nature of work, wages and security, including the effect of the growth of casual and part-time employment, the increased use of contract labour and the erosion of the centralised wage-fixing system, are also important influences on income inequalities. Employment growth has been concentrated in professional, executive, managerial and other high-paid positions and, simultaneously, in the proliferation of casual and part-time work in the secondary labour market (including so-called Macjobs). Between these two poles the number of middle-income positions – such as skilled blue-collar manufacturing industry jobs and clerical white-collar jobs – has tended to be more stable or, in many cases, declining. So wage incomes are becoming more unequal (Borland, Gregory and Sheehan 2001). The result is a more pronounced dualism in the labour market.

It is possible to distinguish two elements in this dualism – changes in occupational structure and changes in rates of pay. Another ANU economist, Michael Keating, a former Secretary of the Department of Prime Minister and Cabinet, says that 'Overall, the picture is one of increasing inequality of earnings over the last 25 years', contrasting with 'a long period of stability or compression of the earnings distribution during most of the twentieth century prior to the mid-1970s' (Keating 2003: 376). Keating's own research suggests that the growing disparities are not primarily because earnings of better-paid workers have risen more rapidly than those of the more lowly paid; rather, there are now just more of the former. In his own words 'It is the highest skilled and paid occupation groups that have expanded relative to the rest' (2003: 385). Keating qualifies this conclusion by conceding that since 1997 there is some evidence of higher-paid occupational groups getting proportionately larger increases in pay, but asserts that the difference is small, notwithstanding other evidence (such as that reviewed in chapter 2 of this book) about the escalation of senior managerial salaries.

Other research on changing wage relativities suggests rather different conclusions. A study commissioned from the Australian Centre for Industrial Relations Research and Teaching, for example, confirmed that lower-paid workers slipped further behind between 1998 and 2004, as wages for the bottom 20 per cent of wage earners rose by an average of only 1.2 per cent per annum, compared with an overall average of 3.6 per cent (O'Malley 2005). Looking over a longer period, the increased dispersion of wage incomes is yet more marked. ABS figures show that in 1985 the worker at the tenth decile of the male earnings distribution received 70 per cent of the median wage, but by 2000 this had fallen to 62 per cent. At the top end, the worker at the ninetieth decile was receiving 62 per cent more than the median wage in 1985, but by 2000 this had risen to 76 per cent. Reviewing these trends, economic journalist Ross Gittins (2004) states that 'The fundamental cause of inequality in our society is the market economy'. It is evidently a market economy in which the structural shifts affecting different occupations are tending to increase wage relativities. Occupational groups in which women are concentrated seem to have been particularly disadvantaged (as noted by Pocock and Masterman-Smith 2005: 127–30).

Further illustrating these growing occupational inequalities, a Productivity Commission study, *The Distribution of Economic Gains of the 1990s*, reported that, while Australians are

> 2.4 times better off than they were 30 years ago, the gap between the rich and the poor has grown as a result of a widening gulf between the high and low wage jobs . . . The wages of blue collar workers relative to highly-skilled white collar workers dropped from 71 to 68 percent between 1987 and 1996, while those of unskilled workers slipped slightly less from 67 to 65 percent of their well-paid white collar counterparts (O'Loughlin 2000).

Industrial relations policy changes interact with the effects of these labour market shifts. They impact on the relative shares of capital and labour in the national income because they affect wage rates (and therefore business costs). They also impact on the degree of income dispersion among those who derive their incomes only from wage labour. In both these respects industrial relations policy is crucial for the political economy of distribution. Indeed, it is not surprising that this has become a major battleground for those concerned about growing inequality in Australia society.

WorkChoices: Whose choices?

In the 1980s the federal Labor government maintained some degree of centralised control over the wage-fixing process but began to accede to the demands of employers (and some of the stronger trade unions) for decentralised enterprise bargaining. The system was working reasonably well, according to the conventional criteria, with, for example, a low incidence of industrial disputation and steady growth in labour productivity. But corporate interests – organised through bodies such as the H. R. Nicholls Society and the Business Council of Australia – were pressing for radical change designed to reduce the power of organised labour (Dabscheck 1990).

The election of the Coalition government led by John Howard provided the opportunity for those more dramatic changes. Its Workplace Relations Bill of 1996 was a portent of more dramatic changes to come. The Bill signalled the intention to move towards more emphasis on individual contracts, known as Australian Workplace Agreements (AWAs). The 1996 Bill was significantly watered down because the government needed the support of the Australian Democrats to get the legislation approved by the Senate. In practice, the uptake of AWAs in the following eight years was very modest, as table 8.1 shows. However, following on from enterprise bargaining, the effect of the 1996 legislation was to further erode the central control through the Industrial Relations Commission that had formerly been a linchpin of the wages system, and which had recognised the inherent inequality in the bargaining position of employers and employees as individuals.

After being re-elected in 2005, and somewhat unexpectedly finding itself with a majority in the Senate too, the Howard government was in a position to make a renewed assault on this institutional heritage. As table 8.1 shows, by 2004 only one-fifth of all employees had their wages determined by the standard awards: so the awards had become, in effect, little more than a social safety net. The *Workplace Relations Act 2005* (Cwlth) – the so-called WorkChoices legislation – reduced the range of safeguards provided by those awards, undermined the collective power of organised labour and provided for a major extension of the use of AWAs. It made it possible for employers effectively to offer contracts to

Table 8.1 Methods of setting pay by sector, May 2004 (% of employees)

Method of setting pay	Private sector	Public sector	All employees
Awards only	24.7	2.3	20.0
Registered collective agreements	24.2	91.8	38.3
Unregistered collective agreements	3.2	0.4	2.6
Registered individual agreements	2.6	1.8	2.4
Unregistered individual agreements	38.5	3.7	31.2

Note: The figures in the private sector and all employees columns do not sum to 100 due to the inclusion of working proprietors of incorporated businesses in the total. These owner–managers account for 5.4 per cent of all employees.

individual workers on a take it or leave it basis. Further redistribution of income from labour to capital and further widening of wage disparities are predictable consequences, as noted by a veritable avalanche of critical commentaries by industrial relations specialists, including the range of contributors to the special 'Whose Choices?' issue of the *Journal of Australian Political Economy* published in December 2005 (King and Stilwell 2005).

The level of the minimum wage in Australia, expressed as a proportion of median wage incomes, has, at nearly 60 per cent (Wooden 2005: 83), been the highest of all the OECD countries. It is unlikely that this will be maintained now that responsibility for setting the minimum wage is shifted from the Industrial Relations Commission to the Australian Fair Pay Commission (AFPC – the somewhat Orwellian-sounding body set up by the Coalition government as part of its 2005 industrial relations changes). Its first decision, in October 2006, was to increase the minimum wage, but few doubt that the purpose of setting up the AFPC – and selecting a particularly right-wing economist as its head – was to reduce the minimum wage relative to other incomes in the longer term.

A significant growth in the number of people who can be described as working poor is already evident, predating the most recent round of IR changes. Casualisation of jobs had been a significant feature of the last decade: by August 2002, 27 per cent of the Australian workforce were in casual jobs, up from 20 per cent in 1991 (Senate Community Affairs References Committee Secretariat 2004; see also Campbell 2000). Such workers are particularly vulnerable because of their lack of guaranteed continuity in employment.

A shift in the balance between full-time and part-time jobs is also ongoing. Industrial relations researchers Ian Watson and John Buchanan note (2001) that full-time employment as a share of the working-age population fell by 20 per cent between 1973 and 1996, representing an effective loss of 2.8 million jobs. During the same period, the share in part-time work rose by 300 per cent. This pattern has continued over the last decade, albeit less dramatically, with part-time employment as a proportion of total employment increasing from 24.8 per cent in 1996 to an estimated 28.6 per cent in August 2006 (ABS 2006d). As Watson and Buchanan note, part-time work can be valuable, particularly in providing employment opportunities for students and those caring for children, but it does not 'provide livelihoods for breadwinners – either male or female – among the unemployed' (2001: 198). Hence, the relative decline of full-time jobs has meant an increase in the number of people who are 'reluctantly stuck' in part-time work. The most recent data show that 24.3 per cent of part-time workers would like to work more hours (ABS 2006d: 5). Moreover, since much of the growth in part-time jobs has been in the services sector, it has not provided suitable employment opportunities for 'that core of long-term unemployed blue-collar workers who have been displaced from manufacturing and infrastructure industries' (Watson and Buchanan 2001: 198).

There is also evidence of a growing gulf between the economic situation of two-income households and no-income households. In the former, typically, both adults (for example, husband and wife) are in paid employment; in the latter both are unemployed (Burbidge and Sheehan 2001). The no-income household's problem is often compounded by the long-term character of their unemployment. Indeed, the problems of the working poor and of continuing long-term unemployment have a common root – the lack of sufficient full-time jobs, despite overall economic growth. This is evidently not soluble through policies to encourage the growth of more low-paid jobs. On the contrary, the desire to create a large low-wage sector in Australia under the banner of a flexible labour market can be expected to further entrench poverty and inequality. Moreover, as Watson and Buchanan (2001: 195) note, in addition to its impact on income disparities, inequality in employment has profound effects on

> the quality of the working life, earnings and career mobility, access to training and protection from workplace hazards. Self-identity is also strongly tied to the work one does. Demeaning work, and poorly paid work, seriously devalues a person's sense of self-worth. Among workers, the low-paid workforce invariably endures the worst outcomes in all these areas – and this comes on top of earning the lowest income.

Neoliberalism applied to labour market policies has become part of the problem, undermining the political possibilities for progressive redistribution from the proceeds of economic growth.

Discrimination

The operation of labour markets also reflects the continuing influence of discriminatory practices that impact on the distribution of employment opportunities and incomes. Discrimination can occur according to gender, ethnicity, age, disability, sexual preference or any number of personal attributes and is often difficult to prove. Discrimination by an employer against job applicants from a particular social group, for example, may be disguised as a legitimate process of selection according to a specific skill or attribute. The segregation of women into jobs requiring 'nimble fingers', common in earlier decades, is an obvious example. At the other end of the spectrum, a woman or recent immigrant who believes a job may have been improperly denied them, may have been overlooked for sound reasons that had nothing to do with their gender or immigrant status. Despite these difficulties, discrimination is important to analyse since its existence directly affects the distribution of economic rewards, including employment, income and access to adequate housing.

Racism is a particular problem with deep roots. The historical development of Australia rested heavily on state-sponsored discrimination based on people's ethnic heritage, with both agriculture and industry exploiting Indigenous Australians and non-Anglo-Celtic immigrants as sources of cheap labour (Steven 2000). The Commonwealth government's white Australia policy prohibited the immigration of non-Europeans and excluded the non-British from owning land (Castles and Vasta 1996). In the 1960s and 1970s there was an official reversal in the attitude towards non-Anglo-Celtic groups: the white Australia policy was abandoned in the late 1960s, racial criteria were removed from the Immigration Act by 1973, and the *Racial Discrimination Act 1975* (Cwlth) made it illegal to discriminate in employment, education or any other aspect of public life on the grounds of race, religion or ethnicity. Yet the legacy persists: as Phil Griffiths (2005) argues, cultivating racism towards immigrants and shifting from the fulsome embrace of multiculturalism to policies that foster a 'new racist offensive' has been a notable feature of the last decade of neoliberal politics. Notwithstanding that offensive, after thirty years of anti-discrimination legislation and affirmative action policies, one might have expected to see substantial improvement in employment outcomes.

Research studies using different methodologies have found mixed results. In the early 1990s, M. D. R. Evans and Jonathan Kelley of the Melbourne Institute of Applied Economic and Social Research found that up to one-third of employers were 'willing to discriminate against immigrants in hiring', and that a similar proportion of workers were prejudiced against immigrants (cited in Forrest and Johnston 1999). Economists Peter Riach and Judith Rich (1991: 245) found that when otherwise equivalent job applications written by Anglo-Celtic or Vietnamese Australians were sent in reply to an advertised vacancy, applicants with Vietnamese names 'encountered discrimination almost six times more frequently than applicants with Anglo-Celtic names'.[1] In contrast, a statistical study by geographers James Forrest and Ron Johnston (1999), using data on occupational segregation and immigrant characteristics, argued that the occupational distribution of

---

[1] Discrimination was deemed to have occurred if one applicant received an invitation to interview while the other did not, or if one applicant received an invitation letter later than the other, indicating the former applicant had been placed lower in the shortlist.

immigrants could be largely explained by disadvantage (arising from differences in the productivity-enhancing skills and attributes, or human capital, of migrants) rather than discrimination (where segregation occurred because of the prejudice of employers or other workers). However, their findings showed variation according to gender and country of origin, with immigrant women and immigrants from Asian and Islamic countries more likely to be unemployed. As Forrest and Johnston noted, this may reflect differences in English proficiency and attitudes to female employment among some immigrant groups. The extent to which the differences are attributable to discrimination is impossible to determine by an examination of statistics alone. As Riach and Rich (2002) have noted, altering the choice of variables and data included in such statistical analyses can produce contradictory results.

A more recent study by Julie Browning and Andrew Jakubowicz (2003) from the Transforming Cultures Research Centre at the University of Technology Sydney (UTS) surveyed specific ethnic community groups to examine the extent to which they had experienced discrimination.[2] It found discrimination on the grounds of perceived ethnic or religious difference to be widespread. Respondents reported increasing harassment in public places as well as discrimination in employment. This was most likely to take the form of exclusion from work or segregation in particular kinds of jobs. Aboriginal communities reported the most severe discrimination, including refusal of work and discrimination in the provision of housing. Respondents from Asian communities reported 'exploitation in small factories where there was little trade union presence, and real fear of losing jobs' (Browning and Jakubowicz 2003: 8). As noted earlier, the extent to which people interpret a more benign process as discrimination is difficult to discern, but the large number of reports of discrimination in Browning and Jakubowicz's study, and their consistent patterns, suggest that it remains a substantial problem.

Discrimination also underpins gender inequality although, like discrimination based on ethnicity, it is often hard to prove at the individual level.

---

[2] The study surveyed community groups and individuals representing Aboriginal, Arabic, Indo-Chinese, South Asian, Pacific Islander, Islamic and Jewish communities in Brisbane, Sydney and Melbourne.

It becomes harder to explain away when the patterns are systemic though. Early feminists commonly argued that the solution to women's unequal economic position would be women's entry into paid work. They fought hard, here and in other countries, to give women equal access to what had previously been mainly a man's world. However, women's increased presence in paid employment over recent decades has evidently not guaranteed their economic, social or political equality, as noted in the preceding chapter. Indeed, as modern feminists often point out, by simply facilitating women's entry into the public sphere without challenging this underlying value system, a subtle form of institutional discrimination has become entrenched. In a study of Australian universities, Kate White (2003: 46) argues that the underrepresentation of women in management roles is the result of a 'heavily male value system' within the upper echelons of these institutions, which effectively excludes the majority of women, that is, the attributes needed to 'get to the top' are 'part of a socialization process that . . . virtually no women participate in', so that the problem is seen to be 'located in women themselves', and the 'solution' is that they must 'become more like men, thereby leaving the university institutions intact even though those institutions are what needs to be changed' (Bagilhole, in White 2003: 52).

In addition to institutional obstacles to promotion, as women have moved into paid employment, they have tended to concentrate in caring professions and other fields seen as natural extensions of women's role in the home. Because these fields have tended to be devalued by the market, the association of a job with women's work tends also to be an association with low status and low rates of pay, irrespective of the crucial social and economic functions performed by workers in these professions. Technological changes are causing significant shifts in some of these patterns, opening up new opportunities for women in sectors such as IT. Sociologist Judy Wacjman (2006: 17) notes that technologies 'can indeed be constitutive of new gender dynamics, but they can also be derivative and reproduce older conditions'. To the extent that women remain concentrated in areas of the labour market where they have less bargaining power – in industries characterised by part-time work or low unionisation – they have also been relatively disadvantaged by the shift from centralised wage determination to enterprise bargaining and individual contracts.

This may explain why the closing of the gender gap in wages, which had been evident during the 1970s and 1980s, has stalled. It is indeed a disappointing dividend for so much social activism and policy changes that have been enacted with the aim of redressing gender inequality. The significant progress in terms of interpersonal relations evidently does not translate automatically into redress of the forms of discrimination that perpetuate gendered economic inequalities. Meanwhile, a double burden of paid work and a disproportionate share of domestic labour is common. It is pertinent to recall the argument of American feminist and author Shulamith Firestone that, since women are biologically geared to rearing and raising children, 'drafting women into the . . . commodity economy fails to deal with the tremendous amount of necessary production . . . now performed by women without pay: Who will do it?' (1970: 235). As chapter 7 of this book noted, it is women who are still doing the bulk of unpaid domestic work. Moreover, such work continues to be undervalued and ignored in national economic accounts: since the performance of these services does not involve wage labour, they are considered, in effect, to be unproductive activities.

Layered on top of these problems are further biases arising from public policies. After a careful review of the Howard government's changes to taxation and family support payments, political economist Elizabeth Hill (2006: 7) concludes that,

> Rather than supporting the economic needs and desires of contemporary families and Australian women, the Howard Government has established a set of economic incentives that reward mothers that adhere most closely to the Howard version of the 'ideal' family – a male-breadwinner household. Women that choose to deviate from this policy norm experience inadequate childcare support and high effective marginal tax rates as they try to deepen their attachment to the labour force.

Land, housing, inheritance

The effect of land and housing markets on economic and social inequality is less direct than the influence of labour markets and of public policies directly addressing welfare and redistribution. It is also a less sensitive issue than discrimination – at least in the sense that participation in 'the national hobby' of land speculation, as urban social scientist Leonie Sandercock (1979) memorably called it, is not necessarily restricted by gender or ethnicity. However, in contemporary Australian society, the operation of land and housing markets has been associated with dramatic redistributions of income and wealth. Inflation in land and housing prices has interacted with the labour market conditions, creating particular difficulties for low- and middle-income households in securing affordable housing, while increasing the wealth of the owners of multiple properties. Also, as noted in chapter 5, housing costs are important in determining the incidence of poverty in Australian society: poverty estimates that omit housing costs tend to be rather conservative, other than for the elderly who, on average, spend less on housing.

A substantial fall in housing affordability has taken place in the last two decades, particularly in the major cities. The squeeze began when rapid rises in land prices in the late 1980s, coupled with very high interest rates, drove home ownership beyond the reach of many Australians and raised the average proportion of income allocated for housing expenditure (National Housing Strategy 1991). The steady growth in land values in the 1990s and the rapid surge in the 2000–3 period then accentuated this process. Home ownership rates have only dipped a little, but this is because relatively low interest rates and ready access to loan finance in the last decade have facilitated entry into the home ownership stakes, albeit at the expense of mounting household debt.

Those who had already become owner-occupiers have not been disadvantaged by these trends: indeed, they have commonly been in a position to benefit from them. Not all their perceived gains are real though. Urban home owners congratulating themselves on the rise in the value of their principal assets are, for the most part, celebrating an illusory gain – unless they are prepared to move away from the cities to rural areas or towns where land and housing values are lower. For those owning multiple properties the gains are real enough though, producing substantial increases in their wealth relative to the rest of the population. By contrast, aspiring home owners on low to middling incomes are further marginalised unless they get substantial financial help from wealthier owner-occupying parents. Rental housing remains the only viable option in many cases, and it is in that sector that there is the greatest incidence of housing stress, defined as a household spending at least 30 per cent of its gross income on housing costs.

The incidence of housing stress is strongly correlated with income. The 2001 Census data show that only 5 per cent of households with weekly income in the $1200–1499 range experienced housing stress, while 23 per cent of those with incomes below $400 and 28 per cent of those in the $400–599 range did so (Yates, Randolph and Holloway 2005: 33). More than half of all households with housing stress had gross incomes below $600 per week. The impact of this stress on different occupational groups is also striking. Of hospitality workers, 27 per cent and 18 per cent of sales assistants were experiencing housing stress, compared with an average of 10 per cent for all households (Yates, Randolph and Holloway 2006: 3).

The incidence of housing stress also has a spatial dimension. This is not surprising because the inflation in land and housing costs has not been uniform between cities, within cities or between city and country areas. One effect has been to accentuate the patterns of locational differentiation between income groups, as described in chapter 6. Just as capital makes capital, locational advantage tends to generate cumulative advantage. Housing in the more sought-after localities becomes yet more highly prized – and yet more highly priced. The revenue base from which local services are provided improves relative to that in localities where lower-income households are clustered. Spatial inequalities thereby intensify as the gulf widens between the inhabitants of upper-income suburbs and the more socioeconomically deprived localities.

Intergenerational shifts in wealth accentuate this tendency because, typically, housing is the largest single component in inheritance, as noted in chapter 3. The absence of any inheritance tax in Australia is a key issue here, leading to greater concentrations of wealth and more limited intergenerational mobility than would otherwise be the case. The abolition of death duties in the various Australian states in the 1960s and 1970s allowed this aspect of economic inequality to become more accentuated. The inflation in housing wealth has evidently compounded this effect even though, as noted in chapter 3, housing wealth remains more evenly distributed than other forms of assets. The connection between inheritance, including the inheritance of land and housing, and economic inequality is an issue that raises particular ethical concerns because inherited income has no obvious justification in terms of productive effort. As such, it links to other concerns about difference in people's economic circumstances that are hard to justify in terms of a liberal notion of a level playing field.

Conclusion

The drivers of economic inequality are multidimensional and deeply rooted. Capitalism as an economic system has an innate tendency towards the reproduction and intensification of inequality. Particular features of the economy in the current period accentuate this tendency. Most prominent among these are the assertion of the power of capital, now organised transnationally, and the influence of neoliberalism on public policy. Giving freer rein to the interests of corporate capital reinforces and legitimises economic inequality. The persistence of economic inequalities based on ethnicity and gender is also notable. The forward march of women in the labour market, resulting from their growing participation rates and greater gender pay equity over the last three decades, has been one of the casualties of the changes in industrial relations policy. Those policy changes, more generally, signal a further shift in the balance of power from labour to capital – with potentially major implications for the relative shares of wages and profits in the national income. Meanwhile, land and housing market conditions are simultaneously facilitating a greater share of property income in the economic surplus.

Are these forces of change inexorable? Should we, as a society, simply accept that the prevailing political economic structures generate cumulatively inegalitarian outcomes? Our response, presumably, depends on the judgements we make about the consequences of greater economic inequality. We have to ask whether the society is becoming happier and whether there is any particular social, economic, environmental or political fallout from economic inequality that should be of public concern. It is from consideration of the causes of inequality to this consideration of its consequences that we now turn.

Chapter Nine

GETTING HAPPIER?

Is an economically unequal society preferable to a more equal one? Some would say that the ultimate test is subjective. Do people in general feel better or worse, happier or unhappier? At one level, this is a complex question of morality and motivation that raises deeper questions about the purpose of life. At another level it is a purely empirical question about what people say when they are asked.

A number of recent social surveys reveal that increasing economic growth, incomes and wealth have not produced a significantly happier society. Summarising the evidence, Richard Layard, a leading economist in the field of happiness research, states that 'People in the West have got no happier in the last 50 years. They have become richer . . . they have longer holidays, they travel more, they live longer, and they are healthier. But they are no happier' (Layard 2003a: 14). The character, causes and consequences of this phenomenon have been extensively probed in the Australian context by Clive Hamilton and other researchers at The Australia Institute in Canberra (Hamilton 2002, 2003c; Hamilton and Denniss 2005; Hamilton and Rush 2006). While some of those concerns go beyond the central theme of this book, the linking question is whether the evident disappointment with material economic progress results from inequality in the distribution of the additional incomes.

Exploring this issue involves a series of sequential steps. This chapter begins by considering the usefulness of the concept of happiness as a measure of social outcomes and examines the correlation between income and happiness. The discussion takes into account the survey evidence on individual perceptions of income and personal happiness, as well as some international comparisons of wellbeing. The specific relationship between happiness and income inequality is then analysed by looking at the evidence and arguments suggesting an inverse relationship. Finally, there is consideration of whether economic inequality undermines people's ability to focus on what makes them happy, including good personal health, spending time with family and friends, doing fulfilling work and having social identity. The purpose of the analysis is to cast light on the correlations and causal connections between income inequality and happiness that have brought us, as a society, to an apparently troublesome impasse.

Don't worry, be happy

Is it possible to establish a clear meaning of happiness as a primary measure of individual and societal wellbeing? Some clarity about the goal of happiness is needed. This is easier said than done because, being a condition that concerns the human state of mind, the concept of happiness is inherently subjective, having different meanings for different people. Orthodox economists cut boldly through this complexity with their assertion of utility as the primary – indeed, exclusive – indicator of each individual's happiness and wellbeing. Utility is the satisfaction derived by individuals from their different patterns of consumption or from different courses of action. It may be regarded as synonymous with happiness, subject to the economists' usual *ceteris paribus* assumption, that is, that other non-material influences on happiness are not affected or are non-existent. Herein lies a paradox because, notwithstanding its claim to be creating positive economics, neoclassical theory itself is thereby centred on an inherently subjective concept. As a basis for orthodox economic theory, utility is not linked to actual studies of wellbeing. This limits the capacity of conventional economics to provide substantive explanations for human behaviour. As Hirata (2001: 7) argues:

> The behavioral theory that has been developed within economics has not been inspired by psychological research or any other sort of empirically

qualified concepts. Rather, it relies primarily on *a priori* axioms that derive their appeal from their theoretical properties. In particular, economics has adopted a conception of behavior that is largely identical with the Hobbesian doctrine of psychological hedonism that states that nature endowed the human mind with but a single motivation which is the attainment of pleasure. Even ostensibly altruistic acts are deemed to be motivated by the ensuing pleasure one experiences.

This tunnel vision aspect of orthodox economic theory causes it to lose sight of a broader concept of material wellbeing. Utility maximisation for the individual and economic growth maximisation for the society are taken as axiomatic. A more comprehensive and critical basis for exploring happiness is needed. Ruut Veenhoven (1984: abstract), editor of the *Journal of Happiness Studies*, argues the latter case, defining happiness as

> the degree to which an individual judges the overall quality of his [*sic*] life-as-a-whole favorably. Within this concept two 'components' of happiness are distinguished: hedonic level of affect (the degree to which pleasant affect dominates) and contentment (perceived realization of wants). These components represent respectively 'affective' and 'cognitive' appraisals of life and are seen to figure as subtotals in the overall evaluation of life, called overall happiness.

In simpler terms, happiness involves feeling good. It requires freedom from want and distress and, over and above that, a positive experience of one's place in society or, more broadly, the universe. Some would argue that its ingredients have a hierarchical form, starting from the basic needs in life and ascending to higher elements of subjectivity and spirituality. The well-established pyramid of needs identified by behavioural psychologist Abraham Maslow can be used to support this interpretation. At the bottom of the pyramid are the basics of life, such as food, housing and material comfort. Next are safety and security, followed by love and belongingness, including the desire to feel accepted by the family and community. After that comes the need for esteem and other people's respect and admiration. At the top comes what Maslow calls 'self-actualisation', where people start enjoying what they have and finding happiness in their own attainments without being influenced by those who are materially better off (Gwynne

1997; de Graaf, Wann and Naylor 2005: 118). Each level of need has to be broadly satisfied before progressing to the next, moving from mere survival to self-fulfilment.

This sort of reasoning would tend to imply a positive correlation between economic circumstances and happiness, but a correlation that diminishes in strength after basic material needs are met. That connection may be less clear if, as Layard (2003a) argues, the causes of happiness are of two types – those with enduring effects and those that produce only transient effects. The question that then arises is: What is that element that can sustain our feeling good? Sources of happiness that are found at the hedonistic level and outside of the human person may be inherently short-lived.

Income and happiness

So, can more money buy more happiness? Popular music lyrics illustrate the diversity of views on this issue, with song titles ranging from 'Money, That's What I Want' to 'Money is the Root of All Evil' and 'Money Can't Buy Me Love'. In practice, the most direct way of finding out whether higher incomes make people happier is to put the question directly to them. Their assessment of their own happiness can then be compared with their personal income and, for whole societies, with changes in national income over time. Many such studies have been done in recent years. The bulk of evidence generated by them indicates that, over time, growing affluence is not delivering corresponding increases in happiness. It seems that no matter how wealthy people are they usually believe they need more income to be happy. Clive Hamilton (2003b: 43) argues that

> most people act as if more money means more happiness. But when people reach the financial goals they aspire to, they do not feel any happier. They therefore raise their threshold of sufficiency even higher, and thus begin an endless cycle.

According to Hamilton, this is a process of 'serial disappointment' that has given rise to the phenomenon of the 'suffering rich' (Hamilton 2003b: 43–4). The prevalence of some such process is confirmed by the results of the 2002 Newspoll survey summarised in table 9.1. As indicated there,

Table 9.1 Attitudes to needs, by income quintile: Responses to the statement 'You cannot afford to buy everything you really need'

	Total	Q1 (lowest)	Q2	Q3	Q4	Q5 (highest)
		Household income quintile				
Agree	62.2	83.7	70.4	62.0	49.2	46.3
Disagree	37.1	16.3	29.6	38.0	50.8	53.7

Note: The study surveyed 1200 individuals. The results were equivalised for household size. Of all respondents, 0.7% refused to answer or said 'don't know'.
Source: Newspoll, previously published in Hamilton 2003a.

62 per cent of respondents said that they could not afford to buy everything they really needed. Significantly, more than a quarter of the wealthiest households surveyed (that is, those with incomes over $70 000 a year) said that they spent 'nearly all of their money on the basic necessities of life' (Hamilton 2003b: 43). Around 49 per cent of respondents with annual incomes of $50 000–69 000 shared this belief. On the other hand, it is interesting to note that over 20 per cent of survey respondents in the lowest-income group (with incomes below $20 000 a year) reported that they had no difficulties in affording everything they really needed. As Hamilton argues, these data suggest that 'above some fairly low threshold, feelings of deprivation are conditioned by expectations and attitudes rather than real material circumstances' (Hamilton 2003b: 44).

Similar studies have been conducted for other wealthy countries and regions, including the USA, Japan and Europe. Layard notes that in the USA, although GDP per head has risen by around 50 per cent since 1975, the proportion of people who claim that they are happy has remained virtually unchanged (Layard 2003a: 14). Similarly, in Japan, the sixfold increase in income per head since 1950 has been accompanied by no significant change in reported levels of happiness. In Europe, the *Eurobarometer* series has found no increase in happiness since the early 1970s. Layard concludes that once a country's average level of income reaches about $15 000 per head, the happiness of its citizens becomes, over time, independent of the average income, although the richer people within those countries still tend, on average, to be happier than the poorest (2003a: 17). So if a given individual in a given country becomes richer, that person is likely to become happier, but 'if the whole society becomes richer, nobody seems to be any happier' (Layard 2003b: 4).

Robert Frank, author of *Luxury Fever* (1999), suggests that one explanation may be that, as people's standard of living increases, they quickly begin to take those new standards for granted. Improvements in material wellbeing may make them happier for a while, but the effect gradually fades away. Several empirical studies have confirmed the existence of this process of adaptation (Diener and Seligman 2004; Layard 2005), which is sometimes called 'habituation'. It applies particularly to modern consumer goods, so that one's expectations of material comfort are increasingly ratcheted up. Thirty years ago central heating, for instance, was considered a luxury, as was the mobile phone less than ten years ago, but today these are viewed as normal requirements, if not essentials, by most people. If people do get used to every new acquisition, as the theory of habituation would suggest, then relentlessly pursuing such material possessions becomes futile. However, the same tendency may not apply to other aspects of life, including time spent with family and friends and the level of autonomy one has at work. These qualitative experiences are quite different to processes of commodity acquisition that are more quantitative in character. Hence, to the extent that rising incomes are associated with a decrease in personal leisure time or job satisfaction, the finding that people's level of happiness is not rising should come as little surprise.

Rising incomes, rising distress

Despite the material affluence and growing average incomes in wealthy countries, it is evident that increasing numbers of people are experiencing depression and anxiety disorders, accompanied by high rates of substance abuse, crime and youth suicide. According to Richard Layard, roughly 14 per cent of people aged under 35 have experienced depression, while in the 1950s the corresponding figure was only 2 per cent (Layard 2003a: 19–20). How to interpret such information is unclear: there may well be an increased willingness to seek help as well as an increased incidence of the problem. But there is also a broader array of indicators of personal and social disorders. Alcohol abuse has increased, for example, with over one-quarter of young white males in the USA reporting that they had experienced problems with alcohol, compared with under 15 per cent of men over the age of 65 who reported that they had ever experienced such problems (Layard 2003a: 20). In Britain, 'a third of all young men have been convicted of a crime by the time they are 30' (Layard 2003a: 21). Layard suggests that these figures are indicators of growing alienation and dissatisfaction with life, with similar trends evident in almost all wealthy nations (Layard 2003a: 20).

Australia is no exception. One survey found that one in every six Australians (17.7 per cent) had experienced a mental illness at some time over the preceding year. The most common forms of illness were anxiety disorders, depression and substance use disorders (Healey 2003). Similarly, in the 2002 National Health Survey, 13 per cent of Australian adults reported experiencing 'high or very high levels of psychological distress' and an additional 23 per cent reported moderate levels (Hamilton and Denniss 2005: 114). In the two weeks prior to the survey, 18 per cent of respondents had used medication for their mental wellbeing (Hamilton and Denniss 2005: 115). Disturbingly, the rate of suicide in Australia, particularly among young males, has consistently been recorded over the last two decades as one of the highest in the world. A number of reports suggest that rates of attempted suicide are even higher among young women (Healey 2002; Taylor *et al.* 2004). The ABS reports that 'during the 1990s . . . suicide became the leading cause of death from injury in Australia' (ABS 2004b: 1).

None of this proves any connection between the incidence of personal disorders and an unequal society, especially in the absence of data connecting changes in income with changes in the intensity of the social problems. Indeed, the various manifestations of social malaise can be found among people in all walks of life – rich and poor, young and old, capitalists and workers alike. That is the point – that social progress is disturbingly elusive. Our current single-dimensional focus on economic growth and ever increasing incomes is not providing the widespread contentment and social wellbeing that had been predicted and expected. If the purpose of the economy is to serve the needs of society, rather than *vice versa*, something has evidently gone wrong.

Income inequality and happiness

Is economic inequality at the root of the weak correlation between income and happiness? Is it the persistence of substantial economic inequalities that accounts for the evident dissatisfaction with material economic progress? Posing such questions pushes the analysis of happiness away from The Australia Institute's emphasis on the general problem of affluence, and refocuses it on the issue of economic inequality that is the central concern of this book. It shifts attention away from aggregate measures of income and happiness to more explicitly distributional concerns.

Why might inequality undermine happiness in society? One explanation is to be found in a somewhat improbable place – orthodox economic theory. As noted earlier, the concept of utility is central to neoclassical economics. One of the core propositions studied by every first year economics student at university is the principle of diminishing marginal utility. Applied to income, this principle states that, as a person's income rises, that person normally receives less additional satisfaction from each extra increment. Thus, the first $10 received by a poor person gives enormous satisfaction: it may mean the difference between starving and eating. But an extra $10 received by someone who already has $1 million would hardly be noticed. So increases in income produce little extra happiness among those who are already materially well off. If this is the case, the failure of increased wealth to generate proportionate increases in wellbeing is not surprising. Indeed, it seems likely that taking from the rich and giving to the poor can be expected to reduce the utility of the former less than it increases the utility of the latter.[1] So, if the principle of marginal utility applies to income, and if interpersonal comparisons of utility are deemed to be legitimate, progressive income redistribution has a strong rationale. By this reasoning, more egalitarian economic arrangements

---

[1] The argument that shifting income from rich to poor would increase total utility was developed by A. C. Pigou (1933). Subsequent neoclassical economists argued that the conclusion was illegitimate because it assumed the possibility of making interpersonal comparisons of utility. In other words, it assumes that we can measure the amount of utility derived from additions to (or subtractions from) income. If, however, only ordinal measures of utility are possible, we cannot infer anything about the total utility of a society. This leads to an agnostic perspective, providing no basis for public policy (Neutze 2000: 201–2). It helps to explain why welfare economics, applying neoclassical theory to normative and policy analysis, has proved to be a conceptual *cul-de-sac* (see Stilwell 1996).

are likely to produce a society in which people are, on average, happier. There is a delicious irony in developing such a conclusion from orthodox economic theory.

Other traditions of political economic thought emphasise the societal context within which individual preferences and aspirations are shaped. A second reason why more income and wealth do not automatically make everybody happier then comes into view – because people tend to compare their situation with that of others. As Karl Marx put it, 'A house may be large or small; as long as the surrounding houses are equally small, it satisfies all of our social demands for a dwelling. But if a palace rises beside the little house, the little house shrinks into a hut' (cited in Frank 1999: 122).

Indeed, there is considerable evidence that people's aspirations, and therefore their satisfaction with their current circumstances, are strongly determined by the reference group to which they compare themselves. Job satisfaction, for example, is lower where there is a higher incidence of promotion among peers (Clark and Oswald 1996). Similarly, several studies of happiness indicate that, beyond a fairly low level of material affluence, income differences relative to reference groups have stronger effects than absolute income. This observation has become known as the 'relative income hypothesis' (Hirata 2001: 36). It undermines the conventional neoclassical economic view, in that it is based on the assumption that people's preferences are independently determined and stable, and that increases in income and commodity consumption will increase utility (Headey and Wooden 2004). On the contrary, if people's preferences are influenced by what others have, increases in income or wealth, beyond a certain point, will generate no necessary increase in satisfaction if the unequal distribution of income and wealth persists.

To illustrate this relative income hypothesis, Clark and Oswald (1996) calculated 'comparison incomes' for British workers, these being the average incomes of people with the same jobs, education, and so on. They found that, while absolute incomes had small effects on satisfaction, comparison incomes had a much greater effect. The smaller the difference between their own incomes and those of people performing comparable jobs, the more satisfied the employees were. The study also found that satisfaction with pay was lower if spouses or other household members earned more (Clark and Oswald 1996). A similar study of graduate students in the USA asked whether they would prefer (a) $50 000 a year while others received half of that or (b) $100 000 a year while others received double that. A majority chose option (a). They evidently thought they would be happy with less than the maximum attainable as long as they were better off than others (Layard 2003b).

Robert Frank (1999) contends that such findings explain why people in the wealthier nations are increasingly locked into a competitive race for the trappings of status and success. This 'luxury fever', he suggests, is making their lives less comfortable and less satisfying. It is an argument that echoes institutional economist Thorstein Veblen's late nineteenth century writing on the subject of 'pecuniary emulation' (Veblen 1899). Veblen argued that the consumption of the wealthy 'leisure class' was fuelled by the quest to display its wealth as a means of attaining social esteem. The profligate consumption patterns of this elite thereby set the aspirational standard for other social groups, notwithstanding the latter's lack of comparable economic means. So social dissatisfaction became endemic – along with the wasteful consumption behaviour of the leisure class. In our era, emulating the lifestyles of the rich and famous is yet more pronounced. Television and other media bring the pictures of those lifestyles into the homes of people in diverse economic and social circumstances, while commercial advertising relentlessly promotes the products necessary for their pursuit.

Another current of political economic analysis that is useful for understanding this connection between inequality and happiness derives from Fred Hirsch, author of the influential book *Social Limits to Growth* (1977). This emphasises that it is relative, rather than absolute, income that increases a person's access to the scarce items that are auctioned off in society to those who can most afford them. Hirsch called these items 'positional goods'. A house in a prestigious residential area is a classic example. The more people who want to buy a house in that locality, the more demand exceeds supply and the higher the prices of the houses will be. This causes the area to become even more exclusive and highly sought-after. So the aspiration of the less wealthy to live in the area is continuously thwarted. By their very nature, positional goods are those goods that we cannot all have. To continue to pursue them in an unequal society is, inevitably, frustrating.

Robert Frank (1999) also argues that increasing relative income tends to skew people's spending patterns towards this kind of conspicuous consumption, in which expensive clothes, cars or housing, for example, are taken as a signal of their competency at work or their social status. If most people could afford these items, other yet more expensive goods would become the sought-after status items. It is a never-ending spiral. Meanwhile, because conspicuous consumption also increases the material aspirations among many of the less wealthy, it makes people increasingly dissatisfied with what they have. Empirical studies support this argument. In a Gallup Poll conducted in the USA, for example, respondents were asked 'What is the smallest amount of money a family of four needs to get along in this community?' Over time, the amounts rose in line with the increase in actual incomes (Layard 2003b: 4). Similar results have been found in other industrialised countries (Layard 2003b; Frank 1999).

It is in this context that the important contribution of the researchers at The Australia Institute can be reinterpreted. Affluenza is the key concept they promote. Hamilton and Denniss use this term to describe this pervasive 'sickness of affluence', drawing on writing from the USA (de Graaf, Wann and Naylor 2005) on the same topic. Hamilton and Denniss (2005: 3) define this as

1 The bloated, sluggish and unfulfilled feeling that results from efforts to keep up with the Joneses.
2 An epidemic of stress, overwork, waste and indebtedness caused by dogged pursuit of the Australian dream.
3 An unsustainable addiction to economic growth.

Hamilton elsewhere argues that economic growth 'not only fails to make people contented, [but it also] destroys many of the things that do' by fostering 'empty consumerism', degrading the natural environment and undermining social cohesion (Hamilton 2003c: x). Nevertheless, most people continue to believe that 'to find happiness they must be richer, regardless of how wealthy they already are' (Hamilton 2003c: xvi). This is thoroughly consistent with the arguments and evidence presented in this chapter.

The significant difference arises in the interpretation of what role economic inequality plays in these processes. According to Hamilton and Denniss, 'to tackle the problem of poverty we must first tackle the problem of affluence' (Hamilton and Denniss 2005: 18). However, the opposite case – that affluenza has its roots in economic inequality and is therefore insoluble without prior attention to the latter – is at least equally arguable. Perhaps the most balanced view is that neither poverty nor affluenza can be solved independently of the other, because it is their relationship that determines people's perceived wellbeing. It is inequality that drives the pursuit of riches and fuels the process whereby others feel more deprived, even if their economic circumstances are improving in absolute terms. It is this relational aspect of income and happiness that is crucial.

As Layard argues, this relational aspect belies the maxim of conventional economics that since 'private actions and exchanges get us to a Pareto optimum where no one could be happier without someone else being less happy . . . the higher the real wage the happier the population' (2003a: 13). Not only does this orthodox economic theory assume that individual actors have perfect information about the choices available to them, it assumes that people's tastes are constant. Hence, 'it fails to realise that our wants (once we are above subsistence level) are largely derived from society . . . To a large extent we want things and experiences because other people have them' (Layard 2003a: 13; see also Layard 2005). The implication is clear – some people getting higher incomes can have adverse consequences for other members of society, making them feel relatively worse off even if their incomes have not actually fallen.

What makes people happy?

Continued striving to attain the material affluence of the most wealthy members of society tends to be self-defeating. It appears as an endless treadmill without progress. Or worse. The pursuit of wealth in an unequal society can adversely affect happiness if it simultaneously undermines the other factors that more reliably increase personal wellbeing.

Why might this potentially negative effect of material affluence arise? It is easy enough to see why, once the basic essentials for survival are met, acquisition of more material goods is not the principal source of greater happiness. As Tim Kasser has argued in his book *The High Price of Materialism*, materialistic values are 'extrinsic' in that they are based on seeking satisfaction from outside one's self. He notes that, not only is aspiring to have more wealth often associated with greater unhappiness, but also that even the successful accumulation of wealth and material possessions 'typically turns out to be empty and unsatisfying' (cited in Gittins 2002: 13). But why might it contribute significantly to *dis*satisfaction, individually and for the society as a whole? Burroughs and Rindfleisch (2002) provide one explanation, arguing that 'a materialistic lifestyle harbors long-term negative consequences', including the unsustainable consumption of natural resources and the breakdown of communities and civic responsibility (2002: 348). Numerous other studies have found that individuals who pursue a materialistic lifestyle generally report lower levels of happiness, life satisfaction and psychological wellbeing, sometimes associated with an increased incidence of depression, anxiety and neuroticism (Burroughs and Rindfleisch 2002; Haddad 2003; Hamilton and Denniss 2005; Wachtel 1983).

So what does make us happy? Intimate, loving relationships with friends and family regularly feature as the primary influence, according to research in the field of happiness studies. Other sources of happiness include being of service to others, finding work that engages your skills and supports your values, being conscious of the gifts in your life and taking the time to renew the spirit and pursue the activities you enjoy (Gittins 2002: 13). These may be commonsense notions, but there is significant evidence that many people do not make achieving them a priority. Robert Lane (2000), for example, argues that materialism itself often undermines the formation of close relationships. As people make material success their first priority, it crowds out the time and energy needed to develop those relationships.

We are all familiar with the adage, 'Time is money', but it seems that more of our time would be better spent taking care of our relationships, health and emotional needs. We need to get off the hedonistic treadmill to cultivate satisfaction that is deeper in value and endurance. The teachings of the Dalai Lama and other spiritual leaders find support from numerous Western psychological researchers on this issue. Mihaly Csikszentmihalyi of the University of Chicago, for example, shows that engaging in activities that have 'flow' is the key to attaining deeper satisfaction. 'Flow' is more about means than ends: it is the state of being fully engaged in what you are doing rather than focusing on the expected outcome. Csikszentmihalyi (1999) concludes that 'Happiness is not something that happens to people but something that they make happen'. Similarly, Hirata emphasises the importance of 'procedural utility' and 'the active and sensible examination' of expectations, rather than maximising the availability of resources, in generating satisfaction with life (2001: 33).

These considerations, although not directly focused on economic inequality, may help to explain why an unequal society is likely to be an unhappier society. They do not gainsay the need to escape from conditions of absolute poverty. Those scraping along at the bottom of the distribution of income surely have a pressing need to secure what material comfort they can. Indeed, they have a reasonable expectation that higher income will contribute to their happiness. However, the efforts of people in other social strata to improve their situation through a dominant, even exclusive, focus on getting that higher income is more predictably self-defeating. It tends to leave insufficient time for building better social relationships and pursuing the activities they enjoy. It is often the perception of relative disadvantage that drives people, even quite affluent people, to pursue more material wealth, well beyond the point at which physical needs are met and at which social relations tend to suffer.

A necessary change in our attitudes to wealth and its distribution is indicated.[2] We cannot be happy if we continue to compare ourselves to those who own or earn more than us or fail to appreciate what we already have. This is the challenge we face as a society – to redress the glaring inequalities that condemn some to poverty while fuelling a pervasive sense of economic insecurity, even among those with all the available material comforts. In this way we can create the economic preconditions for a contented society, albeit not thereby guaranteeing the achievement of that goal nor necessarily redressing the other socioeconomic, environmental and political problems that confront us.

---

[2] A change in our measurement of national economic performance is also implied. The limitations of gross national product (GNP) as a measure of national wellbeing are now widely acknowledged (see Stilwell 2006: 44–6) and experimental alternative measures of a Genuine Progress Indicator are readily available (for example, on the Website of The Australian Institute @ www.tai.org.au). Even the federal Treasury has issued a paper conceding that 'there are better measures of well-being than GDP', although it concludes that 'Happiness as an aggregate social concept is in its embryonic states of development. It is too early to tell if it will ever be useful for policy formulation, though there are reasons to be sceptical' (Coombs 2006: 19).

Conclusion

Poverty is not generally conducive to good health, physically or mentally, but affluence can also be detrimental to human wellbeing. Shifting out of absolute poverty fairly reliably increases happiness. Societies in which large proportions of the population are poor are predictably unhappier, other things being equal (which they seldom are!), than those in which all enjoy the basic material comforts. However, beyond that, there is little evidence of any positive association between material progress, personal happiness and social contentment. More gains on 'the hedonistic index' are potentially to be made through the pursuit of greater equality.

This evidence and argument provide a case for lowering the ceiling as well as raising the floor in the distribution of income and wealth if society as a whole is to become more contented. A failure to do so may make society not only less happy but also more vulnerable to the fallout from growing inequality – manifest as an increasingly worrisome array of economic, social, environmental and political problems.

Chapter Ten

FALLOUT

Inequality has diverse economic, social, political and environmental consequences. There is inherent uncertainty, and therefore endless scope for debate, about the precise nature of these impacts. One can only infer what would be the economic, social, political and environmental outcomes if the degree of inequality were greater or lesser. Such judgements are inescapable in the social sciences. We cannot conduct laboratory experiments to see how any one particular nation would fare differently according to whether it had a more egalitarian or inegalitarian distribution of income and wealth. All we can do is to observe the patterns over time and space and draw inferences about the extent to which economic inequality goes hand in hand with particular economic, social, political and environmental problems.

This chapter reviews some of the principal connections – the fallout from economic inequality. From an *economic* perspective, the key issue is how inequality may affect the capacity of the nation to generate prosperity – through its impact on variables such as labour productivity, the propensity to save, the level of investment and consumption of imported goods. From a *social* perspective, the issue is how inequality bears on the degree of cohesion within the society – the extent to which there are shared values and some sense of a common purpose. *Politically*, the key concerns are how economic inequality sits with the formal democratic commitment to equality of rights and whether it generates pressures on government to implement policies of redistribution. From an *environmental* perspective, the crucial issue is whether inequality impedes the actions that are necessary for attaining ecological sustainability. These concerns warrant careful consideration.

Economic impacts

Apologists for inequality commonly seek to defend it on economic grounds as the prerequisite for a thriving market economy. The preceding chapter has cast doubt on the implied positive connection between economic growth and the happiness of citizens, even those who consume at maximum levels. Different reasons for scepticism arise from questioning whether inequality is actually conducive to economic growth. There are four key questions.

- Is labour productivity enhanced by economic inequality?
- Is the propensity to save greater in a more unequal society?
- Does economic inequality lead to more investment?
- How does economic inequality affect the nation's international trade?

Depending on the nature of these four links, greater economic inequality may be conducive to economic growth, more productive industries and an improvement in the nation's current account – or quite the reverse.

Consider labour productivity first. The conventional wisdom is that productive effort is encouraged by a greater prospect of material gain. On this reasoning, one might regard large economic inequalities as necessary and desirable because they stimulate individuals to try to get ahead by working hard, thereby contributing to improved national economic performance. As noted in the opening chapter of this book, this is the incentivation argument that is commonly posited by proponents of neoliberal ideologies and policies. From this perspective, the ideal situation would be one where there are steeply rising income profiles for each career path, large wage inequalities between skilled and unskilled jobs and low marginal rates of income taxation. These are the circumstances in which incentivation could be expected to flourish, leading to greater productive efforts by each individual and higher productivity for the economy as a whole. It is a set of expectations that needs to be set against some important qualifications and contrary observations.

First, surprising as it may seem, orthodox economic analysis provides no general support for the view that economic inequality enhances productive effort. According to the standard neoclassical economic theory of how people allocate their time, higher rewards per hour of work tend to have two contradictory effects. There is a 'substitution effect', because high pay rates increase the incentive for people to substitute work for leisure. There is also an 'income effect', because less hours of work need to be undertaken to generate any particular level of income when wage rates are higher. This income effect of higher wage rates leads people whose preference for leisure is strong to reduce their hours of work. So, the net outcome of the substitution and income effects depends upon the particular form of each individual's preferences and choices between income and leisure. No generalisation is possible. A more unequal society may cause some to work harder and some to work less, but there is no reason to presume that the aggregate effects are positive.

Second, there are other non-pecuniary motivations for hard work and increased productivity. Personal financial reward is not the only carrot. This is especially the case in contemporary employment conditions where work often involves collective effort in a team, a degree of loyalty to the company or some personal identification with the employing organisation. In these circumstances the driving forces of personal fulfilment and social status may be as important as the prospect of immediately enhanced income, particularly for professionals, managers and creative workers. Likewise, for scientific and technical workers, invention and innovation often involve an element of personal ingenuity and challenge that is its own source of motivation. This is not to deny the importance of the pecuniary factor as an incentive to personal effort, but to situate it as one element in a broader social–institutional context.

In practice, there is no systematic evidence of a positive connection between economic inequality and superior macroeconomic performance. Indeed, operating in the opposite direction is a tendency for inequality to adversely affect the cooperative relationships that are necessary for 'the complementarity of equity and growth' (Manning 2001: 194). People's willingness to participate cooperatively in the creation of social wealth depends on their expectation that the benefits of cooperation will be fairly shared. But these fair shares are recurrently threatened by class conflict and other social divisions. Entrenched inequalities can therefore undermine the necessary conditions for efficiency, productivity and growth within the private or public sectors of the economy. So instead of there being an efficiency–equity trade-off, inequity may endanger efficiency. Research on cross-country comparisons lends some support to this latter view: some countries with relatively egalitarian income distributions perform better in terms of economic growth rates than do more inegalitarian nations (Kuttner 1984; Boreham, Dow and Leet 1999: 124–30). At the macroeconomic scale, incentivation evidently does not work reliably enough to provide a sound basis for national economic policy.

What about the incentive to save? Would that be enhanced or retarded by greater economic inequality? One might expect the former because rich people generally tend to save a higher proportion of their income than do the poor. However, there is no general reason why total savings would be greater with a very inegalitarian distribution (where only the rich can afford to save) than with an egalitarian distribution (where many more people would have the capacity for modest savings). It is an empirical question, the outcome of which is shaped by social and institutional factors, such as the demographic profile and the extent to which the workforce is covered by compulsory occupational superannuation schemes. Interest rates and tax rates may also be important influences on rates of saving. Lowered taxation of personal income derived from interest on savings, for example, could increase economic inequality (since the rich generally save more) as well as enhance the total volume of saving. However, if saving is largely a residual left over after consumption spending needs are satisfied, the aggregate level of saving (as distinct from the institutional form in which savings are held) may be quite insensitive to changes in interest rates and taxes on the income from interest.

In any case, increased savings are not necessarily conducive to improved national economic performance. They could be helpful in reducing dependence on foreign borrowing (although that outcome could also be achieved in other ways, such as through the more systematic mobilisation of the savings in superannuation funds for domestic investment). However, as

Keynesian economists properly remind us, if people set out to save more (from any given level of income) their saving tends to reduce the aggregate demand for goods and services, leading to a reduced national income that then depresses their capacity to save. It is investment rather than saving that is the driving force of the economy. Or, to use James Meade's memorable metaphor, it is the dog called 'investment' that wags its tail called 'saving', and not the other way around (Meade 1975: 62).

So, is there any reason to believe economic inequality stimulates investment? If so, the macroeconomic argument for inequality would be significant. As with savings, the determinants of investment are complex. Analytical studies have, typically, identified the dominant influence of factors such as expected levels of demand, prevailing and expected interest rates and levels of capacity utilisation in business (see Toner 1988; Harcourt 2001: 266–9). The degree of business confidence, reflecting what Keynes termed the 'animal spirits' of the investors, is also critical. Economic inequality could bear indirectly on that, making investors more optimistic if they expected the distribution of income to be further skewed away from wages towards profits – towards their particular class interests. In that case, if economic inequality were to produce more buoyant animal spirits among business-people, it could well generate more enthusiasm for investment; however, it would not do so if the more unequal income distribution were to simultaneously undercut the demand for goods and services on which the incentive to invest depends. Investment depends crucially upon the expected level of consumer spending, and lower-income groups spend higher proportions of their incomes than do higher-income groups.

None of this is to deny that economic inequality has a deep connection with the process of capital accumulation. Indeed, the precondition for capital accumulation in a capitalist economy is the class relationships associated with ownership and control of the means of production. However, a perpetual tension is embedded in the relationship between capital accumulation and distributional inequality. This tension – what Marxian political economists identify as a pervasive contradiction – arises because of the dual role of wages in a capitalist economy. Low wages are conducive to reduced costs of production but they simultaneously undermine the demand for the goods and services produced. High wages generate demand but at the expense of raising costs of production. So there is no one level of wages – and, by extension, no overall distribution of income – that is continuously optimal for the accumulation of capital.

Pursuing this issue further, it is also pertinent to question the particular type of incentives that economic inequality generates. It may be, for example, that the incentives for private capital accumulation encourage speculative or other financial endeavours that do not add directly to wealth creation in the economy as a whole. Indeed, this tendency, variously described as 'profits without production' (Melman 1983) and 'casino capitalism' (Strange 1986), has been increasingly evident in the last quarter century as the hypermobility of financial capital on a global scale has opened up ever more opportunities for speculative gain without actually producing tangible commodities. These are circumstances in which economic inequality grows but does little or nothing to improve the material economic conditions of people in general. It is a pertinent reminder that the personal incentive to get rich should not be confused with generating conditions for improved national and international economic performance.

The final economic consideration relates to the connection between economic inequality and international trade. Would more economic inequality increase or reduce the amount of goods imported and therefore affect the severity of the balance of payments constraint on growth? Given the importance of international trade and, particularly in the Australian case, the steady growth of the nation's current account deficit during the last two decades, this important issue warrants more attention than it has received in economic research. Of course, both rich and poor people consume imported goods. While the former often spend their money on big ticket items such as French champagne and European luxury cars, the latter buy cheap manufactured goods from China and other countries where production costs undercut those of Australian producers. But the wealthy also buy some of the cheap imported goods. They may also spend a higher proportion of their income on locally produced services, ranging from private education to hairdressing and fitness classes. So, the relationship between income inequality and trade patterns is complex. Analytically, the key issue is whether a dollar taken from the poor and given to the rich would lead to more or less imports. If the proportion of consumer spending going on imported goods tends to be greater for people in upper-income groups than for people in lower-income groups, economic inequality tends to worsen the problem of the current account deficit and thereby constrains national economic growth.[1]

Social impacts

What about the social consequences of economic inequality? These may be ultimately more important than the direct economic connections, partly because, in the long run, the effective functioning of the economy depends on particular social preconditions – social capital, social cohesion and social mobility, for example. The links are subtle and complex. No fixed or automatic relationship exists between economic position, social status, class consciousness and personal behaviour; however, to the extent that economic inequality reduces the integration of different social groups and the density of social networks, it can be expected to undermine the conditions for social stability (Wilkinson 1996). As Stuart Rees, a pioneer of peace and conflict studies in Australia, emphasises, there is also an inexorable link between social justice and peace – and, conversely injustice and violence (Rees 2003: 222–57). In the extreme case, the juxtaposition of a marginalised underclass and an affluent elite is conducive to the periodic recurrent breakdown of social order. As the UN Human Development report has noted, differences in income inequality across countries are closely associated with differences in rates of crime and violence (United Nations 2000).

The situation in some American cities, where the rich take refuge from the underclass by living in security-patrolled gated communities, is already starting to be replicated Down Under. As anticipated by French social scientist Andre Gorz (1985), the situation is one in which

---

[1] This negative impact of economic inequality on the current account deficit was demonstrated by research undertaken by Australian political economist Phil Raskall (1992), but no comparable recent studies seem to have been undertaken. In October 2006 one of the authors of this book contacted fifteen of the country's leading applied economists – in Sydney, Canberra and Melbourne – but none could suggest any relevant studies. It seems that distributional concerns are not high on the agenda for Australian macroeconomists.

pauperism and over-abundance go hand in hand, where organised society
marginalises and represses a dispossessed social majority: slum dwellers in the
shadows of skyscrapers precariously surviving on crime and the underground
economy.

The costs of social conflict in such a context are a high price to pay for the
market freedoms that generate economic inequality. The costs of policing,
law courts and jails become particularly burdensome for governments in
these circumstances. So, too, do the costs to individuals – for their expenditures on personal and household security devices and on insurance. More
and more economic resources are used, individually and collectively, for
social control.

Expenditures on transfer payments are also a heavy fiscal burden for
government in an unequal society. Social security payments escalate – in
Australia in 2002–3 they reached 43 per cent of all federal government budget outlays. Figures from the Australian Bureau of Statistics also show that
the proportion of Australians of workforce age claiming income support
was 21.6 per cent in 2002, up from 14.1 per cent in 1989. Over the same
period, income support as a percentage of GDP increased from 6.3 per cent
to 7.5 per cent (Argyrous and Neale 2003). Not all social security claimants
are poor, however. The major expansion of family payments by the Howard
government, for example, is more geared to childbearing households than
the poor. The major beneficiaries of the big package of tax and family payments changes in the 2004–5 federal budget were families on high incomes
(NATSEM 2004). Meanwhile, the fiscal strains associated with government
expenditures are often sheeted home to the problem of 'welfare dependency'
(Smyth and Wearing 2002: 227).

Welfare dependency?

Critics of current arrangements for welfare provision argue that the system has expanded to a point where it supports substantial numbers of
people who could, and should, support themselves. The inference is that
welfare provision encourages people to rely on state handouts rather
than on seeking paid full-time employment, and that improving the living standards of the poor therefore involves 'stronger work incentives,

not higher benefits' (Saunders 2004: 1; see also Saunders 2005: 95). Jocelyn Newman, former Minister for Family and Community Services in the Howard government, referred to 'a destructive and self-indulgent welfare mentality' (cited in Saunders 1999: 9).

Certainly, the culture of poverty may have an attitudinal dimension. The well-documented cycle of how people respond to unemployment is a case in point. Their initial optimism and enthusiasm about getting another job is often followed by anxiety, pessimism and, eventually, resignation to failure. As despair and hopelessness set in their capacity for taking initiatives to seek opportunities for material improvement atrophies. Not wanting to work may then be a means by which they ultimately come to terms with their own circumstances, in effect redefining their personal goals so that they do not appear as failures. The inadequacy of appropriate employment opportunities thereby creates the behavioural changes and attitudinal characteristics of the so-called dole bludgers.

It is not surprising that these concerns about welfare dependency have focused disproportionately on Indigenous communities, given their general economic disadvantage and marginalised status in Australia. Noel Pearson, the prominent Aboriginal lawyer and activist, has been a major figure in the public debate, arguing that 'the current mode of delivery of welfare services to Aboriginal people is deeply antithetical to their interests and wellbeing' (Martin 2001: vii). There are three key propositions here. The first is that the provision of welfare payments with no demands for reciprocity and responsibility on the part of welfare recipients has generated passivity and dependence within Aboriginal societies. The second is that this passivity and dependence become entrenched, vitiating possibilities of initiatives that might break the vicious cycle, tending instead to foster self-destructive and dysfunctional practices. Third, a solution requires structural change, including the development of new institutions for Aboriginal governance. It is through these formal and informal Aboriginal institutions, according to Pearson's argument, that 'the principles of reciprocity and individual responsibility necessary to leach the "poison" from welfare resources can be instituted and implemented' (Martin 2001: vii). These are controversial propositions that continue to be strongly debated among those concerned with welfare and the wellbeing of Indigenous communities (see, for example, Armstrong 2005).

The more full-frontal attack on welfare dependency in Australia has come from the federal government. After the Coalition gained office in 1996, more obligations were placed upon welfare recipients, including the introduction and extension of work for the dole schemes and tighter controls on job search requirements for those on unemployment benefits. These schemes do not necessarily have the intended impacts. Roger Patulny, from the Social Policy Research Centre at the University of New South Wales, notes that behind such measures is the belief that 'welfare in the form of unemployment benefits undermines the motivation to work' (2004: 5). He questions the implication that these policies 'inspire individuals with a new motivation to engage civically as well as economically' (2004: 6). Similarly, if the focus of efforts to tighten eligibility rules for income support is to catch 'welfare cheats', the emphasis of welfare policies becomes skewed towards minimising the possibility that benefits will be provided to the undeserving rather than helping those who are legitimately in need. Patulny notes that 'Failure to catch the cheats may undermine motivation to social participation – but equally, so might failure to redress social deprivation' (2004: 6). The cumulative effect is increased public suspicion of those on welfare and a corresponding increase in their sense of exclusion.

Proponents of neoliberal policies typically argue that the level of unemployment benefit needs to be set very low so as to provide an incentive to enter the workforce. Indeed, the maximum rate of unemployment benefits has been consistently below the poverty line, as noted in chapter 5. Michael Raper, former president of the Australian Council of Social Service, argues that expecting such a low rate of benefit to incentivise recipients to find work blames the individuals involved and also presupposes the existence of suitable available jobs. From that critical perspective, low rates of income support are more likely to increase poverty and financial hardship than to increase the movement of welfare recipients into paid work. Evidently, the social problems associated with inequality and poverty are inexorably bound to the character of welfare policy. As such, they are inextricably political in character.

Political impacts

Politically, economic inequality creates distinctive tensions. Perhaps the most profound is the tension between the political principles of democracy and the economic principles of capitalism. As liberal economist Arthur Okun noted many years ago, modern societies have political institutions that claim to provide 'universally distributed rights and privileges that proclaim the equality of all citizens', while the economic institutions 'generate substantial disparities among citizens in living standards and material welfare' (Okun 1975). The uncomfortable tensions thereby generated are reflected in the contrast between 'one person one vote' as the organising principle in the political sphere and 'one dollar one vote' as the key principle in the economic sphere. In practice, the latter tends to dominate, even to subvert, the former. To quote Okun again, 'Money is used by some big winners of market rewards in an effort to acquire extra helpings of those rights that are supposed to be equally distributed'. This is a polite way of referring to corruption. It is because economic inequality concentrates resources and class power that the wealthy have the means to capture political institutions to serve their interests at the expense of any broader national interest. Corporate donations to political parties – especially by urban developers seeking a permissive response to their building proposals – are one of the more blatant examples of this process.

The posited connection between capitalism and democracy, repeatedly asserted by neoliberals such as Milton Friedman, looks ever more shaky where substantial economic inequality prevails. Notwithstanding some broad historical association between the development of freedom of the marketplace and freedom of the ballot box, the tendency of the former to produce inequalities that constrain the latter is deeply problematic. Money may not be able to buy extra political rights directly, but it can buy services (including expensive legal representation) that generate social and political advantages. Poorer people's effective rights are more constrained by their inability to purchase those services. So the formal equality of rights before the law has an uneasy relationship, to say the least, with the existence of pervasive economic inequalities.

Such concerns have generated recurrent demands on governments to implement policies of progressive redistribution. But the capacity of governments to respond is limited by the vested interests associated with the class structure on which the capitalist economy depends. Ah, there's the rub. Given the association, albeit imperfect, between those vested interests and party political loyalties, it is not surprising that the accommodation by government to demands for progressive redistribution is inconsistent. Indeed, there is some evidence that economic inequality systematically biases democratic responsiveness. Research in the USA, based on surveys of voters' opinions, shows that 'when Americans with different income levels differ in their policy preferences, actual policy outcomes strongly reflect the preferences of the most affluent but bear virtually no relationship to the preferences of poorer or middle-income Americans' (Gilens, 2005). In other words, rich people's opinions influence policy, poor people's don't. This is the fundamental political economic contradiction – that economic inequality generates challenges to basic democratic principles that the state in capitalist society is recurrently unable to resolve.

Such political economic tensions have international as well as national dimensions. As previously noted, a high proportion of economic resources within individual nations is currently allocated to spending on security measures to cope with the social conflicts arising from major economic inequalities. A similar tendency now operates worldwide, especially since the catastrophic terrorist attacks on New York and Washington on 11 September 2001. Terrorism, and international conflict in general, have complex roots, of course; however, they evidently derive at least partly from perceptions that global economic inequalities are the product of imperialism and exploitation. One might hope that long-term solutions may be found in concerted action to redress these causal factors, but to date, the dominant response has been to divert more economic and social resources into military, security and border protection activities. One could hardly have more conclusive, and unwelcome, proof that an unequal society is an insecure society. The costs of coping with its consequences are onerous – economically, socially, politically and environmentally.

Environmental impacts

The relationship between economic inequality and environmental problems is being increasingly recognised. This is important because there are sound reasons to expect an economically unequal society to also be a society in which the propensity for environmental damage is greater and the likelihood of remedial policies is less. Those with high incomes and therefore the ability to pay can continue to consume increasingly scarce 'environmental goods' (such as clean air, water and energy) even though the prices for these goods are rising (either as a direct result of the resource scarcity itself or as an indirect result of taxes imposed by governments to discourage consumption of those goods). In an economically unequal society access to environmental resources cannot be effectively regulated through a price mechanism because the price mechanism simply translates economic inequalities into ecological inequalities that may, in the last resort, determine access to the resources necessary for human survival (see Beder 2006: 174–278 and Rosewarne 2002 for more general critiques of mainstream environmental economic theory and policies).

There is also a more indirect connection between inequality and environmental degradation, resulting from the impact of economic inequality on social values and political processes. It is illustrated by the American economist Ken Boulding's memorable proposition that 'the presence of pollution is symptomatic of the absence of a community' (Boulding 1971: 169). Environmental consciousness is enhanced by a sense of shared and collective interests, which is more likely to exist in an egalitarian society than in one with deep economic and social divisions.

The connection between environmental concerns and economic inequality has also come to be recognised on an international scale. Because many environmental problems are global in character, their resolution requires agreement on appropriate remedial policies between poor and rich nations. Achieving that agreement has proven to be recurrently difficult, not least because the policies are often seen to require the poorer countries to tighten their belts to deal with global resource depletion and pollution problems not primarily of their own making. Not surprisingly, that is unacceptable to them. It is the resource and energy requirements of the more affluent nations that have contributed disproportionately to global environmental stress. Developing nations, typically, aspire to similar standards of living and resent being denied, on ecological grounds, what the more affluent nations have already achieved. So, like environmental problems and economic inequalities within a nation, environmental problems on a global scale cannot readily be redressed independently of measures to rein in the international economic inequalities.

The goal of ecological sustainability is both crucial and elusive. It is inconceivable that it could be achieved without dramatic changes to patterns of production, consumption and transportation, nationally and globally. That is why it is necessarily linked to concerns about social justice. Only when people perceive the need to act as if they are all in the same boat, incurring reasonable equality of sacrifice for the common good, are they likely to embrace policies designed to change the forms of production, consumption and transportation that cause environmental stress.

Inequality and public health

Poverty and affluence can both be unhealthy. Extremes of deprivation and overindulgence, expressed in patterns of food consumption and other social behaviours, are each associated with poor health outcomes and premature death. There is also growing evidence that the incidence of health problems, and hence the cost of providing adequate health services, is related to the extent of economic inequality.

Epidemiological evidence linking ill health with poverty is well established (see Wilkinson 1994). Historically, the incidence of tuberculosis illustrated this predictable connection. The poor diet and unhealthy housing that commonly characterise poverty have causal connections with a wide array of other health conditions. In Australia this shows up today in significant differences in the average life expectancy of people living in rich and poor regions. A male born between 1998 and 2000 and living in the Central Darling local government area of New South Wales has an estimated life expectancy of 13 years less than a male born at the same time and living in the affluent suburb of Mosman on Sydney's north shore (Royal Australian College of Physicians report, cited by Cresswell 2005). The Central Darling's population includes a relatively high proportion of Aboriginal people with low incomes and poor health.

The link between health and inequality, rather than poverty, is less immediately obvious, but is now documented by significant research (see Wilkinson 1996, 2005; Wilkinson and Pickett 2006). These studies generally show that, in cross-country comparisons, greater income inequality is associated with lower life expectancies and higher mortality rates. Evidently, once the economic development of a nation has reached a stage that can ensure basic material living standards for most, if not all, of its citizens, further increases in economic growth do not necessarily improve health outcomes. In these more affluent countries, where the prime causes of death are no longer infectious but degenerative diseases, relative (rather than absolute) incomes have become one of the major determinants of health.

Why do relative differences in income, rather than absolute material standards, lead to higher rates of disease and death? The leading researcher in this field, R. G. Wilkinson, argues that the answer lies in the psychosocial impacts of inequality, including 'social stress, poor social networks, low self-esteem, high rates of depression, anxiety, insecurity [and] the loss of a sense of control' (Wilkinson 1996: 5). Hence, while an uneven income distribution is associated with a higher incidence of 'all of the broad categories of causes of death', including 'cardiovascular diseases, infections, respiratory diseases and cancers', the relationship is most pronounced in the greater prevalence of stress-related diseases, 'alcohol-related deaths, homicide and accidents' (Wilkinson 1996: 4). Stress-related conditions can include 'infections, diabetes, high blood pressure, heart attack, stroke, depression and aggression' (Wilkinson and Marmot 2003: 13). The threats to economic security and social cohesion that neoliberal policies tend to exacerbate can be a compounding factor (Coburn 2000).

This relationship between a markedly uneven distribution of income and the increased prevalence of social causes of death points to a particularly problematic consequence of greater economic inequality.

Conclusion

The modern social, economic and political challenge is how to reconcile the individual pursuit of wealth with broader social goals. Historically, the great claim of the capitalist economy is that it has harnessed that individual self-interest for the purpose of economic progress. The resulting economic growth has transformed living standards and social expectations. But this growth has come at a significant cost in terms of environmental damage, resource depletion and other externalities. More and more people are questioning the logic and sustainability of this economic arrangement. As noted in the preceding chapter, economic inequality, in addition to generating significant economic, social, political and environmental problems, also has negative consequences for people's subjective assessment of how well they are doing.

This chapter has shown that economic inequality has some further, awesome consequences. It can obstruct the achievement of improvement in economic performance while it simultaneously undermines social cohesion, corrupts democratic political processes and impairs the possibilities of dealing with the looming environmental crisis. These are powerful grounds for seeking to rein in, if not reverse, the forces currently intensifying economic inequalities. The fallout from increasing inequality is too hazardous. Ultimately, what is at stake is our capacity to live together in an economically prosperous, socially harmonious, politically democratic and ecologically sustainable manner. Redirecting public policy to the pursuit of more egalitarian social outcomes seems an increasingly necessary response. Hence the question: 'What is to be done?'

Chapter Eleven

WHAT IS TO BE DONE?

Economic inequality is properly a concern for public policy. Its adverse impacts on economic efficiency, social cohesion and environmental sustainability make it necessarily so. A good society is one characterised by a collective concern with social justice and a capacity to act in pursuit of that objective. That this case even has to be made is symptomatic of the pervasive influence of neoliberalism during the last two decades, subordinating the concern with economic inequality to narrower concerns with economic efficiency and growth, and casting doubt on the capacity of the state to act in pursuit of common goals. The proponents of incentivation have also ignored the ways in which egalitarian policies can contribute to efficiency and growth in practice. As the authors of an American book, *The Winner-take-all Society*, note, 'Much of the rivalry for society's top prizes is both costly and unproductive' (Frank and Cook 1995: viii). It is time to change direction.

What can – and should – be done? This chapter focuses first on individual responses to inequality, looking at the tension between personal striving to get rich, and other personal choices, such as philanthropy and downshifting. The discussion then turns to what governments can do to redistribute income towards the poor, focusing particularly on taxes and government expenditures that could ameliorate economic inequalities. Employment policies then come into the spotlight, recognising that universal access to useful and reasonably remunerated employment is crucial for the economic basis of a more equitable society. Finally, consideration is given to whether more fundamental social changes are necessary, including strategies to impose ceilings as well as floors on the distribution of income and wealth, and the possibility of a change in the dominant values of society towards more egalitarian aims and practices.

Do it yourself?

For most people, most of the time, economic inequality is a social given, taken as part of the predetermined structures within which we lead our individual lives. So the usual response to inequality is one of acceptance rather than challenge. Personal progress results from operating within the system rather than from seeking to change it. The purposive individual seeks to get into the top range of income and wealth, or at least into a higher range, whether by hard work, further education and training, financial speculation or prayer for a lucky Lotto win. So the quest for upward mobility rather than societal change is the characteristic personal behaviour – and in a consumerist society more is seldom enough.

That said, there are significant exceptions. Two quite different forms of individual response to economic inequality warrant particular attention. One is philanthropy – the use of personal wealth to support good causes, usually through foundations established to manage and allocate the funds. Some such good causes are aimed at reducing poverty, but not all philanthropic activity alleviates economic inequality. Much of it goes to the support of the arts and culture, support of elite educational institutions, scientific research, and so on. In the USA the era of the robber barons spawned a tradition of philanthropy led by business leaders such as Rockefeller and Carnegie. The two wealthiest Americans today – multibillionaire Bill Gates and investor 'folk hero' Warren Buffett – maintain that strong tradition. Individuals such as these can, and do, use some of their wealth – however it be derived – in a manner that conveys substantial social benefit, even though it may not redress the systemic origins of economic inequality. Australia has no comparably strong philanthropic tradition. Drawing on research by the

Asia–Pacific Centre for Philanthropy and Social Investment at Swinburne University, Daniel Petre (2005) notes that Australian donors have typically given less than 4 per cent of their wealth and infers that, overall, 'the most wealthy allocate less than 1 per cent of their wealth to philanthropy'.

The other relevant individual response is downshifting. Growing numbers of people are evidently opting out of the relentless process of competition to increase their wealth – by taking lower-paid but less stressful or less time-consuming jobs. In effect, they are voting with their feet against the dominant trend towards a richer but more unequal society. A study carried out for The Australia Institute found that, when asked whether Australian society placed 'too much emphasis on money and not enough emphasis on the things that really matter', 83 per cent of survey respondents agreed we did (Hamilton and Mail 2003: 8). As the authors of this study argue,

> Australians are working longer and harder than they have for decades and are neglecting their families and their health as a result. So while they say they do not have enough money, many Australians also say that money-hunger conflicts with their deeper values and preferences (Hamilton and Mail 2003: 8).

Some are responding to this tension not just by expressing their personal disquiet when answering social surveys, but also by actually opting out of the pursuit of more material affluence, making voluntary changes to their lifestyles that involve earning and consuming less. Such downshifting can take various forms, ranging from changes in occupation and the length of working hours to the characteristic seachange and treechange shifts away from big city living. The Australia Institute researchers estimate that 23 per cent of Australians aged between 30 and 59 have downshifted since the early nineties. That figure rises to over 30 per cent if the definition of downshifting is expanded to include those people returning to study or establishing their own businesses. Moreover, the trend towards downshifting appears to have been increasing in recent years (Hamilton and Mail 2003: 9). Over 90 per cent of respondents who had downshifted reported that they were happy with the change, although 15 per cent reported that they were finding the money loss very hard (Hamilton and Mail 2003: 11).

A bold interpretation of downshifting would see it as leading, in effect, to a social revolution against an increasingly wealthy society bedevilled by the fallout from economic inequality. Such an interpretation seems unrealistic, however well intended, and likely to founder on the rocks of experience. Similar mixtures of prescription and wishful thinking by analysts of social change have previously been frustrated in practice – one thinks back, for example, to Robert Reich's book, *The Greening of America*, with its romantic assessment of the power of the anti-consumerist counterculture of the 1970s. A more cautious interpretation of downshifting would be to regard it as an embryonic element in the quest for better balance between material and non-material elements affecting personal wellbeing. Indeed, such concerns about how to achieve work–life balance are becoming increasingly widely voiced (Pocock 2003).

What is significant about individual responses is that they signal the need for change to the dominant economic model. The emphasis in these responses on personal responsibility and locally focused action is also admirable. But individual actions are no substitute for concerted strategies to tackle the root causes of economic inequality. For that latter purpose systematic government policies are necessary: only the state has the formal power to implement and enforce legislation, and the fiscal capacity to produce significant changes in the distribution of income and wealth.

Redistributive policies

What can governments do? They face an initial choice between a politics of recognition and a politics of redistribution (as described by Fraser 1995). The former acknowledges the different circumstances and needs of the various subgroups, especially minorities within society, while the latter emphasises a commitment to redistribution of income and wealth across the whole society. The two are not radically different in practice, as proponents of the two approaches acknowledge (Fraser and Honneth 2003). In both cases, the onus is on governments to lead the way by formulating policies that redress unwarranted and socially unacceptable inequalities. Such policies can operate on both the ceilings and floors in the distribution of income and wealth, and thereby reduce disparities in economic opportunity.

Taxation is the most obvious policy instrument. Its basic function is to raise revenue to finance government expenditure, but how this is done has a major bearing on the degree of economic inequality. It hardly needs to be said that the Australian taxation system is currently very limited as a means of achieving egalitarian objectives, as noted in chapter 8. The wide array of allowances against income tax (so-called tax expenditures) reduces a nominally progressive income tax scale to one that is less progressive in practice. The gulf between the top marginal income tax rate and the company tax rate provides a strong incentive to conceal individual income as company income. Moreover, tax revenues collected from individual corporations are often very low in practice because of the widespread use of tax minimisation schemes. The dividend imputation system allows individuals' income from share ownership to be effectively tax-free, although the income is taxed previously when it accrues as company profits. Capital gains taxes are offset by the deductions allowed for inflation and the exemptions accorded to owners of owner-occupied properties. There is an absence of wealth taxes, other than those on land that are levied by state and local governments. There is no inheritance tax.

These various features of the tax system in Australia make it not markedly progressive in practice, to put the point mildly. Tax avoidance and evasion further limit its effectiveness, notwithstanding the worthy efforts of the Australian Taxation Office (ATO). The difficulties are of long-standing. As Australia's leading tax economist noted nearly three decades ago, 'The essential problem is not to make the rich pay high rates of tax or even to pay more tax: it is to make the rich pay any tax at all' (Mathews 1980). One study of Sydney suburbs found that the proportion of income paid in tax (after taking account of allowances against tax and exemption from tax on dividend incomes because of the imputation system) was actually *lower* in affluent north shore suburbs such as Palm Beach than in working class areas (Cleary 1990). More recent evidence indicates no fundamental change. An ATO 2000 estimate, for example, found that '100 wealthy individuals continue to avoid about $800 million in tax', and that one of Australia's billionaires had claimed a taxable annual income of just $12 524 (Albanese 2000: 15).

International comparison shows that Australia was a little below middle-ranking among OECD nations in terms of the extent to which tax arrangements reduced the inequality of 'market incomes' during the 1990s (Tiffen and Gittins 2004: 138, table 8.7). Subsequent changes to tax policies by the Australian government have tended to make the outcomes more regressive. The decision in 1999 to introduce the Goods and Services Tax was particularly significant in this respect: it was heralded at the time as an epoch-making reform, its proponents arguing, among other things, that it would generate more tax revenues from those with the largest spending power because an expenditure tax, unlike an income tax, cannot be readily avoided. However, as a flat-rate tax on goods and services, the GST bears less heavily on high-income recipients than would a genuinely progressive income tax. So the reduction in the income tax that was introduced as a compensation to the public for the introduction of the GST meant an overall reduction in the formal progressivity of the tax system.

As noted in chapter 8, the Howard government's decision – also in 1999 – to reduce capital gains taxes also had a markedly regressive effect on income inequalities. In effect, it halved the tax on income from capital relative to income from labour. So 1999 was a watershed year for distributional inequity of after-tax incomes. Equally striking in terms of regressive distributional effects were the income tax changes announced in the 2005–6 federal budget. The tax cuts were worth around $7 a week to someone on an income of $55 000 per year, but $42 a week to those on $80 000 or more. This starkly illustrates of the abandonment of egalitarian goals in the design of the tax system.

The obvious challenge for proponents of a more equitable society is to reverse these regressive tax changes. This presents no major technical problem: there are numerous tax reforms that could redress economic inequalities if there were the political will to do so (as described by Harding 1999; Smith 1999; Leigh 2006). The income tax scale could be made more progressive. The capital gains tax rate could be restored to the pre-1999 cuts level. Tax expenditures could be reduced. The company tax rate could be aligned with the top marginal income tax rate. The tax exemptions applying to family trusts – commonly used as a general means of tax avoidance – could be eliminated.

A more fundamental shift would be to put greater emphasis on taxation policies affecting the ownership of resources. These are potentially more effective than income taxation in tackling economic inequality. As argued earlier in this book, who owns what substantially determines who gets what. For any given pattern of wage rates, profit rates, rents and rate of interest, the distribution of income depends on the degree of inequality of ownership of the labour, land and capital resources that produces these incomes. Concentrated ownership generates greater income inequality: a less concentrated ownership would lead to a more equitable distribution of income even without any changes in wage rates, profit rates, rents, interest rates and income tax rates. So taxes levied directly on wealth could have radically redistributive effects in the long term.

At present increases in wealth are subject to capital gains tax, but this applies only when assets are sold and thereby converted into income. An annual wealth tax (for example, on asset holdings of more than $1 million) would more effectively capture some of that private wealth for public purposes. Inheritance taxes could also capture part of the unearned incomes that perpetuate economic inequality intergenerationally. Australia is currently unusual in having no wealth or inheritance taxes.[1] Tax economist Julie Smith calls them 'Pay-as-you-can' and 'Pay-as-you-go' taxes (Smith 1999: 95). Their introduction would, over time, impart more flexibility in the composition of the capital-owning class without undermining the property relationships on which the continued functioning of the capitalist economy depends. The extra tax revenues could then be used to finance government spending on public education, public housing, health, transport infrastructure and other services that could help to create more equality of opportunity throughout society, as well as contributing to a better quality of life.

Policies to introduce wealth or inheritance taxes would, of course, be resisted. Strong vested interests are at issue, not to mention the widespread belief that such taxes negate the rights of the elderly regarding the disposition of their property. Whether there would be inefficiencies generated by inheritance taxes, or wealth taxes more generally, is a moot point though;

---

[1] The United Kingdom, for example, has an inheritance tax of 40 per cent of the value of estates over £385 000 (approximately A$900 000).

it would largely depend on whether the precise form of the taxes created incentives for the concealment of wealth in non-productive forms. Finally, it needs to be noted that, in the Australian case, the reintroduction of inheritance taxation would require a federal government initiative because it was beggar-thy-neighbour competition between the state governments that propelled the dismantling of the inheritance taxes that existed prior to the 1970s. No state government can be expected to go it alone now in reintroducing inheritance taxation; in any case, it is logically a nationwide issue requiring uniformity of taxation provisions.

A national land tax?

Landowners capture unearned income at the expense of the rest of the community. They benefit from rising land values that are, typically, the product of social processes rather than individual effort. Residential and commercial land values usually increase when new public infrastructure is built nearby. Landowners can also receive tremendous windfalls when their land is rezoned to allow more intense development. Yet more fundamentally, the driving force causing higher land values, particularly in urban areas, is the nature of the urban growth process itself. While demand for sites for residential or commercial activities is continually growing, the supply remains fixed, so the result is a long-run tendency for inflation in land values. Without adequate taxation on land to recoup this social dividend, the rising land values resulting from the community's productive efforts add to existing landowners' wealth, while those unable to afford land are further excluded from the market.

These processes are a major contributor to economic inequality. They have a dubious ethical basis too: those fortunate enough to have owned land in desirable areas capture the economic surplus at the expense of those making a productive contribution to its creation, and at the expense of future generations saddled with higher prices for access to urban land and housing.

The case for using land tax to counter these adverse features of property markets is well established (see, for example, Day 1995, 2005; Stilwell and Jordan 2004; Laurent 2005). Levied on the site value of the land, land tax creates a disincentive for hoarding unused land and a means of stabilising land prices by reducing the attraction of real estate for speculative investment. Tax analyst Terry Dwyer has estimated that, as the value of land resources in Australia grew between 1988–9 and 1998–9, the potential income from land ownership rose from $75.4 billion to $132.6 billion, an increase of 76 per cent, faster than the 68 per cent growth of total taxes from all sources collected over that same period (Dwyer 2003). The inference is that existing taxes – mainly on individual incomes, company profits and consumer expenditures – are not keeping up with the growth of the economic surplus captured by landowners.

Each of the state governments and the government of the Australian Capital Territory already levy a land tax, but land used for owner-occupied housing is exempted in all cases. Local government rates are also, in effect, land taxes because they are usually levied on the unimproved capital value of properties, although the form of these rates varies considerably from locality to locality. To be effective in addressing economic inequality, a land tax must be uniform nationwide. This would prevent property speculators from simply shifting their investments interstate to reduce their land tax liabilities. One option, then, would be to replace the current array of state and territory land taxes and local government rates with a nationally uniform land tax scheme. Such a scheme could be linked to a reform of local government finance. Replacing the existing local government rates with an apportionment to local governments from a uniform land tax could be an economically efficient – and electorally attractive – reform.

More radically, a nationally uniform land tax scheme could be linked to a replacement of the existing local and state and territory governments by regional governments (as advocated in Stilwell 2000: 260–6), which could provide an institutional and fiscal basis for more balanced regional development. In general land tax can be expected to generate more revenue from those regions where land price inflation is most pronounced. So the metropolitan areas would tend to be more highly taxed than nonmetropolitan areas, particularly rural areas, which would favour regional decentralisation of population and industry. That tendency would be further accentuated if additional revenue from a more comprehensive system of land taxation were used for regional redistribution, such as financing better infrastructure and services in non-metropolitan areas, thereby linking tax reform with regional policy. Using land tax revenue to substantially expand the supply of public housing is another means of directly linking the policy to the redress of economic and social stresses in the housing market.

Turning from tax reform to government expenditure, other possibilities for ameliorating inequalities arise. Targeting government expenditures to the needy has immediate appeal as the most obvious way of meeting this objective. Indeed, this has been a persistent theme in social security policy reforms in recent decades, as the principle of universality in welfare provision has given way to a more means-tested approach. International comparisons suggest that Australia has been 'top of the table' in terms of the share of government transfers going to the poorest 30 per cent of households (Tiffen and Gittins 2004: 138, table 8.6). While this is impressive, the conventional way of tackling poverty, based on the postulate that it is deficient income proportional to need that causes primary poverty,[2] is superficial and lacks an indepth understanding of the contributory factors. It has led to a policy focus on simply creating an income safety net, rather than policies to address 'accumulated disadvantage ' (Saunders 2005: 79). The shallowness of this proposition avoids investigation of the underlying causes of poverty and further restrains the consignment of responsibility.

Assessing how government expenditures in general impact on distributional inequalities is extraordinarily complicated. It is necessary, for example, to estimate the distribution of the benefits deriving from collectively provided services, ranging from health and education to defence and transport. This cannot be done without making an array of simplifying assumptions. Still, the most thorough research on this subject suggests that, taking account of the incidence of tax as well as government expenditure transfers, there is substantial redistribution between men and women and between rich and poor, and scope for much more (Harding 1999, 2006; Harding, Lloyd and

[2] 'Primary poverty is determined according to whether income is above or below a poverty line that reflects what is required to meet needs. Despite the reservations surrounding how and where to set the poverty line, the method is based on an objective assessment of income in relation to need' (Saunders 2002: 157).

Warren 2004; Steketee 2005). Evidently, the design of an effective social wage and social security system, together with the form that the tax system takes, can have a significant impact on the degree of economic inequality.

Yet all policies of tax and welfare reform – important as they are – remain constrained by their redistributive logic. They are aimed at modifying a pre-existing distribution of income. The alternative is to more directly change that pre-tax distribution. Therein lies a more radical approach to the redress of economic inequality.

Getting to the source

Policies aimed at modifying the pattern of market rewards get more directly to the source of economic inequalities. The relative shares of labour and capital in the national income, the pattern of wage rates and the distribution of income from profits, executive salaries, professional fees, interest and rents, all come under consideration. The question is, what can be done to operate on these variables? It must be conceded that the government's capacity to directly control pre-tax incomes, other than where they arise from capital and labour employed in the public sector, is limited; however, there is a range of potentially significant indirect policy measures. Indeed, most government policies – ranging from the determination of interest rates to the setting of tariffs on imported goods – have an impact on the distribution of pre-tax incomes. A government with a strong commitment to creating a more equitable society would monitor the distributional effects of its various macroeconomic and microeconomic policies – in effect, conducting an ongoing social justice audit on all aspects of public policy.

Incomes policy is the most obvious of the various policies bearing directly on the pattern of economic rewards. As such, it warrants particular attention. Incomes policy affects the pre-tax distribution of income through the determination of wage rates relative to incomes derived from capital and land. Australia is unusual in having had a distinctive institutional framework for this sort of policy, principally because of the key role played by the Australian Industrial Relations Commission (AIRC). Historically, the AIRC (formerly the ACAC) has implemented policies that have had a bearing on the overall shares of the national income going to wages and salaries, and on the extent of inequality among those receiving wage incomes. The Labor government's Accord with the trade unions in the 1980s institutionalised these elements as part of a broader process of national economic management. It was a significant and unprecedented initiative in the development of an Australian incomes policy (described more fully in Stilwell 1986). However, the Accord subsequently became narrowed to a policy of wage restraint, and the introduction of enterprise bargaining in 1993 reduced the extent to which equity concerns rather than bargaining power determined wage outcomes. The advent of the Coalition government in 1996 saw the start of a sustained assault on the role of the AIRC as an instrument for incomes policy, culminating in the WorkChoices reforms introduced in 2005.[3] This latest set of policy changes undermines the possibilities for ameliorating the inequalities inherent in market processes and shifts the power relationship in wage determination processes yet more firmly to the interests of employers.

A policy shift in the opposite direction is what is advocated here. Restoring the share of the wages in the national income and reducing the inequalities among recipients of wage incomes are the dual themes. Is this a realistic possibility? Public debate in Australia has been strongly influenced by the neoliberal belief that decentralisation of wage determination processes, giving freer rein to market processes and thereby boosting profits, is the only way to achieve international competitiveness and economic growth. However, a recent report commissioned by the Academy of Social Sciences in Australia (ASSA) shows that the 'coordinated market economies' of northern Europe have performed 'just as well on these measures as the 'liberal market economies' of the USA, the UK and Australia (cited by Briggs

---

[3] These reforms see some of the responsibilities of the AIRC, including its role in determining minimum wage rates, transferred to the new Australian Fair Pay Commission. This Commission is comprised of five members, hand-picked by the government, including two academic economists and representatives of business and employees. Considering the composition of the Commission, industrial relations experts, almost without exception, anticipated that it would adopt a neoliberal perspective and reduce minimum wage rates in the expectation of increasing the number of private sector jobs (see Briggs *et al.* 2006). But, as even one supporter of industrial relations reform has argued (Wooden 2005), reducing minimum wages will not reliably have this effect unless matched by corresponding reductions in welfare payments. Even then, the outcome is doubtful because, as Keynes argued, wage cuts tend to reduce the aggregate expenditures on which economic expansion depends.

et al. 2006). Significantly, the more coordinated market economies have performed appreciably better in terms of equity. Based on this evidence, Briggs *et al.* argue that Australia should embrace a policy of 'coordinated flexibility' in wage determination, combining enterprise bargaining, broader framework agreements and the retention of coordinated minimum wages and standard awards. This would more effectively protect workers' interests, although not necessarily reverse the shift in income shares from labour to capital.

The setting of the minimum wage rate is a particular concern. Briggs *et al.* argue that those determining minimum wages should avoid the pitfalls of the low-wage approach taken by the USA, where there has been an expansion of poorly paid, insecure jobs, particularly in the service sector. Not only are these jobs characterised by low pay, but also by a high rate of turnover and little prospects for career advancement. Productivity has been poor: between 1990 and 1996, for example, productivity growth rates in the services sector in the USA were one-tenth of those in the equivalent sector in the more managed German economy (Briggs *et al.* 2006: 17). The current industrial relations policy threatens to lead Australia in a similar direction.

A preference for the American model is implicit in the widely publicised proposal by the five Australian economists for reduction of the minimum wage, compensated by income tax credits for low-waged workers (Dawkins 1999; Keating 2001). The underlying belief is that faster employment growth would be facilitated by wage reduction, at least at the bottom end of the earnings distribution. The research by Michael Keating, discussed in chapter 8, purports to provide supporting evidence by showing that wage differentials have been relatively consistent in the last decade, notwithstanding the push for more labour market flexibility (Keating 2003). On this reasoning, more dramatic institutional change is needed now to generate employment growth. Lower wage rates, compensated by tax credits, are the preferred mechanism.

It is an odd chain of reasoning and, not surprisingly, it has been subjected to various criticisms (for example, Watson 1998–9; Borland 2001: 224–5; Nevile 2001). Such a policy would push more of the cost of employing labour from employers onto the state. It would create more incentive for labour-intensive methods of production, when most commentators (including Keating) emphasise that there is more long-term potential for growth in the high-skill, high-technology sectors of the economy. Keynesian economic reasoning also suggests that the aggregate demand effects of wage reduction on employment levels could be perverse, unless the policy relied primarily on increasing the export of cheaply produced commodities – which would be difficult because there are many other low-cost players in that game, especially in China, the countries of South-East Asia and the Indian subcontinent. Finally, as a policy ostensibly designed to reduce economic inequalities, it is somewhat bizarre to advocate increasing earnings differentials by lowering minimum wages.

The alternative to the low-wage policy is to restore a living wage policy, taking into account workers' needs by setting minimum wages at a level 'which allows wage earners to be self-reliant and not dependent on government transfers to protect them from poverty' (Briggs *et al.* 2006: 16). The living wage would be calculated to 'provide someone who works full-time year-round with a decent standard of living as measured by the criteria of the society in which he/she lives' (Waltman, in Briggs *et al.* 2006: 18). Proponents of this policy approach also claim that it would likely lead to better quality jobs, better morale and higher productivity, as well as eradicating the incidence of poverty among working people (Briggs *et al.* 2006).

Australia is well positioned to pursue such a strategy, having already developed the necessary institutional infrastructure. The AIRC and the industrial tribunals could be empowered to make the assessments of living standards on which the level of the living wage would be based. There is a precedent for such assessments: the Social Policy Research Centre at the University of New South Wales has developed personal expenditure 'Budget Standards' that identify the requirements for 'modest, but adequate' indicative incomes (as noted by Briggs *et al.* 2006: 35). An interesting suggestion also comes from Jerold Waltman, professor of Political Science at the University of Southern Mississippi, who argues that increases in a minimum living wage should be linked to earnings in the top 5 per cent of the population. The incomes floor would thereby be linked to movements of the highest incomes rather than to average incomes. As Briggs *et al.* suggest, such a link would certainly 'focus the attention of policy makers on the source of any undue "wage pressures" and on those best able to restrain their earnings' (Briggs *et al.* 2006: 35).

Guaranteed minimum income?

The principle of establishing an income level necessary for the avoidance of poverty has been widely accepted in Australia. Historically, the award system of wage determination embodied a belief that workers' incomes should be linked to their needs for a decent standard of living and to employers' capacity to pay. The foundation of this living wage principle was the Arbitration Commission's judgement of 1907 – the famous Harvester decision – that established the notion of the family wage as a basis for wages policy. This was defined as the income necessary for a typical male breadwinner to keep himself and his family of three children at a reasonable living standard. That particular benchmark is obviously inappropriate today, given the increased participation of women in paid work and the greater diversity of household types that now prevail. Some such benchmark is necessary though, if the wages system is to serve social goals as well as the more narrowly defined concerns of the economic marketplace. It is necessary to ensure that the general level of wage incomes is consistent with socially accepted living standards.

Quite different arrangements would be needed to provide a minimum income for all households, not just a minimum wage. The case for some such guaranteed minimum income that is not conditional on employment is also of long standing. The *Henderson Report* proposed it as a means of eradicating poverty in Australia (Henderson 1975). The distinguished British philosopher Bertrand Russell (1917) had earlier advocated it, among other reasons, as a means whereby society could facilitate greater artistic and cultural development by liberating those with creative talents from the need for regular wage labour. Today its rationale would also be to recognise the diversity of important but otherwise unpaid activities – personal care, community organisation, further education and skills development, for example. It would provide social security without administrative complexity and without the personal intrusions associated with policing a selective welfare state. As such, it has political appeal to both the libertarian Left and Right. In an economic system based on advanced modern technology it makes less and less sense to proceed on the assumption that income must be directly tied to a conventional concept of work.

The five economists' proposal for tax credits for low-wage workers in Australia can be considered as an application of this guaranteed minimum income principle. However, as argued in this chapter, its neoliberal economic rationale is to facilitate wage reduction, so it cannot reasonably claim a place in a progressive political economy of distribution. A more radical interpretation of the guaranteed minimum income principle emphasises the direct payment by government of a 'basic income' to all citizens, with no work test, means test or assets test (McDonald 1995, 2005; Harding 1999; Glynn 2006: 180–3). As Rob Watts (2006: 35) puts it,

> Basic Income would necessitate the sweeping away of all the current plethora of welfare and social support schemes, and their replacement with a single, simple, no doubt wonderfully electronic, transfer of funds on a weekly basis to every citizen in the country.

The welfare state already has to cope with massive and recurrent redistribution: a basic income system would destigmatise the process. Such a system could also eliminate many of the complexities within the present system of targeted state welfare provisions and provide a general social safety net that does not depend on each individual's capacity to demonstrate eligibility for selective assistance. Its economic feasibility would depend on how much was saved in existing welfare state expenditures by shifting to the new system. Its effectiveness would depend on the level at which the minimum income has been set: a high level, apart from being a major drain on state spending, could have significant work disincentive effects, but a very low level would still leave people vulnerable to absolute poverty. As with Goldilocks, it is a situation requiring not too little, not too much, but just right.

In addition to recognising the key role a living wage policy could play in national economic management and income distribution, a more fully fledged incomes policy warrants consideration. Such a policy would mean greater regulation of incomes from profit, executive salaries, professional fees, interest and rents, as well as incomes from wages. This would be a much taller order. However, the effectiveness and durability of even a wages policy, let alone a more broadly-based incomes policy, depends on it promising and delivering what is perceived to be a fair share in the rewards from economic activity. So the more broadly-based approach is important, and the means for extending incomes policy to include non-wage incomes are not difficult to envisage. The status of executive salaries as tax-deductible business expenses, for example, could be terminated where those executive salaries are more than, say, ten times average weekly earnings. That would provide a strong incentive for companies to rein in the executive remuneration levels that have risen so steeply in recent years. As for other non-wage incomes, governments can control incomes derived from interest payments through monetary policy (in conjunction with the Reserve Bank), professional fees could be made subject to similar regulation as wages, while income from rents is affected by the impact of policies affecting the demand and supply of housing, such as the provision of public housing or subsidies for home ownership.

These are elements of a broader incomes policy could be constructed through the more coordinated use of existing policy instruments. International experience indicates that incomes policies of this sort are possible and that they can be effective in macroeconomic management and income redistribution (see Kuttner 1984, 1997). Regulating income from profit seems to be the principal problem in practice. Orthodox economists would say that any attempt to control profit is incompatible with the functioning of capitalism as an economic system. Indeed, because profit is inherently an economic surplus, it is difficult to regulate without undermining the essential dynamic of business activity. So be it, a socialist might respond, although it then becomes necessary to prescribe the transitional arrangements necessary for moving towards an alternative, non-capitalist economic system that is not subject to that constraint. Even accepting capitalist principles, though, profit is not sacrosanct. It can be – and is – made subject to company taxation. Moreover, the uses made of profit – whether distributed as dividends to shareholders or reinvested in the business, for example – are amenable to the influence of government policies. Putting higher company tax rates on distributed profits than on undistributed profits, for example, could be a means of encouraging reinvestment of profits, thereby expanding and modernising productive capacity and generating more employment in the economy.

Jobs for all

Full employment is a necessary economic foundation for a more equitable society. As noted in chapter 5, there is a strong correlation between the incidence of unemployment and poverty, particularly where the unemployment is long-term. Any rational economic system would mobilise its unemployed people to produce the goods and services necessary to satisfy the society's needs – and there are plenty of socially useful jobs to be done. Capitalism is not economically rational in this sense, as Keynesian economists and radical political economists have recurrently emphasised. Its labour markets can be in equilibrium while unemployment persists. Nor does economic growth necessarily eradicate the imbalance. Even after fifteen years of continually rising GDP, the official unemployment rate in Australia remained at around 5 per cent of the workforce in 2006. ABS survey data suggest that, taking account of underemployment and concealed unemployment, the actual rate may be nearly treble the usual published rate – an estimated 14.8 per cent rather than the official 5.1 per cent in 2005 (Garnaut 2005a: 1).

The costs of this persistent unemployment are high in social and economic terms as well as opportunity costs – the goods and services forgone by leaving human resources idle. Estimates of these costs have been made by, for example, John Langmore and John Quiggin (1994) and Martin Watts (2000). Fortunately, there is no shortage of policy instruments for reducing, if not eradicating, the problem. These include fiscal and monetary policies, trade and industry policies, public sector job creation and policies for the redistribution of working time. Some have already been implemented, of course – they are part of the standard toolkit of economic management – but the persistence of the unemployment problem is indicative of their inadequate development. The failure to generate growth in full-time jobs is of particular concern, given the evidence (reviewed in chapter 6) of the higher incidence of poverty among those with casual and part-time jobs. As Bob Gregory's research has shown, only one-quarter of all net job creation in the decade between 1990 and 2000 involved full-time jobs, and almost all of these were casual (Gregory 2002). This pattern persists and poses particular challenges to policy makers.

Some policies for full employment can operate through facilitating faster growth of job opportunities in the private sector. To use established jargon, they 'flatten the speed bumps' on the road to economic growth, such as those caused by the current account deficit, inflationary tendencies, inadequate capital capacity, workforce skills mismatch and regional imbalance in labour markets (Stilwell 2000: 183). Industry policies, incomes policies, investment policies (such as steering superannuation funds into targeted national investment priorities), education and training policies, and regional policies are the corresponding interventions. Emphasising policies for faster employment growth is not wholly compatible with prioritising social goals other than increased production of material goods and services, but it can be made compatible with redistributive policies. These policies have never been well integrated in Australia.

Other job-creation measures can operate through extending public sector employment, using the capacity of the state to act as employer of last resort. Keynesian economists have recurrently stressed the importance of government taking the lead in redressing unemployment, and this is the most direct means of doing so. A group of economists at the University of Newcastle have been particularly vigorous in promoting this view – that all unemployed people should be guaranteed employment, albeit at wage rates below those normally prevailing in both public and private sectors (Mitchell 1999, 2000). Public sector jobs in general can be engines of economic growth, as they have been throughout earlier phases of Australian economic history, although employer of last resort policies raise key questions about what wage rate is appropriate and what degree of compulsion is to be applied to the unemployed in ensuring their compliance.

There is much to be learnt from overseas experience with employment policies such as these (as emphasised by Dow, Boreham and Leet 1999). Among other things, a careful study of overseas experience refutes the belief that the best way to create jobs is by allowing wage inequalities to widen – as in the case of the USA. After an exhaustive comparison of that model with the European economies – commonly said to have higher unemployment levels because of their market rigidities – David Howell (2002: 236) concludes that

> There is a less elegant but more convincing story to be told about the declining economic well-being of the less skilled in developed countries, a story in which low-skill workers have borne the brunt of weak aggregate demand, sectoral and demographic shifts, increased mobility of production and financial capital, and labour market deregulation.

Achieving full employment is not straightforward in current political economic conditions but that is no reason to abandon the objective. Simultaneously, there is much to be said for rethinking carefully what 'jobs for all' and 'full employment' actually involve. Policies for redistributing work, for example, through shortening the working day or the working week, warrant particular attention (Hayden 1999; Woldring 1997). There is a long-standing tradition of social thought seeking 'liberation from toil' through technological progress that reduces the time each of us needs to spend in paid employment (see, for example, Russell 1935). Over the last decade, Andre Gorz (1999) has been a particularly powerful advocate of more flexible working-time arrangements whereby employees can vary their patterns of part-time and full-time work, further education and leisure.

It is not that work is unnecessary or unimportant. Geoff Dow argues the case for more of it, particularly to produce the additional goods and services needed for a good society, for example, in education, health, transport and other public infrastructure and services (Dow 2001: 140–1). The challenge for us, as a society, is how best to facilitate and remunerate socially useful work and to share it more equitably. We need to find a balance, not just in personal work–life choices, but also in relation to broader societal concerns – recognising the ecologically unsustainable and personally unsatisfying character of the current priority given to economic growth.

A related consideration is the nature of work itself. Although the primary focus of this book is on inequality of rewards, there is a parallel set of concerns about inequalities in the character of the work experience. The quality of work depends on multiple characteristics – levels of skill, work effort, worker autonomy and discretion, risk and rewards, for example. British labour market researcher Frances Green emphasises that the patterns of change – whether towards more skilled work or towards work intensification, for example – are quite variable between nations (Green 2006). Australia sits near the top of the international league-table in terms of the average annual hours worked per employed person (1814 hours in 2003, compared with 1429 in Germany and 1337 in Norway). It sits near the bottom in terms of growth of wages per employee over the period 1975–2002. 'Overworked and underpaid Down Under' is the obvious inference. How to translate the benefits of technological progress into improved lives for working people is a challenge that evidently still needs resolution, along with continuing concerns such as discrimination in employment.

Dealing with discrimination

Policies that help to eradicate discriminatory practices – whether individual or institutional – are essential in any program for greater economic equality and social mobility. Racism and sexism, as impediments to this equality of opportunity, are often deep-seated and not readily responsive to top-down edicts. Legislative requirements, such as equal pay and affirmative action, have reduced some of the formal barriers to equal participation by women in economic life. Major obstacles remain, as noted in chapter 7, including labour market segmentation, and inadequate childcare facilities. Similarly, while discrimination on the grounds of race has been made illegal, the disadvantage the people of non-Anglo-Celtic background, particularly Indigenous Australians, commonly face in the labour market has not been overcome. People with personal handicaps also experience the limits on their full participation in the economy very acutely. Public sector employers can play a leading role by acting as exemplars in employment practices to deal with these concerns. More generally, redress of discrimination needs to be part of a long process of public education and reform.

The improved public provision of childcare and the enforcement on private sector employers of requirements for the provision of work-based childcare can contribute directly to improving women's access to employment. Still more fundamental is the need to tackle the institutional discrimination that arises in connection with women's reproductive roles. If women engaging in childbirth and childrearing are economically disadvantaged as a result, the question that follows is how the economic system should be reorganised in order to prevent such disadvantage. If women who, for example, choose to have children need to interrupt their careers in order to do so, what must society do in order to ensure that they are not disadvantaged in employment, income or career prospects when they then return to work? Moreover, if women (or men) have family responsibilities outside of their paid work, how do expectations of workers need to be reassessed in order to accommodate and adequately value that vital social and economic role? Such questions take as a starting point the necessary but unpaid work that women actually do, and ask how the economy must be structured in order to reflect that reality. This would involve a re-evaluation of the nature of work and its remuneration, and a recognition that mothers, carers and unpaid domestic workers are 'economic actors in the mainstream' (Waring 1996: 58).

If discrimination according to gender and ethnicity is not redressed, it tends to be self-perpetuating. As Australian research over two decades ago has shown (Connell *et al.* 1982), the process starts early among young people in schools. Mary Bluett, president of the Victorian branch of the Australian Education Union, gives a more recent example when she notes the impact that having a male principal and a largely female staff tends to have on perpetuating beliefs about gender and power among young children (Dunn 2003). Attitudes about ethnicity are also shaped by institutional practices and are often cumulatively reinforced. The concentration of a particular ethnic minority among the unemployed, for example, fuels beliefs that they are, in general, unemployable. Tackling discrimination requires constant vigilance and monitoring, with particular reference to the media, educational institutions and workplaces. It is not purely attitudinal though: such an approach must also address the real economic inequalities that continue to pervade Australian society.

Conclusion

There are numerous policy instruments that could create a less unequal distribution of income and wealth if there were the political will to implement them. A more progressive system of taxation and government expenditure, incomes policy and policies bearing on the ownership of wealth, including its intergenerational transmission, are among the possibilities. A more broadly-based land tax could be a particularly potent means of creaming off the prodigious wealth that is currently captured by landowners as a result of land price inflation in the major cities, simultaneously generating more revenues to fund public infrastructure. Policies designed to tackle economic inequality also need to focus on job creation, the redistribution of work and the sources of discrimination that continue to impede equality of opportunity.

Even this big package of possible policy initiatives is far from fully comprehensive. As Hugh Stretton, that marvellously persistent advocate for a fairer Australian society, emphasises, there is a yet broader array of avenues through which equity can be sought – policies relating to housing, health, education, childcare, work, pensions, social security and natural resources, for example (Stretton 2005). As noted in chapter 6, urban and regional policies can also usefully contribute to more egalitarian outcomes.

Of course, redistributive measures that go against the interests of the principal wealth holders can be expected to provoke vigorous opposition. The wealthy, understandably, seek to defend their economically privileged position by whatever means are available. The battle lines are not always clear cut though. Some wealthy people, albeit few and far between, engage in philanthropy. Others, perceiving the advantages of substituting leisure and environmental quality for part of their income, have been downshifting. It would be unrealistic to expect the interests of the principal owners and managers of industrial and financial capital to be similarly malleable, but the advocacy and promotion of policies for progressive redistribution can have the effect of generating changes in attitudes and expectations. This may help to put the possibility of more equitable socioeconomic arrangements higher on the political agenda.

Chapter Twelve

PROSPECTS

Could we have a more egalitarian society? In Australia, as in other countries where neoliberal policies have been in vogue in recent decades, the political will to tackle economic inequality has been conspicuously lacking. Governments have implicitly formulated their policy priorities on the assumption that economic inequalities facilitate productivity and economic growth. The evidence and arguments presented in preceding chapters in this book indicate good reasons to challenge this assumption. Extreme inequalities in income and wealth may actually undermine economic efficiency. Moreover, they contribute to an array of broader social, environmental and political problems – undermining social cohesion, public health, political legitimacy and environmental responsibility. They also impede the development of a more generally contented society. If people's perception of their happiness is judged according to what they have relative to others, then substantial economic inequality is a recipe for widespread social discontent.

Individuals can, and do, respond to these problems, sometimes by opting out of the endless pursuit of greater material wealth and seeking more balance in their personal lives between work and income, leisure and personal fulfilment. Individual responses do not substantially change the distributional inequalities though. More effective action, including redistribution through taxes and public expenditures, must come from governments, and through employment and incomes policies that not only guarantee a decent wage for the less well off, but also limit the excessive remuneration of the already affluent. Examples of these policies were considered in the preceding chapter. But public policy initiatives themselves take place in a broader social context. Their successful adoption will depend on a fundamental values shift in our society. This chapter explores the prospects.

Perpetuating inequality

The changing patterns of economic inequality in Australia over the last couple of decades have some clear general features. There has been a redistribution of income shares from labour to capital. Some groups, such as business executives, have been particularly big winners, rewarding themselves with prodigious executive remuneration packages. The income inequalities have flowed into yet greater disparities in the distribution of wealth. Moreover, since those at the top of the distribution hold more of their wealth in income-generating forms, such as shares and property, the inequalities are perpetuated over time. The total wealth owned by those on the *BRW*'s rich 200 list has nearly quadrupled over the last decade, with the entry price being raised to a cool $196 million by 2006. Meanwhile, at the other end of the scale, poverty has continued to grow in relative terms. Those most affected, including the unemployed, Indigenous Australians, people with disabilities and the working poor, are marginalised and left behind. Spatial inequalities are also becoming more entrenched, as housing costs in the most desirable areas lock out all but the most affluent elites, while many rural and regional areas battle with processes of economic decline.

These trends are not easily reversed. The power and economic resources of the winners are not usually directed at resolving the difficulties of the losers. There is also a pervasive mythology about economic inequality that vitiates effective action aimed at its reduction.

A book on this subject written over a decade ago by one of the current authors (Stilwell 1993) argued that the beliefs impeding commitment to remedial, egalitarian policies are of four types. These impediments are worth reconsidering because, in general, they seem to have become more entrenched in the meanwhile. First is the belief that *major inequalities don't exist*. This is the problem of limited understanding, sometimes a problem of denial. The myth of Australia as a classless society and misconceptions about the effectiveness of redistributive policies are manifestations of this tendency. Second is the belief that *major inequalities do exist but are unsystematic.* Social position is interpreted in terms of luck rather than class or other economic biases that impede equality of opportunity. Third is the belief that *major inequalities do exist and are systematic but are justified.* Many and varied justifications may be posited: 'people get what they deserve', 'productivity and effort are the determinants of income differentials', 'social mobility ensures equality of opportunity' and 'inequalities associated with ethnicity and gender reflect innate characteristics'. For any, or all, of these reasons remedial policy interventions are regarded as unwarranted. Finally, there is the belief that *major inequalities do exist, are systematic and unjustified, but are not crucially important.* This may be the effect of, for example, extreme patriotism diverting concern away from intranational inequalities or the attitude of fatalism by which underprivileged groups sometimes reconcile themselves to their disadvantaged socioeconomic position.

To the extent that these beliefs are widespread, they undermine the social precondition for vigorous intervention and political change, but they are not absolute obstacles to progressive reform. Ultimately, they operate through shaping the pattern of public opinion, and public opinion is diverse and changeable. The neoliberal think tanks certainly act on that belief, relentlessly disseminating propaganda that is conducive to inequality and hostile to welfare (Mendes 2003; Cahill 2005). However, despite those efforts and their frequent embrace by the mainstream media, the evidence about current Australian attitudes to economic inequality is far from discouraging.

What do the people think?

A pervasive feature of Australian social surveys is widespread support for egalitarian ideals. As briefly noted in the opening chapter of this book, evidence from the latest Australian Survey of Social Attitudes (AuSSA) showed that almost 82 per cent of Australians consider the gap between high and low incomes to be too large. The concern with excessive income disparities is, predictably, greatest among those at the bottom of the scale, but even among the highest-income earners, a majority think that economic inequality has gone too far.

Table 12.1 Attitudes to economic inequality in Australia, 1984–2003; per cent of the population who consider that income differences in Australia are too large

1984*	1987*	1994*	2003**
62	61	66	84
(*n* = 2988)	(*n* = 1569)	(*n* = 1453)	(*n* = 4165)

* Data from National Social Science Survey (NSSS). NSSS asked respondents whether they agree that 'There is too much of a difference between rich and poor in this country'.
** Data from the Australian Survey of Social Attitudes (AuSSA). AuSSA asked respondents if the gap between those on high and low incomes is too large or too small.
Source: Pusey & Turnbull 2005: 174.

It remains a puzzle why, according to survey evidence from the same source, there is stronger support for a more equal income distribution than for government policy to actively pursue that goal. One wonders who, if not government, is expected to be the agent of redistribution. Maybe people think companies should pay their top executives less and pay their non-managerial workers more, but the question of how this might be encouraged or enforced remains unresolved. Evidently, a preference for greater equality but a distrust of government's capacity to produce it leaves us somewhat in limbo when it comes to the politics of creating a more egalitarian society. The widespread disquiet about the current extent of economic inequality is not matched by any consensus on what to do about it.

Other survey evidence indicates that public concern about inequality has increased over time. Comparing the responses from the 2003 AuSSA to earlier surveys of attitudes to income inequality, social researchers Pusey and Turnbull (2005) show that opposition to substantial income inequality in Australia seems to have become more widespread. The evidence, reproduced here as table 12.1, shows that there was a significant increase between 1994 and 2003 in the number of respondents who thought that income differences were too large. The wording of the survey questions in 2003 was a little different from that in earlier surveys, as noted at the foot of table 12.1, which inhibits a strong conclusion on this issue. However, it seems plausible to posit that the experience of economic inequalities over the last decade is

Table 12.2 Attitudes to income redistribution in Australia, 1984–2003; per cent of the population who think that income should be redistributed

1984[1]	1987[2]	1987[1]	1993[2]	1994[1]	1996[2]	2001[2]	2003[3]
51	46	39	51	41	47	56	46
($n = 2979$)	($n = 1778$)	($n = 1631$)	($n = 2948$)	($n = 1449$)	($n = 1725$)	($n = 1949$)	($n = 3986$)

[1] Data from National Social Science Survey (NSSS).
[2] Data from Australian Election Study (AES); NSSS and AES asked respondents if income and wealth should be redistributed to working people.
[3] Data from the Australian Survey of Social Attitudes (AuSSA). AuSSA asked respondents if government should redistribute income from the well off to the less well off.
Source: Pusey & Turnbull 2005: 175.

reflected in growing disquiet about the outcome. The latest AuSSA shows a slight decrease in the number of people who think that income inequality is too large, down from 84 per cent in 2003 to 82 per cent in 2005. Future surveys will reveal whether this marks a change in direction or just a temporary dip in the trend towards greater concern.

Changes in attitudes to income redistribution are less marked. Table 12.2 reproduces the evidence from Pusey and Turnbull (2005) on the number of survey respondents favouring redistribution. Again, some of the variation may be the result of the different wording of earlier surveys, as noted at the foot of table 12.1, but the general pattern shows no consistent trend up or down, which confirms that the increase in public concern about income inequality has not been matched by increasing support for the redistribution of incomes by government. In 2003 the percentage of respondents who favoured redistribution was 46 per cent, just below the average of all eight surveys studied, at 47 per cent. Pusey and Turnbull (2005: 175) conclude that 'despite a rising perception of inequality, redistribution of income and wealth is no more popular than it ever was'. The most recent AuSSA survey shows that support for redistribution has fallen over the last two years, slipping back to around 39 per cent by 2005. The enigma persists – the population remains more or less evenly divided on the question of redistribution, even though most think incomes are too unequal.

So can we realistically anticipate stronger support for policies to reduce economic inequalities? There is some evidence that a process of change is already under way. Clive Hamilton's investigations into the growing discontent with affluenza and the incidence of downshifting, for example, lend some support to this view. Phil Raskall, another veteran analyst of economic inequalities in Australian society, argues that there is growing interest in change, with many Australians sharing a concern that 'far too much emphasis is being put on improving the economy and too little on creating a better society' (Raskall 2003: 5). Even Michael Keating – one of the five economists proposing a lower minimum wage and tax credits – has come out strongly advocating higher taxes to deal with inequality and provide 'the public expenditure necessary to sustain our civilised society' (Keating 2004: 2).

While surveys and opinion polls indicate a widespread preference for increased social spending, and even a willingness to pay the taxes necessary to fund it, politicians continue to prioritise tax cuts and to shy away from redistributive policies. This was particularly evident during the 2004 federal election campaign, in which both the Labor and Liberal Parties emphasised the Australian public's tax burden, and vied with each other with their promises of tax cuts to 'reward hard work' (Australian Labor Party 2004; Liberal Party of Australia 2004). As federal treasurer for over a decade, Peter Costello has been particularly focused on emphasising tax cuts rather than more progressive redistribution; the Labor Party has yet to offer a clearly differentiated alternative.

In summary, there is an evident tension between widespread public disquiet about the extent of economic inequality and the reluctance of our political leaders to embrace policies that could generate more egalitarian outcomes. While there are significant attitudinal barriers to the redress of economic inequality in Australia, they are not shared by a significant proportion of the population. The more basic problem lies in the way Australian attitudes are interpreted or represented at the political level. Changing that requires a social and political movement with a different vision for Australian society and the political will among the nation's leadership to embrace these concerns.

A way forward?

Policies for a more egalitarian society need to be part of a broader program of economic, social and environmental management. Creating growth and more equitable distribution of employment opportunities through appropriate fiscal, monetary, industry and trade policies is an obvious case in point. Ensuring an adequately financed program of government expenditures on public housing, social security, health and education is another. These are the preconditions for greater equality of access to economic opportunities. A genuinely progressive tax system is needed to generate the necessary revenues. Likewise, environmental and energy polices that ensure the sustainability of the natural environment are necessary for combating the tendency for environmental goods to become accessible only to those with ability to pay. Intergenerational equity in access to environmental assets is a key tenet of the case for ecological sustainability – so that future generations are not denied access to environmental assets by the rapacious activities of the present generation. The inherent connection between the objectives of ecological sustainability and social justice comes through strongly in this sort of thinking about new directions for public policy.

Making progress in these policy areas is not simple, of course. As with all progressive political, economic and social change, there is a need for critique, vision, strategy and organisation. We need a critique of the prevailing situation, vision about the characteristics of a better society, a strategy for getting from here to there, and political organisation to bring about the transition (Stilwell 2000, chapter 2). These are difficult requirements, but not impossibly difficult. The strong and growing support for the Green Party in Australia, for example, reflects concerns about issues of social justice and economic efficiency – interpreted as using our economic resources effectively to serve social goals – as well as concerns about environmental quality. The Greens have become an important political vehicle for change. This bodes well for the development of critique, vision, strategy and organisation.

There are other significant pressure points, too. The trade union movement periodically shows its capacity to embrace industrial and social reforms as well as protection of the immediate interest of current union members – but it could do more. Under the leadership of Greg Combet, the ACTU has shown that it can effectively represent the interests of the workforce in general, especially when faced with a threat such as that posed by WorkChoices. Meanwhile, a broad array of non-governmental organisations is actively pursuing alternative political agendas, challenging the dominant neoliberal orthodoxy and the associated obsessions with material acquisitiveness and economic growth.

We live at a time when more people can be expected to question the point of further affluence for the already affluent. It is increasingly apparent that it is neither fulfilling nor sustainable. The coherence and security of society are likely to be of increasing concern, too. Egalitarian ideas and policy practices are crucial in these circumstances. As Layard notes, much of policy over last twenty years has been focused on rewarding 'individual performance, rather than providing an adequate general level of pay and stressing the importance of the job and the promotion of professional norms and professional competence' (2003b: 15). It is not surprising that so many people's primary concern has been with getting a bigger personal slice of the incomes and wealth – through capital gains and other unearned incomes, if possible – rather than creating better overall social outcomes. The limits of this strategy, and its social and environmental fallout are now evident.

The impact of the dominant neoliberal ideologies and policy practices has been to increase competition, not cooperation. In terms of human happiness this is a zero sum game since, above a certain threshold, happiness does not increase with rising actual income, but with rising relative income. The latter often involves sacrificing those things that ultimately contribute more to personal wellbeing. For all these reasons, as well as the continuing need to tackle the problem of poverty, the redress of economic inequality is central to the achievement of a good society.

SOCIAL ATTITUDES TO ECONOMIC INEQUALITY

Table A.1 Attitudes of different income groups to gap between high and low incomes, per cent, by gross annual income of respondent

	$0–$15 599	$15 600–$36 399	$36 400–$77 999	$78 000 or more	Total
	%	%	%	%	%
Much too large	39.0	37.6	32.3	15.1	34.4
Too large	44.3	49.8	50.0	44.7	47.7
About right	8.6	9.0	11.9	31.7	11.8
Too small	1.1	0.2	0.4	1.8	0.7
Much too small	0.2	0.2	0.1	0.0	0.1
Can't choose	6.9	3.3	5.3	6.6	5.3
Total	100	100	100	100	100

Source: Wilson *et al.* (2006).

Table A.2 Attitudes of different income groups to the statement, 'Ordinary working people do not get a fair share of the nation's wealth', per cent, by gross annual income of respondent

	$0–$15 599	$15 600–$36 399	$36 400–$77 999	$78 000 or more	Total
	%	%	%	%	%
Strongly agree	19.7	19.6	13.6	3.9	16.4
Agree	45.3	45.7	46.2	35	44.8
Neither agree nor disagree	19.8	20.3	22.1	22.8	20.9
Disagree	10.4	10.2	14.8	33.5	13.8
Strongly disagree	0.7	0.9	1.6	4.5	1.4
Can't choose	4.0	3.3	1.6	0.3	2.8
Total	100	100	100	100	100

Source: Wilson *et al.* (2006).

Table A.3 Attitudes of different income groups to the statement, 'Government should redistribute income', per cent, by gross annual income of respondent

	$0–$15 599	$15 600–$36 399	$36 400–$77 999	$78 000 or more	Total
	%	%	%	%	%
Strongly agree	13.0	11.2	7.9	3.0	10.0
Agree	30.4	29.4	28.8	21.9	28.8
Neither agree nor disagree	22.6	25.6	25.9	18.0	24.0
Disagree	24.0	24.7	25.7	38.3	26.1
Strongly disagree	4.3	4.9	9.1	16.8	7.1
Can't choose	5.7	4.2	2.5	2.1	4.0
Total	100	100	100	100	100

Source: Wilson *et al.* (2006).

COMPARISON OF EQUIVALENCE SCALES

This table shows differences between the Henderson study's weighting of different types of household for the purpose of calculating the incidence of poverty and that used in the more recent study by NATSEM. Some such weighting is necessary in order to impose a single poverty line measure on households with different demographic composition. As the table below shows, the differences in weighting are relatively minor, but even small differences can bear significantly on estimates of the overall proportion of people in poverty.

Table B.1 Comparison of equivalence scales utilised in the *NATSEM Report* (2004) and the *Henderson Reports (1975) on Poverty*.

NATSEM (a)		Henderson (b)	
Unit	Index	Index	Unit
Single person	0.48	0.43	Single person, not working
Single parent, 1 child	0.62	0.58	Single parent, not working, 1 child
Couple, no children	0.71	0.71	Couple, 1 working, no children
Couple, 2 children	1	1	Couple, 1 working, 2 children
Couple, 4 children	1.29	1.29	Couple, 1 working, 4 children

Source: (a) Lloyd *et al.* (2004a: 3); (b) Henderson (1975: 13).

BIBLIOGRAPHY

Aarons, L. 1999, *Casino Oz: Winners and Losers in Global Capitalism*, Goanna Books, Sydney.

Aitkin, D. 2005, *What Was it all For? The Reshaping of Australia*, Allen & Unwin, Sydney.

Albanese, A. 2000, 'Casino Oz – the odds are not that even', *Sydney Morning Herald*, 1 March, p. 15.

Altman, J. & Hunter, B. 1998, 'Indigenous Poverty', in R. Fincher and J. Niewenhuysen (eds), *Australian Poverty: Then and Now*, Melbourne University Press, Melbourne pp. 238–57.

Anderson, T. 2002, 'The Political Economy of Human Rights', *Journal of Australian Political Economy*, no. 50, December, pp. 200–27.

Argy, F. 2003, *Where to From Here? Australian Egalitarianism Under Threat*, Allen & Unwin, Sydney.

— 2006, *Equality of Opportunity in Australia: Myth and Reality*, discussion paper no. 85, The Australia Institute, Canberra.

Argyrous, G. & Neale, M. 2003, 'The "Disabled" Labour Market: The disability support program and unemployment', *Journal of Australian Political Economy*, no. 51, June, pp. 5–28.

Armstrong, M. 2005, 'Aborigines: Problems of race and class', in R. Kuhn (ed.), *Class and Struggle in Australia*, Pearson Longman, Sydney.

Atkinson, A. B. 1972, *Unequal Shares: Wealth in Britain*, Allen Lane, The Penguin Press, London.

— 1983, *The Economics of Inequality*, Clarendon Press, Oxford.

— 2004, 'The Luxembourg Income Study (LIS): past, present and future', *Socio-economic Review*, vol. 2, no. 4, pp. 165–90.

— & Leigh, A. 2006, *The Distribution of Top Incomes in Australia*, Australian National University Centre for Economic Policy Research, discussion paper no. 514, March.

Australian Broadcasting Corporation Online 2004, 'ACOSS says Capital Gains Tax Cuts Favour the Rich',19 July. Accessed online @ http://www.abc.net.au/am/content/2004/s1156695.htm, 20 July 2006.

—Online (2006) 'Police Minister to visit troubled Wadeye', 22 May. http://www. abc.net.au/news/newsitems/200605/s1644085.htm, 3 December 2006.

—2006, 'Police Minister to visit troubled Wadeye', ABC News Online, 22 May. Accessed online @ http://www.abc.net.au/news/ newsitems/200605/s1644085.htm, 12 September 2006.

Australian Bureau of Statistics (ABS) 1984, *Income and Housing Survey, Income Units, Australia, 1981–82 (6523.0)*, Commonwealth of Australia, Canberra.

—1989, *1986 Income Distribution Survey, Income Units, Australia (6523.0)*, Commonwealth of Australia, Canberra.

—1993, *1990 Survey of Income and Housing Costs and Amenities, Income Units, Australia (6523.0)*, Commonwealth of Australia, Canberra.

—2001, *Labour Force, New South Wales and Australian Capital Territory, 2001 (6201.1)*. Accessed online @ http://www.abs.gov.au/ausstats/abs@.nsf/7884593a920277 66ca2568b5007b8617/21ee576cdc2c46dbca256889000f701a!OpenDocument, 27 April 2005.

—2001b, *Government Benefits, Taxes and Household Income, Australia (6537.0)*, Commonwealth of Australia, Canberra.

—2002a *Labour Force, Victoria, 2001 (6202.2)*. Accessed online @ http://www.abs. gov.au/ausstats/abs@.nsf/7884593a92027766ca2568b5007b8617/af160e3d-2e1647a8ca2568bd0010a421!OpenDocument, 27 April 2005.

—2002b, *Education and Training Indicators, Australia (4230.0)*. Accessed online @ http:// www.ausstats.abs.gov.au/Ausstats/subscriber.nsf/Lookup/3EC41B1520088D8 ACA256C85007B00AF/$File/42300_2002.pdf, http://www.abs.gov.au/ausstats/ abs@.nsf/7884593a92027766ca2568b5007b8617/83bcf9372ebbeb7dca2568bd00 13504d!OpenDocument, 28 July 2005.

—2003a, 'Family and Community Services: Services in remote Aboriginal and Torres Strait Islander communities', in *Australian Social Trends 2003*. Accessed online @ http://www.abs.gov.au/AUSSTATS/abs@.nsf/allprimarymainfeatures/ 2356424 C275E3E45CA256EB400035395?OpenDocument, 30 March 2005.

—2003b, *Australian Census Analytic Program: Counting the Homeless, 2001(2050.0)*. Accessed online @ http://www.ausstats.abs.gov.au/ausstats/free.nsf/Lookup/ 5AD852 F13620FFDCCA256DE2007D81FE/$File/20500_2001.pdf, 30 March 2005.

—2003c, *Labour Force, Australia (6203.0)*. Accessed online @ http://www.abs.gov. au/ausstats/abs@.nsf/7884593a92027766ca2568b5007b8617/3e9949111cc4b424ca 2568bd00133b6a!OpenDocument, http://www.abs.gov.au/ausstats/abs@.nsf/ 7884593a92027766ca2568b5007b8617/83bcf9372ebbeb7dca2568bd0013504d! OpenDocument, 2 August 2005.

—2004a, *Census of Population and Housing: Australia in Profile, A regional analysis, 2001 (2032.0)*. Accessed online @ http://www.abs.gov.au/ausstats/abs@. nsf/7884593a92027766ca2568b5007b8617/e13b99ab214baa25ca2568890021fb16! OpenDocument, 27 April 2005.

— 2004b, *Australian Social Trends, Health – Mortality and morbidity: injuries, 2003 (4102.0)*. Accessed online @ http://www.abs.gov.au/AUSSTATS/abs@.nsf/ allprimarymainfeatures/2356424C275E3E45CA256EB400035395?OpenDocument, 30 March 2005.

— 2005a, *Household Income and Income Distribution, Australia, 2003–04 (6523.0)*. Accessed online @ http://www.abs.gov.au/AUSSTATS/abs@.nsf/Productsby-Catalogue/5F4BB49C975C64C9CA256D6B00827ADB?OpenDocument, 18 September 2006.

— 2005b, *Employee Earnings and Hours, Australia, May 2004 (6306.0)*. Accessed online @ http://abs.gov.au/AUSSTATS/abs@.nsf/ProductsbyCatalogue/2764 1437D6780D1FCA2568A9001393DF?OpenDocument, 18 September 2006.

— 2005c, *Deaths, Australia 2004 (3302.0)*. Accessed online @ http://www.abs.gov.-au/ausstats/abs@.nsf/7884593a92027766ca2568b5007b8617/9f986bcf971716a2-ca256889000cc7b0!OpenDocument, 12 September 2006.

— 2005d, *Australian Labour Market Statistics (6105.0)*. Accessed online @ http://www.ausstats.abs.gov.au/ausstats/subscriber.nsf/Lookup/D3D7FAA735-DDA645CA25703B00774A0B/$File/41020_2005.pdf, 16 August 2005.

— 2005e, *Household Expenditure Survey, Australia: Detailed Expenditure Items, 2003–04. Table 2. Gross Income Quintile, Household expenditure on goods and services (6535.0.55.001)*, Data Cube. Accessed online @ http://www.ausstats.abs.gov.au/ausstats/subscriber.nsf/Lookup/113D4D69731156ECC A257059007F72A0/$File/6535055001_2003_04.xls, 25 August 2005.

— 2005f, *Employee Earnings and Hours, May 2004 (6306.0)*. Accessed online @ http://abs.gov.au/AUSSTATS/abs@.nsf/productsbyCatalogue/27641437D6780D1F CA2568A9001393DF?OpenDocument, 9 November 2006.

— 2006a *Australian System of National Accounts, 2005–06 (5204.0)*. Accessed online @ http://www.abs.gov.au/AUSSTATS/abs@.nsf/ProductsbyCatalogue/1109-53FFA28D4E52CA2572110002FF03?OpenDocument, 9 November 2006.

— 2006b, *Household Wealth and Wealth Distribution, Australia, 2003–04 (6554.0)*. Accessed online @ http://www.abs.gov.au/AUSSTATS/abs@.nsf/Productsby ReleaseDate/ABDECB2B70579A67CA25715C001A3C71?OpenDocument, 4 May 2006.

— 2006c, *Consumer Price Index, Australia, Mar 2006 (6401.0)*. Accessed online @ http://www.abs.gov.au/ausstats/abs@.nsf/e8ae5488b598839cca25682000131612 /938da570a34a8edaca2568a900139350!OpenDocument, 6 July 2006.

— 2006d *Australian Labour Market Statistics, Oct 2006 (6105.0)*. Accessed online @ http://www.abs.gov.au/AUSSTATS/abs@.nsf/DetailsPage/6105.0Oct%202006? OpenDocument, 9 November 2006.

— 2006e, *Average Weekly Earnings, Australia, February 2006 (6302.0)*. Accessed online @ http://www.abs.gov.au/AUSSTATS/abs@.nsf/DetailsPage/6302.0Feb%202006? OpenDocument, 16 June 2006.

— 2006f, *Australian Labour Market Statistics, April 2006 (6105.0)*. Accessed online @ http://www.abs.gov.au/AUSSTATS/abs@.nsf/DetailsPage/6105.0Apr%202006? OpenDocument, 16 June 2006.

— 2006g, *Labour Force, Australia, May 2006 (6202.0)*. Accessed online @ http://www.abs. gov.au/AUSSTATS/abs@.nsf/DetailsPage/6202.0May%202006?OpenDocument, 16 June 2006.

— 2006h, *Labour Force, Australia, Spreadsheets, June 2006, table 03. Labour force status by sex (6202.0.55.001)*. Time series spreadsheet. Accessed online @ http://www.abs.gov.au/AUSSTATS/abs@.nsf/DetailsPage/6202.0.55.001Jun%202006? OpenDocument, 11 August 2006.

— 2006i, *Employee Earnings, Benefits and Trade Union Membership, Australia, August 2005 (6310.0)*. Accessed online @ http://abs.gov.au/AUSSTATS/abs@. nsf/ ProductsbyCatalogue/99E5614783415356CA25713E000F92B1? OpenDocument, 21 September 2006.

Australian Institute of Health and Welfare 2002, *Medical Labour Force 2002*, National Health Labour Force Series, no. 30. Accessed online @ http://www. aihw.gov.au/publications/hwl/mlf02/mlf02.pdf, 17 August 2005.

Australian Labor Party 2004, *Labor's Tax and Better Family Payment Policy: Rewarding Hard Work*. Accessed online @ http://www.alp.org.au/policy/prosperity/ taxfamilypayment.php, 24 September 2004.

Australian Stock Exchange 2005, *Australia's Share Owners: An ASX study of share investors in 2004*. Accessed online @ http://www.asx.com.au/about/pdf/2004_ share_ownership_booklet.pdf, 24 March 2006.

Australian Vice-Chancellors' Committee 2005, *AVCC Member Vice-Chancellors*. Accessed online @ http://www.avcc.edu.au/content.asp?page=/about_avcc/current_ office_holders/avcc_members.htm, http://www.abs.gov.au/ausstats/abs@.nsf/ 7884593a92027766ca2568b5007b8617/83bcf9372ebbeb7dca2568bd0013504d! OpenDocument, 28 July 2005.

Badcock, B. 1984, *Unfairly Structured Cities*, Basil Blackwell, Oxford.

Baker, J. 1987, *Arguing for Equality*, Verso, London.

Baum, S. 2003, 'Socio-economic Advantage and Disadvantage Across Australia's Metropolitan Cities', paper presented at State of Australian Cities National Conference, Sydney, 2–5 December. Accessed online @ http://www.uws.edu.au/ about/acadorg/caess/uf/conference#3, 17 October 2005.

— 2004a, 'Measuring Socio-Economic Outcomes in Sydney: An analysis on Census data using a general deprivation index', *Australian Journal of Regional Studies*, vol. 10, no. 1, pp. 105–28.

— 2004b, 'The Socio-Spatial Structure of Australia's Metropolitan Regions', *Australian Journal of Regional Studies*, vol. 1, no. 2, pp. 157–79.

Baxter, J. 1997, 'Gender equality and participation in housework: A cross-national perspective', *Journal of Comparative Family Studies*, vol. 28, no. 3, Autumn, pp. 220–48.

— & Wright, E. O. 2000, 'The Glass Ceiling Hypothesis: A comparative study of the United States, Sweden, and Australia', *Gender and Society*, vol. 14, no. 2, April, pp. 275–94.

Beder, S. 2006, *Environmental Principles and Policies*, UNSW Press, Sydney.

Bell, S. (ed.) 2000, *The Unemployment Crisis in Australia: Which way out?* Cambridge University Press, Melbourne.

Birrell, B. & Seol, B. 1998, 'Sydney's ethnic underclass', *People and Place*, vol. 6, no. 3, pp. 16–29.

Bittman, M., England, P., Sayer, L., Folbre, N. & Matheson, G. 2003, 'When Does Gender Trump Money? Bargaining and time in household work', *American Journal of Sociology*, vol. 109, no. 1, pp. 186–214.

Blau, F. D. & Kahn, L. M. 2000, 'Gender differences in pay', *Journal of Economic Perspectives*, vol. 14, no. 4, Fall, pp. 75–99.

Bloodworth, S. 2005, 'Women, class and oppression', in R. Kuhn (ed.), *Class and Struggle in Australia*, Pearson Longman, Sydney.

Boreham, P., Dow, G. & Leet, M. 1999, *Room to Manoeuvre: Political aspects of full employment*, Melbourne University Press, Melbourne.

Borland, J. 2001, 'Unemployment', in J. Nieuwenhuysen, P. Lloyd and M. Mead (eds), *Reshaping Australia's Economy; Growth with Equity and Sustainability*, Cambridge University Press, Cambridge.

—, Gregory, B. & Sheehan, P. 2001, 'Inequality and Economic Change', in J. Borland, B. Gregory and P. Sheehan (eds), *Work Rich, Work Poor: Inequality and economic change in Australia*, Centre for Strategic Economic Studies, Victoria University, Melbourne.

Boulding, K., 1971, 'Environmental Quality – Discussion', *Papers and Proceedings of the American Economic Association*, May, p. 169.

Bradbury, B. 2003, *Child Poverty: A review*, policy research paper no. 20, Department of Family and Community Services, Canberra.

Briggs, C., Buchanan, J. & Watson, I. 2006, *Wages Policy in an Era of Deepening Wage Inequality*, Academy of the Social Sciences in Australia, occasional paper 1/2006, policy paper 4, Canberra.

Broomhill, R. & Sharp, R. 2005, 'The Changing Male Breadwinner Model in Australia: A new gender order?', in *Labour & Industry*, vol. 16, no. 1, August, pp. 105–27.

Browning, J. & Jakubowicz, A. 2003, *What Can We Say About Racism in Australia?*, Racism Monitor Report, discussion paper no. 1. Accessed online @ http://www.fairgo.net/reports.html, 25 September 2006.

Bryan, D. & Rafferty, M. 1999, *The Global Economy in Australia*, Allen & Unwin, Sydney.

Bryson, L. & Thompson, F. 1972, *An Australian Newtown: Life and leadership in a working-class suburb*, Penguin, Ringwood.

Burbidge, A. & Sheehan, P. 2001, 'The Polarisation of Families', in J. Borland, B. Gregory and P. Sheehan (eds), *Work Rich, Work Poor: Inequality and economic change in*

Australia, 2001, Centre for Strategic Economic Studies, Victoria University, Melbourne.

Burgess, J. 2005, 'Exploring Job Quality and Part-time Work in Australia', *Labour & Industry*, vol. 15, no. 3, April, pp. 29–40.

Burke, P. 1998, 'The Poverty of Homelessness', in R. Fincher and J. Nieuwenhuysen (eds), *Australian Poverty: Then and now*, Melbourne University Press, Victoria.

Burrell, S. 2006a, 'Sydney loses title of wealth capital', *Sydney Morning Herald*, 4–5 March, p. 1.

— 2006b, 'Sydney loses its shine to old rival', *Sydney Morning Herald*, 4–5 March, p. 4.

— & O'Sullivan, J. 2006, 'Millions ride shares rocket to riches', *Sydney Morning Herald*, 21 March, p. 1.

— & Patty, A. 2006, 'Logged Out: Why every Australian family needs the internet', *Sydney Morning Herald*, News Review, June, pp. 24–5.

Burroughs, J. E. & Rindfleisch, A. 2002, 'Materialism and well-being: A conflicting values perspective', *Journal of Consumer Research*, December, vol. 29, issue 3, pp. 348–71.

Business Review Weekly 2004, 'BRW Rich 200', *Business Review Weekly*, 20 May–14 July.

— 2006a, 'BRW Rich 200', *Business Review Weekly*, 18 May–21 June.

— 2006b, 'BRW Young Rich', *Business Review Weekly*, 14 September–18 October.

Butlin, N. 1983, *Trends in Australian Income Distribution: A first glance*, working paper no. 17, Department of Economic History, Australian National University, Canberra.

Button, J. & Stevenson, A. 2004, 'Property boom splits nation', *Age*. Accessed online @ http://www.theage.com.au/articles/2004July2009/1089000352014.html?from/storylhs&oneclic k/true, 6 October 2004.

Cahill, D. 2005, 'The Right Values in Education: Neo-liberal think tanks and the assault upon public schooling', *Overland*, vol. 179, pp. 9–14.

Campbell, I. 2000, 'The Spreading Net: Age and gender in the process of casualisation in Australia', *Journal of Australian Political Economy*, no. 45, June, pp. 68–99.

Chalmers, J., Campbell, I. & Charlesworth, S. 2005, 'Part-time Work and Caring Responsibilities in Australia: Towards an assessment of job quality', *Labour & Industry*, vol. 15, no. 3, April, pp. 41–66.

Chin, S.-F., Harding, A. & Tanton, R. 2006, *A Spatial Portrait of Disadvantage: Income Poverty by Statistical Local Area in 2001*, paper presented at ANZRSAI Conference, Beechworth, 26–9 September.

Clark, A. E. & Oswald, A. J. 1996, 'Satisfaction and Comparison Income', *Journal of Public Economics*, vol. 61, no.3, pp. 359–81.

Cleary, P. 1990, 'In Palm Beach the Clever Dicks Pay 19% Tax', *Sydney Morning Herald*, 14 December.

Coates, S., Vidler, S. & Stilwell, F. 2004, 'Editors' Introduction, Special issue on superannuation', *Journal of Australian Political Economy*, no. 53, June, pp. 5–12.

Coburn, D. 2000, 'Income Inequality, Social Cohesion and the Health Status of Populations: The role of neoliberalism', *Social Science and Medicine*, no. 51, pp. 135–46.

Collins, J., Gibson, K., Alcorso, C., Castles, S. & Tait, D. 1995, *A Shop Full of Dreams: Ethnic small business in Australia*, Pluto Press, Sydney.

Commonwealth of Australia 2006, *Parliament of Australia*. Accessed online @ http://www.aph.gov.au/index.htm, 11 August 2006.

Connell, R. W., Ashenden, D. J., Kessler, S. & Dowsett, G. W. 1982, *Making the Difference: Schools, families and social division*, George Allen & Unwin, Sydney.

Connell, R. W. & Messerschmidt, J. W. 2005, 'Hegemonic Masculinity: Rethinking the concept', *Gender and Society*, vol. 19, no. 6, December, pp. 829–59.

Connolly, C. & Hajaj, K. 2002, *Financial Exclusion and Social Exclusion*, Financial Services Community Policy Centre, University of New South Wales, Sydney, March.

Coombs, G. 2006, 'Wellbeing and Happiness in OECD Countries', *Economic Roundup*, Australian Treasury, Canberra, May, pp. 11–21.

Cottle, D. & Keys, A. 2004, 'The Monopolisation of the Australian Funeral Industry', *Journal of Australian Political Economy*, no. 54, December, pp. 32–44.

Cresswell, A. 2005, 'Health chasm between rich, poor widening' *Australian*, 7 March.

Crikey 2006, *From CRW to BRW*. Accessed online @ http://www.crikey.com.au/articles/2006/05/18-1515-8426.print.html, 25 May 2006.

Csikszentmihalyi, M. 1999, 'If We Are So Rich, Why Aren't We Happy?', *American Psychologist*, October, vol. 54, no. 10. Accessed online @ http://sparta.rice.edu/~erinm/Mihaly.html, 17 October 2005.

Curthoys, A. 2000, 'Gender Studies in Australia: A history', *Australian Feminist Studies*, vol. 15, no. 31, pp. 19–38.

Dabscheck, B. 1990, 'The BCA's Plan to Americanise Australian Industrial Relations', *Journal of Australian Political Economy*, no. 27, November 1990, pp. 1–15.

Daly, A., Kawaguchi, A., Meng, X. & Mumford, K. 2006, 'The Gender Wage Gap in Four Countries', *Economic Record*, vol. 82, no. 257, June, pp. 165–76.

Daly, A., McNamara, J., Tanton, R., Harding, A. & Yap, M. 2006, *Indicators of Social Exclusion for Australia's Children: An analysis by state and age group*, paper presented at the University of Queensland Social Research Centre Opening Conference, 18–19 July.

Davidson, K. 1987, 'J. K. Galbraith and the New Economics', *Sydney Morning Herald*, 24 February.

Davis, W. 1982, *The Rich: A study of the species*, Sidgwick & Jackson, London.

Dawkins, P. 1999, 'A plan to cut unemployment in Australia: An elaboration of the "five economists"' letter to the Prime Minister, 28 October 1998', Mercer – Melbourne Institute, *Quarterly Bulletin of Economic Trends*, no. 1, pp. 48–59.

— 2001, 'The "five economists' plan": The original ideas and further developments', *Australian Journal of Labour Economics*, vol. 5, no. 2, pp. 203–30.

—, Freebairn, J., Garnaut, R., Keating, M. & Richardson, C. 1998, 'Dear John, How to create more jobs, an open letter', *Australian*, 26 October.

Day, P. 1995, *Land: The elusive quest for social justice, taxation reform and a sustainable planetary environment*, Australian Academic Press, Brisbane.

— 2005, *Hijacked Inheritance: The triumph of dollar Darwinism?*, Copyright Publishing, Brisbane.

Department of Education, Science and Training 2005, *Students 2004 (full year): Selected Higher Education Statistics*. Accessed online @ http://www.dest.gov.au/sectors/ higher_education/publications_resources/profiles/students_2004_selected_higher_ education_statistics.htm, 20 February 2007.

Department of Immigration and Multicultural Affairs 2006, *Population Flows: Immigration aspects 2004–05 Edition*. Accessed online @ http://www.immi.gov. au/media/publications/statistics/popflows2004-5/index.htm, 12 September 2006.

Diener, E. & Seligman, M. 2004, 'Beyond Money: Towards an economy of well-being', *Psychological Science in the Public Interest*, vol. 5, no. 1.

Dieter, H. 2006, 'Australia's Bilateral Trade Agreement with the United States: Significant drawbacks, few gains?', *Journal of Australian Political Economy*, no. 57, June, pp. 85–111.

Dilnot, A. 1990, 'The distribution and composition of personal sector wealth in Australia', *Australian Economic Review*, no. 89, pp. 33–40.

Doughney, J., Macdonald, F., Pyke, J., Lyon, A., Leahy, M. & Rea, J. 2004, *Lifelong economic well-being for women*. Summary paper: 'What women want', report commissioned by Security4Women consortium. Accessed online @ http://www.security4women. com/documents/What%20Women%20Want%20Summary%20July%202004.pdf, 25 August 2005.

Dow, G. 2001, 'Book Review', *Journal of Australian Political Economy*, no.47, June, pp. 138–42.

— 2002, 'Neoliberal Corporate Governance of the Australian Economy', in S. Bell (ed.), *Economic Governance and Institutional Dynamics*, Oxford University Press, Melbourne.

—, Boreham, P. & Leet, M. 1999, *Room to Manoeuvre: Political aspects of full employment*, Melbourne University Press, Melbourne.

Downer, A. 2002, 'Australia's Overseas Aid Program 2002–3', Statement by Minister for Foreign Affairs, Commonwealth of Australia, Canberra, 14 May, table 2.

Dunn, A. 2003, 'For men, school is definitely out', *Age*, 8 February. Accessed online @ http://www.theage.com.au/articles/2003 February 2007/1044579934724.html, 16 August 2005.

Dwyer, T. 2003, 'The Taxable Capacity of Australian Land and Resources', *Australian Tax Forum*, vol. 8, no. 1.

Eardley, T. 2000, 'Working But Poor? Low pay and poverty in Australia', *Economic and Labour Relations Review*, vol. ll, no.2, pp. 308–38.

Easterlin, R. A. 1995, 'Will raising the incomes of all increase the happiness of all?', *Journal of Economic Behavior and Organization*, 27, 35–47.

— 2004, *Diminishing Marginal Utility of Income: A caveat.* Accessed online @ http://www.bpress.com/cgi/viewcontent.cgi?article=1004&context=usclwps, 20 February 2007.

Eckersley, R. 1998, 'Perspectives on Progress: Economic growth, quality of life and ecological sustainability', in R. Eckersley (ed.), *Measuring Progress: Is life getting better?* CSIRO, Melbourne.

Economic Planning Advisory Commission (EPAC) 1995, *Income Distribution in Australia: Recent Trends and Research*, commission paper no. 7, Australian Government Publishing Service, Canberra.

England, P. 2005a, 'Gender Inequality in Labor Markets: The role of motherhood and segregation', *Social Politics*, vol. 12, no.2, Summer, pp. 264–88.

— 2005b, 'Emerging Theories of Care Work', *Annual Review of Sociology*, vol. 31, pp. 381–99.

—, Budig, M. & Folbre, N. 2002, 'Wages of Virtue: The relative pay of care work', *Social Problems*, vol. 49, no. 4, November, pp. 455–73.

Equal Opportunity for Women in the Workplace Agency (EOWA) 2006, *2006 EOWA Australian Census of women in Leadership*, Equal Opportunity for Women in the Workplace Agency, Sydney.

Fagan, R. H. & Webber, M. 1994, *Global Restructuring: The Australian Experience*, Oxford University Press, Melbourne.

Federal Court of Australia 2006, 'List by appointment date of current judges'. Accessed online @ http://www.fedcourt.gov.au/aboutct/jj_seniority.html, 16 June 2006.

Federal Treasury 2004, *Economic Roundup, Summer 2004–05*. Accessed online @ http://www.treasury.gov.au/documents/958/PDF/full.pdf, 31 March 2006.

— 2006, *Economic Roundup, Summer 2006*. Accessed online @ http://www.treasury.gov.au/documents/1087/PDF/Summer_2006_Economic_Roundup.pdf, 31 March 2006.

Fincher, R. & Nieuwenhuysen, J. 1998, 'Introduction', in R. Fincher and J. Nieuwenhuysen (eds), *Australian Poverty: Then and now*, Melbourne University Press, Melbourne.

Fincher, R. & Saunders, P. (eds) 2001, *Creating Unequal Futures? Rethinking poverty, inequality and disadvantage*, Allen & Unwin, Sydney.

Firestone, S. 1970, *The Dialectic of Sex: The case for feminist revolution*, William Morrow and Company, New York.

Flatau, P. *et al.* 2006, 'The effectiveness and cost-effectiveness of homelessness prevention and assistance programs', positioning paper, Australian Housing and Urban Research Institute, Western Australian Research Centre, September.

Folbre, N. & Nelson, J. A. 2000, 'For Love or Money – Or Both?', *Journal of Economic Perspectives*, vol. 14, no. 4, Fall, pp. 123–40.

Forrest, J. & Johnston, R. 1999, 'Disadvantage, Discrimination and the Occupational Differentiation of Migrant Groups in Australia', *International Journal of Population Geography*, no. 5, pp. 277–96.

Frank, R. 1999, *Luxury Fever: Why money fails to satisfy in an era of excess*, The Free Press, New York.

— & Cook, P. 1995, *The Winner-Take-All Society: How more and more Americans compete for ever fewer and bigger prizes, encouraging economic waste, income inequality, and an impoverished cultural life*, The Free Press, New York.

Frankel B., 2002, 'Financialisation', in S. Bell (ed.), *Economic Governance and Industrial Dynamics*, Oxford University Press, Melbourne.

Fraser, N. 1995, 'From Redistribution to Recognition? Dilemmas of justice in a "postsocialist" age', *New Left Review*, no. 212, July/August, pp. 68–93.

— & Honneth, A. 2003, *Redistribution or Recognition?: A political–philosophical exchange*, Verso, London.

Frey, B. & Stutzer, A. 2002, *Happiness and Economics: How the economy and institutions affect human well-being*, Princeton University Press, Princeton.

Friedman, M. 1962, *Capitalism and Freedom*, University of Chicago Press, Chicago.

Garnaut, J. 2005a, 'Keen to work, a million lost in the system', *Sydney Morning Herald*, 12–13 March.

— 2005b, 'Landlords and speculators reap billions from tax rule changes', *Sydney Morning Herald*, 19 April.

— 2006, 'Australia, you're rolling in it', *Sydney Morning Herald*, 27 March, p. 1.

Geoghegan, A. 2006, 'Macquarie Bank CEO reaps rewards as profits rise', *The World Today*, 16 May, ABC Online. Accessed online @ http://www.abc.net.au/worldtoday/content/2006/s1639712.htm, 25 May 2006.

Gibilisco, P. 2003, 'A Just Society Inclusive of "People with Disabilities"', *Journal of Australian Political Economy*, no. 52, December, pp. 128–42.

Gibson-Graham, J. K., Resnick, S. & Wolff, R. 2001, *Re/presenting Class: Essays in postmodern Marxism*, Duke University Press, Durham and London.

Gilding, M. 1997, 'Gender Roles in Contemporary Australia', in K. Pritchard Hughes (ed.), *Contemporary Australian Feminism*, Addison Wesley Longman, Melbourne.

— 1999, 'Superwealth in Australia: Entrepreneurs, accumulation and the capitalist class', *Journal of Sociology*, vol. 35, no. 2, August, pp. 169–81.

Gilens, M. 2005, 'Inequality and Democratic Responsiveness', *Public Opinion Quarterly*, vol. 69, no. 5, pp. 778–96.

Gittins, R. 2002, 'Take time out from economic rationalism to smell the roses', *Sydney Morning Herald*, 18 September, p. 13.

— 2004, 'We can't blame CEOs for the rich–poor divide', *Sydney Morning Herald*, 9 June.

— 2005a, 'WorkChoices more about class war than economics', *Sydney Morning Herald*, 21 November.

— 2005b, 'Treasurer's tax cut justification a bit rich', *Sydney Morning Herald*, 18 May, p. 17.

Gleeson, B. 2006, *Australian Heartlands: Making space for hope in the suburbs*, Allen & Unwin, Sydney.

— & Low, N. 2000, *Australian Urban Planning: New challenges, new agendas*, Allen & Unwin, Sydney.

Glover, J., Harris, K. & Tennant, S. 1999, *A Social Health Atlas of Australia*, 2nd edn, vol. 1.1. Accessed online @ http://www.publichealth.gov.au/tables/austable.pdf, 12 May 2005

Glynn, A. 2006, *Capitalism Unleashed: Finance, globalisation and welfare*, Oxford University Press, Oxford.

Gorz, A. 1985, *Paths to Paradise: On the Liberation from Work*, Pluto Press, London.

— 1999, *Reclaiming Work: Beyond the wage-based society*, Polity Press, London.

de Graaf, J., Wann, D. & Naylor, T. H. 2005, *Affluenza: the all-consuming epidemic*, 2nd edn, Berrett-Koehler, San Francisco.

Gray, I. & Lawrence, G. 2001, *A Future for Regional Australia: Escaping global misfortune*, Cambridge University Press, Cambridge.

Green, F. 2006, *Demanding Work: The paradox of job quality in the affluent economy*, Princeton University Press, Princeton.

Gregory, R. G. 1993, 'Aspects of Australian and US Living Standards: the disappointing decades 1970–1990', *Economic Record*, vol. 69, pp. 61–76.

— 2002, 'It's full-time jobs that matter', *Australian Journal of Labour Economics*, vol. 5, no. 2, pp. 271–8.

— & Hunter, B. 1995, 'The Macro-economy and the Growth of Income and Employment Inequality in Australian Cities', Discussion Paper 325, Centre for Economic Policy Research, Australian National University, Canberra.

Greig, A., Lewins, F. & White, K. 2003, *Inequality in Australia*, Cambridge University Press, Cambridge.

Griffiths, P. 2005, 'Racism: Whitewashing the class divide', in R. Kuhn (ed.), *Class and Struggle in Australia*, Pearson Longman, Sydney.

Gwynne, R. 1997, *Maslow's Hierarchy of Needs*. Accessed online @ http:// web.utk. edu/~gwynne/maslow.htm, 25 May 2005

Haddad, L. 2003, 'Towards a Ceiling on Personal Income and Wealth', unpublished paper, Faculty of Economics and Business University of Sydney, Sydney.

Hägerström, J. 2003, *Perspectives on 'Race'/Ethnicity and Class in Feminism (in an Educational Context)*, paper presented at Gender and Power in the New Europe, 5th European Feminist Research Conference, 20–4 August, Lund University, Sweden.

Hakim, C. 2002, 'Lifestyle Preferences as Determinants of Women's Differentiated Labor Market Careers', *Work and Occupations*, vol. 29, no. 4, November, pp. 428–59.

Hamilton, C. 2002, 'Economics in the Age of Consumer Capitalism', *Journal of Australian Political Economy*, no. 50, December, pp. 130–6.

— 2003a, 'Real and Imagined Hardship in Australia', *Journal of Australian Political Economy*, no. 52, December, pp. 42–57.

— 2003b, 'The Politics of Affluence', *Arena Magazine*, no. 64, April–May, pp. 43–6.

— 2003c, *Growth Fetish*, Allen & Unwin, Sydney.

— 2006, 'What's Left? The death of social democracy', *Quarterly Essay*, 21, pp. 1–69.

— & Denniss, R. 2005, *Affluenza: When too much is never enough*, Allen & Unwin, Sydney.

— & Mail, E. 2003, 'Downshifting in Australia', The Australia Institute Discussion Paper no. 50, January. Accessed online @ http://www.tai.org.au/documents/dp_fulltext/DP50.pdf, 20 February 2007.

— & Rush, E. 2006, 'The Attitudes of Australians to Happiness and Well-being', web paper, September, The Australia Institute, Canberra.

Harcourt, G. C. 2001, 'Post Keynesian Thought', in G. C. Harcourt, *50 Years a Keynesian and Other Essays*, Palgrave Macmillan, London.

Harding, A. 1999, 'The Burdened Middle: Income inequality and welfare reform', in M. Carman and I. Rogers (eds), *Out of the Rut: Making Labor a genuine alternative*, Allen & Unwin, Sydney.

— 2002, *Trends in Income and Wealth Inequality in Australia*, NATSEM, University of Canberra, Canberra.

— 2006, 'Who Benefits? Income Redistribution by Government', *EcoDate*, vol. 20, no. 3.

—, Greenwell, H. & Blake, M. 2002, *Income Distribution Report: AMP–NATSEM Income and Wealth Report*, 1, February. Accessed online @ http://www.amp.com.au/display/file/0,2461,FI37391%255FSI3,00.pdf?filename=natsem_issue1.pdf, 20 February 2007.

—, Kelly, S. & Bill, A. 2003, *Income and Wealth of Generation X: AMP-NATSEM Income and Wealth Report*, 6, November. Accessed online @ http://www.amp.com.au/group/3column/02449,CH7497%255FNI12855%255FSI3,00.html, 6 April 2005.

—, Lloyd, R. & Greenwell, H. 2001, *Financial Disadvantage in Australia*, Report by NATSEM for The Smith Family, Sydney.

—, Lloyd, R. & Warren, N. 2004, *The Distribution of Taxes and Government Benefits in Australia*, paper presented at the Conference on the Distributional Effects of Government Spending and Taxation, Levy Economics Institute, 15 October. Accessed online @ http://www.natsem.canberra.edu.au/publications/papers/cps/cp04/2004_008/cp2004_008.pdf, 7 October 2005.

—, Yap, M. & Lloyd, R. 2004, *Trends in Spatial Income Inequality, 1996–2001: AMP–NATSEM Income and Wealth Report*, 8, September. Accessed online @ http://www.natsem.canberra.edu.au/publication.jsp?titleID=OP0410, 4 May 2005.

Harvey, D. M. 1989, *The Urban Experience*, Basil Blackwell, Oxford.

Harvey, M. 2006, 'Lib flays own side over childcare', *Herald Sun*, 15 May. Accessed online @ http://www.heraldsun.news.com.au/printpage/0548119135404,00.html, 16 May 2006.

Hawtrey, K. 2002, *A New Proposal to Expand Housing Supply*. Accessed online @ http://www.chp.org.qu/parity/articles/results.chtml?filename_num=00140, 20 February 2007.

Hayden, A. 1999, *Sharing the Work, Sparing the Planet: Work time, consumption and ecology*, Between the Lines, Toronto.

Headey, B., Marks, G. & Wooden, M. 2005, 'The Structure and Distribution of Household Wealth in Australia', *Australian Economic Review*, vol. 38, no. 2, pp. 159–75.

Headey, B. & Wooden, M. 2004, 'The Effects of Wealth and Income on Subjective Well-Being and Ill-Being', *Economic Record*, vol. 80, s1, pp. S24–S33.

Healey, J. (ed.) 2002, *Suicide and Self-harm, Issues in Society*, vol. 166, The Spinney Press, Thirroul.

—(ed.) 2003, *Mental Health, Issues in Society*, vol. 190, The Spinney Press, Thirroul.

—(ed.) 2005, *Wealth and Inequality, Issues in Society*, vol. 226, The Spinney Press, Thirroul.

Henderson, R. 1975, *Poverty in Australia: First main report April 1975, Australian Government Commission of Inquiry into Poverty*, Australian Government Publishing Service, Canberra.

High Court of Australia n.d., 'Justices'. Accessed online @ http://www.hcourt.gov.au/justices.html, 16 June 2006.

Hill, E. 2006, 'The Ideology and Politics of Work and Family Policy in Australia 1996–2006: Subverting women's economic security', paper presented to 15th Annual Conference on Feminist Economics, University of Sydney, Sydney, July.

Hirata, J. 2001, *Happiness and Economics: Enriching economic theory with empirical psychology*. Accessed online @ http://johannes-hirata.de/research_master.htm, 25 May 2005.

Hirsch, F. 1977, *Social Limits to Growth*, Routledge and Kegan Paul, London.

Hollier, N. (ed.) 2004, *Ruling Australia: The power, privilege and politics of the new ruling class*, Overland, in association with Australian Scholarly Publishing, Melbourne.

Holton, R. J. 1998, *Globalization and the Nation-State*, St. Martin's Press, New York.

Horin, A. 2000, 'One child in seven is living in poverty', *Sydney Morning Herald*, 27 July, p. 2.

—2006, 'Mums the only women for Coalition', *Sydney Morning Herald*, 4 March.

Howell, D. 2002, 'Increasing Earnings Inequality and Unemployment in Developed Countries: Markets, institutions and the "unified theory"', *Politics and Society*, vol. 30, no. 2, pp. 193–242.

Human Rights and Equal Opportunity Commission, Sex Discrimination Unit 2005, 'Striking the Balance: Women, men, work and family', discussion paper. Accessed online @ http://www.hreoc.gov.au/sex_discrimination/strikingbalance/docs/STB_Final.pdf, 17 August 2005.

Hunter, B. 1999, 'Three nations, not one: Indigenous and other Australian poverty', CAEPR working paper no. 1. Accessed online @ http://dspace.anu.edu.au/handle/1885/40532?mode=simple, 12 September 2006.

Irvine, J. 2005, 'Incomes rise but still a gender gap', *Sydney Morning Herald*, 18 November.

Jackson, R. 1992, 'Trends in Australian Living Standards Since 1980', *Australian Economic History Review*, vol. XXXII, no. 1, pp. 24–46.

Jefferson, T. & Preston, A. 2005, 'Australia's "Other" gender Wage Gap: Baby boomers and compulsory superannuation accounts', *Feminist Economics*, vol. 11, no. 2, July, pp. 79–101.

Johnson, D. 1996, 'Poverty Lines and the Measurement of Poverty', *Australian Economic Review*, 1st quarter, pp. 110–26.

Jones, E. 2005, 'Liquor Retailing and the Woolworths–Coles Juggernaut', *Journal of Australian Political Economy*, no. 55, June, pp. 23–47.

Jones, F. 1975, 'The Changing Shape of Australian Income', *Australian Economic History Review*, vol. XV, no. 1, pp. 21–34.

Kaldor, N. 1955–6, 'Alternative Theories of Distribution', *Review of Economic Studies*, vol. 23, pp. 83–100.

Keating, M. 2003, 'The Labour Market and Inequality', *Australian Economic Review*, vol. 36, no. 4, pp. 374–96.

— 2004, 'The Case for Increased Taxation', occasional paper 1/2004, Academy of the Social Sciences in Australia, Canberra.

Kelly, S. 2002, *Levels, Patterns and Trends of Australian Household Savings*, Report prepared by NATSEM for the Financial Planning Association. Accessed online @ http://pandora.nla.gov.au/pan/32331/20030110/www.fpa.asn.au/images/userimages/fpa/savingsreport0902.pdf, 20 February 2007.

— 2005, 'Inter-generational Transfer of Wealth – "Great Expectations"', Conference Paper CPO508. Accessed online @ http://www.natsem.canberra.edu.au/publications/papers/cps/cp05/cp2005_008/cp2005_008.pdf, 6 April 2006.

Kempen, E. T. V. 1997, 'Poverty pockets and life chances: On the role of place in shaping social inequality: The changing spatial order in cities', *American Behavioral Scientist*, November–December, vol. 41, no. 3, pp. 430–50.

Keynes, J. M., 1951, *The General Theory of Employment Interest and Money*, Macmillan, London (first published 1936)

King, A. 1998, 'Income Poverty Since the Early 1970s', in R. Fincher and J. Nieuwenhuysen, (eds), *Australian Poverty: Then and now*, Melbourne University Press, Melbourne.

King, J. & Stilwell, F. 2005, 'The Industrial Relations "Reforms": An introduction', *Journal of Australian Political Economy*, no.56, December, pp. 5–12.

Knibbes, G. 1916, *Private Wealth of Australia*, McCarron Bird, Melbourne.

Kohler, M., Connolly, E. & Smith, K. 2004, *The Composition and Distribution of Household Assets and Liabilities: Evidence from the 2002 HILDA survey*, Reserve Bank of Australia Bulletin. Accessed online @ http://www.rba.gov.au/PublicationsAndResearch/Bulletin/bu_apr04/bu_0404_1.pdf, 28 February 2005

Kuhn, R. (ed.) 2005, *Class and Struggle in Australia*, Pearson Longman, Sydney.

Kuttner, R. 1984, *The Economic Illusion: False choices between prosperity and social justice*, Houghton Mifflin, Boston.

—— 1997, *Everything for Sale: The virtues and limits of markets*, Alfred A. Knopf, New York.

Lamb, F. 2005, 'Race chasm still yawns, study finds', *Sydney Morning Herald*, 12 July.

Lane, R. 1991, *The Market Experience*, Cambridge University Press, New York.

—— 2000, *The Loss of Happiness in Market Democracies*, Yale University Press, New Haven.

Langmore, J. & Quiggin, J. 1994, *Work for All: Full employment in the nineties*, Melbourne University Press, Melbourne.

Latham, M. 1998, *Civilising Global Capital: New thinking for Australian labor*, Allen & Unwin, Sydney.

—— 2003, *From the Suburbs: Building a nation from our neighbourhoods*, Pluto Press, Sydney.

Laurent, J. (ed.) 2005, *Henry George's Legacy in Economic Thought*, Edward Elgar, Cheltenham.

Layard, R. 2003a, 'What is happiness? Are we getting happier?', in *Happiness: Has social science a clue?*, Lecture 1, Lionel Robbins Memorial Lectures 2002/03, London School of Economics and Political Science, London, 3 March.

—— 2003b, 'Income and happiness: rethinking economic policy', in *Happiness: Has social science a clue?*, Lecture 2, Lionel Robbins Memorial Lectures 2002/03, London School of Economics and Political Science, London, 4 March.

—— 2003c, 'How can we make a happier society?', in *Happiness: Has social science a clue?*, Lecture 3, Lionel Robbins Memorial Lectures 2002/03, London School of Economics and Political Science, London, 4 March.

—— 2005, *Happiness: Lessons from a new science*, Penguin, New York.

Leigh, A. 2005, 'Deriving Long-Run Inequality Series from Tax Data', *Economic Record*, vol. 81, no. 255, August, pp. 558–70.

—— 2006, 'The Political Economy of Tax Reform in Australia', *Public Policy*, vol. 1, no. 1, pp. 52–60.

Liberal Party of Australia 2004, *The Howard Government's Plan for a Stronger Australia*. Accessed online @ http://www.liberal.org.au/documents/Howard_Government_Catalogue.pdf, 24 September 2004.

Light, I. 2005, 'The Ethnic Economy', in N. Smelser and R. Swedberg (eds), *The Handbook of Economic Sociology*, Princeton University Press, Princeton and Oxford.

Lloyd, R., Harding, A. & Greenwell, H. 2001, 'Worlds Apart: Postcodes with the highest and lowest poverty rates in today's Australia', paper presented to the

National Social Policy Conference, July, Sydney. Accessed online @ http://www. natsem.canberra.edu.au/publications/papers/cps/cp01/2001_005/cp2001_005.pdf, 4 May 2005.

Lloyd, R., Harding, A. & Payne, A. 2004a, 'Australians in poverty in the 21st century', paper prepared by NATSEM for 33rd Conference of Economists, 27–30 September. Accessed online @ http://www.natsem.canberra.edu.au/ publication.jsp?titleID/CP0407, 4 April 2005.

Lloyd, R., Yap, M. & Harding, A. 2004b, 'A spatial divide? Trends in the incomes and socioeconomic characteristics of regions between 1996 and 2001', paper presented to the 28th Australian and New Zealand Regional Science Association International Annual Conference, Wollongong, 28 September–1 October. Accessed online @ http://www.natsem.canberra.edu.au/publications/papers/cps/cp04/2004_005/cp2004_005.pdf, 28 April 2005.

Lundberg, F. 1969, *The Rich and the Super Rich: A Study in the Power of Wealth Today*, rev. edn, Thomas Nelson and Sons, London.

McDonald, A. 1995, *Unemployment Forever? Or a support income system and work for all?*, A. & D. McDonald, Urangan.

— 2005, *Do Economists Care?*, A. McDonald, Urangan.

McGregor, C. 1997, *Class in Australia*, Penguin, Ringwood.

Macklin, J. 2002, 'Postcodes for Prosperity: The link between location, education and employment', speech given at Towards Opportunity and Prosperity Conference, 5 April, Melbourne. Accessed online @ http://www.melbourneinstitute.com./conf/top2002/pdffiles/MacklinJenny5B.pdf, 28 April 2005.

McLean, I. & Richardson, S. 1986, 'More or Less equal? Australian income distribution in 1933 and 1980', *Economic Record*, no. 62.

McMahon, S. 2006, 'Myer chief's $18 m pay revealed', *Sydney Morning Herald*, 9 February.

McManus, P. & Pritchard, B. 2000, 'Introduction', in B. Pritchard and P. McManus (eds), *Land of Discontent: The dynamics of change in rural and regional Australia*, UNSW Press, Sydney, pp. 1–13.

McQueen, H. 1974, 'The Myth of Equality', *Heresies*, ABC, Sydney.

Maddock, R., Olekalns, N., Ryan, J. & Vickers, M. 1984, 'The Distribution of Income and Wealth in Australia 1914–80, An introduction and bibliography', *Source Papers in Economic History*, no.1, Australian National University, Canberra.

Manning, P. 2001, 'Equity with Growth', in J. Nieuwenhuysen, P. Lloyd and M. Mead (eds), *Reshaping Australia's Economy: Growth with equity and sustainability*, Cambridge University Press, Cambridge.

Mares, P. 2002, *Borderline: Australia's response to refugees and asylum seekers in the wake of the Tampa*, 2nd edn, UNSW Press, Sydney.

Martin, D. 2001, 'Is welfare dependency "welfare poison"? An assessment of Noel Pearson's proposals for Aboriginal welfare reform', *Technical Report Discussion*

Paper, no. 213, Centre for Aboriginal Economic Policy Research, Australian National University, Canberra. Accessed online @ http://www.anu.edu.au/caepr/ Publications/DP/2001_DP213.pdf, 20 February 2007.

Mathews, R. 1980, The Structure of Taxation, in Australian Institute of Political Science (ed) *The Politics of Taxation*, Hodder and Stoughton, Sydney.

Mayne, S. 2005, 'The CRW list: We find another five missing multi-millionaires', *Crikey Daily*, 25 May. Accessed online @ http://5m3r.blogspot.com/2005/05/10-of-28-kennedy-nsw-budget-crw-rich.html#2005/05/23–1736-3238, 22 September 2006.

Meade, J. 1975, 'The Keynesian Revolution', in M. Keynes (ed.), *Essays on John Maynard Keynes*, Cambridge University Press, Cambridge.

Meagher, G. 2003, *Friend or Flunkey? Paid domestic workers in the new economy*, UNSW Press, Sydney.

Melbourne Institute of Applied Economic and Social Research 2006, *Poverty Lines: Australia, March quarter*, 2006, University of Melbourne, Melbourne. Accessed online @ http://melbourneinstitute.com/labour/inequality/poverty/Poverty%20lines%20Australia%20March%202006.pdf, 26 September 2006.

Melman, S. 1983, *Profits Without Production*, Knopf, New York.

Mendes, P. 2003, 'Australian Neoliberal Think Tanks and the Backlash Against the Welfare State', *Journal of Australian Political Economy*, no. 51, June, pp. 29–56.

Mill, J. S. 1965, *Principles of Political Economy*, Augustus M. Kelley, New York, first published 1848.

Mishel, L., Bernstein, J. & Allegretto, S. 2005, *The State of Working America 2004/2005*, Economic Policy Institute, ILR Press, Ithaca.

Mission Australia 2004, 'Poverty: Young people and children in Australia', in J. Healey (ed.), 'Wealth and Inequality', *Issues in Society*, vol. 226, The Spinney Press, Thirroul.

Mitchell, W. F. 1999, 'Full Employment Abandoned: the Macroeconomic Story', in M. Carman and I. Rogers (eds), *Out of the Rut: Making Labor a Genuine Alternative*, Allen & Unwin, Sydney.

— 2000, 'The Job Guarantee in a Small Open Economy', in E. Carson and W. F. Mitchell, (eds), *The Path to Full Employment and Equity*, supplement to *The Economics and Labour Relations Review*, vol. 11, pp. 10–25.

Murphy, B. 1979, 'Who's Running Australia: Portraits of the ruling class', *Tribune*, Sydney.

Murphy, P. & Watson S. 1997, *Surface City: Sydney at the Millennium*, Pluto Press, Sydney.

Murray, G. 2001, 'Interlocking Directorates: What do they tell us about corporate power in Australia?', *Journal of Australian Political Economy*, no. 47, June, pp. 5–26.

Murray, L. 2006, 'Why $21 m Moss Gathers Australia's Biggest Wage', *Sydney Morning Herald*, May 17, pp. 1–2.

mydr.com.au 2005, 'Youth Suicide in Australia: An issue that cannot be ignored'. Accessed online @ http://www.mydr.com.au/default.asp?article=3275, 6 June 2005.

National Housing Strategy 1991, *The Affordability of Australian Housing*, Issues Paper 2, AGPS, Canberra.

NATSEM 2004, 'Four-fifths of budget tax cuts and family payment increases received by families with children – and three-fifths of families receive no benefit', media release, 14 May.

Neutze, G. M. 2000, 'Economics, Values and Urban Australia', in P. N.Troy (ed.), *Equity, Environment, Efficiency*, Melbourne University Press, Melbourne.

Nevile, J. 2001, 'Evidence or Assumptions? The basis of the five economists' case for wage cuts', in E. Carlson and W. F. Mitchell (eds), *Achieving Full Employment*, Supplement to the *Economic and Labour Relations Review*, vol. 12, pp 131–48.

New South Wales Office of Industrial Relations 2004, *A History of Pay Equity*. Accessed online @ http://www.workandfamily.nsw.gov.au/payequity/history.html, 2 August 2005.

Northwood, K., Rawnsley, T. & Chen, L. 2002, 'Experimental Estimates of the Distribution of Household Wealth, Australia, 1994–2000', *Working Papers in Applied Econometrics*, no. 2002/1, cat no. 1351.0, Australian Bureau of Statistics Canberra.

O'Connor, K., Stimson, R. J. & Baum, S. 2001, 'The Regional Distribution of Growth', in J. Nieuwenhuysen, P. Lloyd and M. Mead (eds), *Reshaping Australia's Economy: Growth with equity and sustainability*, Cambridge University Press, Cambridge.

O'Dwyer, L. 2001, 'The Impact of Housing Inheritance on the Distribution of Wealth in Australia', *Australian Journal of Political Science*, vol. 36, no. 1, pp. 83–100.

Okun, A. 1975, *Equality and Efficiency: The big tradeoff*, Brookings Institution, Washington.

O'Leary, J. & Sharp, R. (eds) 1991, *Inequality in Australia: Sharing the Cake*, William Heinemann, Melbourne.

O'Loughlin, T. 2000, 'Gap between rich and poor grows', *Sydney Morning Herald*, 15 November.

O'Malley, N. 2005, 'PM's wages bonanza eludes most workers', *Sydney Morning Herald*, 29 August, p. 6.

— 2006, 'Cops are tops in the pay league – until they hit 20', *Sydney Morning Herald*, weekend edition, 6–7 May, p. 3.

Osborne, P. 2006, 'Pressure over childcare', *Australian*, 15 May. Accessed online @ http://www.theaustralian.news.com.au/printpage/0594219141101,00.html, 16 May 2006.

O'Sullivan, M. and Askew, K. (2006) 'Telstra's Secret Pay Deals Under Fire', *Sydney Morning Herald: Business*, 14 November.

Patulny, R. 2004, *Social Capital and Welfare: Dependency or Division? Examining Bridging Trends by Welfare Regime, 1981 to 2000*, SPRC Discussion Paper no. 138 [Accessed online @] http://www.sprc.unsw.edu.au/dp/DP138.pdf, 20 April 2006.

Peatling, S. 2005, 'Too busy to tackle child care crisis', *Sydney Morning Herald*, August 5. Accessed online @ http://smh.com.au/news/national/too-busy-to-tackle-childcare-crisis/2005 August 2003/1122748703200.html, 12 August 2005.

Peel, M. 1995, *Good Times, Hard Times*, Melbourne University Press, Melbourne.

— 2003, *The Lowest Rung: Voices of Australian poverty*, Cambridge University Press, Cambridge.

Peetz, D. 1998, *Unions in a Contrary World: The future of the Australian trade union movement*, Cambridge University Press, Cambridge.

— 2006, *Brave New Workplace: How individual contracts are changing our jobs*, Allen & Unwin, Sydney.

Pen, J. 1971, *Income Distribution*, Penguin, Harmondsworth.

Petre, D. 2005, 'It's a bit rich: the wealthy can give far more', *Sydney Morning Herald*, 5 April.

Pietsch, S. 2005, 'To have and to hold on to: wealth, power and the capitalist class', in R. Kuhn (ed.), *Class and Struggle in Australia*, Pearson Longman, Sydney.

Piggott, J. 1987, 'The distribution of wealth in Australia – A survey', *Economic Record*, vol. 60, pp. 252–65.

Pigou, A. 1946, *The Economics of Welfare*, 4th edn, Macmillan, London (originally published 1933).

Pocock, B. 2003, *The Work/Life Collision: What work is doing to Australians and what to do about it*, The Federation Press, Sydney.

— & Masterman-Smith, H. 2005, 'WorkChoices and Women Workers', *Journal of Australian Political Economy*, no. 55, December, pp. 126–44.

Podder, N. & Kakwani, N. 1976, 'Distribution of Wealth in Australia', *Review of Income and Wealth*, Series 22, March, pp. 75–92.

Preston, A. & Burgess, J. 2003, 'Women's Work in Australia: Trends, issues and prospects', *Australian Journal of Labour Economics*, vol. 6, no. 4, December, pp. 497–518.

Pritchard, B. 1994, 'Finance Capital as an Engine of Restructuring: The 1980s merger wave', *Journal of Australian Political Economy*, no. 33, June, pp. 1–20.

Pritchard Hughes, K. 1997, 'Feminism for beginners', in K. Pritchard Hughes (ed.), *Contemporary Australian Feminism*, Addison Wesley Longman, Melbourne.

Probert, B. 1997, 'Women's working lives', in K. Pritchard Hughes (ed.), *Contemporary Australian Feminism*, Addison Wesley Longman, Melbourne.

Productivity Commission 2004, *First Home Ownership*, Report no. 28, Commonwealth of Australia, Melbourne. Accessed online @ http://www.pc.gov.au/inquiry/housing/finalreport/housing.pdf, 12 May 2005.

Pusey, M. 1991, *Economic Rationalism in Canberra: A Nation-Building State Changes its Mind*, Cambridge University Press, Melbourne.

— 2003, *The Experience of Middle Australia*, Cambridge University Press, Cambridge.

— & Turnbull, N. 2005, 'Have Australians Embraced Economic Reform?', in S. Wilson, G. Meagher, R. Gibson, D. Denemark and M. Western (eds), *Australian Social Attitudes: The first report*, UNSW Press, Sydney.

Quiggin J. 2002, 'Economic Governance and Microeconomic Reform', in S. Bell (ed.), *Economic Governance and Institutional Dynamics*, Oxford University Press, Melbourne.

Randolph, B. 2004, *Renewing the Middle City: Planning for stressed suburbs*, Urban Frontiers Program, issues paper no. 15, University of Western Sydney, Sydney. Accessed online @ http://www.uws.edu.au/download.php?file_id/6426/ Issues_Paper_no.15.pdfmimetype/application/pdf, 27 April 2005.

— & Holloway, D. 2002, 'The Anatomy of Housing Stress in Sydney', *Urban Policy and Research*, vol. 20, no. 4, pp. 329–56.

Raskall, P. 1992, 'The Import Content of Household Expenditure by Income', SSEI Working Paper series, Centre for Applied Economic Research and the Social Policy Research Centre, University of New South Wales, Sydney.

— 2003, 'The truth about Australia's inequality and how to tackle it', *Australian Socialist*, vol. 12, no. 2, pp. 4–6.

Rees, S. 2003, *Passion for Peace*, UNSW Press, Sydney.

Riach, P. A. & Rich, J. 1991, 'Testing for racial discrimination in the labour market', *Cambridge Journal of Economics*, no. 15, pp. 239–56.

— 2002, 'Field Experiments of Discrimination in the Market Place', *Economic Journal*, no. 112, November, pp. 480–517.

Ricardo, D. 1962, *On the Principles of Political Economy and Taxation*, Dent, London (first published 1817).

Rodrigo, D. 2003, 'Circuits of Advantage and Disadvantage', unpublished Honours thesis, School of Economics and Political Science, University of Sydney, Sydney.

Rogers, M. F. & Jones, D. R. 2006, *The Changing Nature of Australia's Country Towns*, Centre for Sustainable Rural Communities, Bendigo.

Rooney, M. 2006, 'Making Poverty Visible', *Overland*, no. 184, Spring, pp. 41–7.

Rosewarne, S. 2002, 'Towards an Ecological Political Economy', *Journal of Australian Political Economy*, no. 50, December, pp. 179–99.

Rubinstein, W. 2004, *The All-time Australian 200 Rich List*, Allen & Unwin, Sydney, in association with *Business Review Weekly*.

Russell, B. 1917, *Roads to Freedom*, George Allen & Unwin, London.

— 1935, *In Praise of Idleness*, George Allen & Unwin, London.

Sandercock, L. 1979, *The Land Racket: The real costs of property speculation*, Silverfish Books, Canberra.

Saunders, P. 1993, 'Longer Run Changes in the Distribution of Income', *Economic Record*, vol. 69, no. 207, pp. 355–64.

— 1998, 'Setting the Poverty Agenda: The origins and impact of the *Henderson Report*', in R. Fincher & J. Nieuwenhuysen (eds), *Australian Poverty: Then and Now*, Melbourne University Press, Melbourne.

— 2002, *The Ends and Means of Welfare: Coping with economic and social change in Australia*, Cambridge University Press, Cambridge.

— 2003, *Examining Recent Changes in Income Distribution in Australia*, Social Policy Research Centre Discussion Paper no. 130. Accessed online @ http://www.sprc. unsw.edu.au/dp/DP130.pdf, 27 October 2004.

— 2005, *The Poverty Wars*, UNSW Press, Sydney.

— 2006, *The Costs of Disability and the Incidence of Poverty*, Social Policy Research Centre, Discussion Paper no. 147, University of New South Wales, Sydney.

— 2006a, *A Perennial Problem: Employment, Joblessness and Poverty*, Social Policy Research Centre, Discussion Paper no. 146, University of New South Wales, Sydney.

— & Adelman, L. 2005, *Income Poverty, Deprivation and Exclusion: A comparative study of Australia and Britain*, Social Policy Research Centre, Discussion Paper no. 141, University of New South Wales, Sydney.

— & Bradbury, B. 2006, 'Monitoring Trends in Poverty and Income Distribution: Data, methodology and measurement, *Economic Record*, vol. 82, pp. 341–64.

Saunders, P. [CIS] 1999, 'Families, welfare and social policy', in *Family Matters*, Australian Institute of Family Studies, no. 54 Spring(Summer. Accessed online @ http://www.aifs.gov.au/institute/pubs/fm/fm54ps.pdf, 2 May 2005.

— 2002a, 'Can we trust official statistics?', Centre for Independent Studies, Sydney. Accessed online @ http://www.onlineopinion.com.au/view.asp?article=1863, 4 August 2004.

— 2004, 'Why ACOSS Is Wrong To Be Complacent About Welfare Dependency', in *Issue Analysis*, no. 51, Centre for Independent Studies, Sydney. Accessed online @ http://www.cis.org.au/IssueAnalysis/ia51/ia51.pdf, 20 April 2005.

— & Tsumori, K. 2002, *Poverty in Australia: Beyond the Rhetoric*, Policy Monograph no. 57, Centre for Independent Studies, Sydney.

Schneider, M. 2004, *The Distribution of Wealth*, Edward Elgar, Cheltenham.

Scutella, R. & Wooden, M. 2004, 'Jobless Households in Australia: incidence, characteristics and financial consequences', *Economic and Labour Relations Review*, vol. 14, no. 2, pp. 187–207.

Sen, A. K. 1985, *Commodities and Capabilities*, North-Holland, Amsterdam.

— 1997, *On Economic Inequality*, Oxford University Press, Oxford.

Senate Community Affairs References Committee 2003, *Official Committee Hansard. Reference: Poverty and Financial Hardship*, 28 May. Accessed online @ http://www.aph.gov.au/hansard/senate/commttee/S6516.pdf, 28 April 2005.

— 2004, *A hand up not a hand out: Renewing the fight against poverty. Report on poverty and financial hardship*, Commonwealth of Australia, Canberra. Accessed online @ http://www.aph.gov.au/senate/committee/clac_ctte/completed_inquiries/2002–04/poverty/report/report.pdf, 18 April 2005.

Sexton, E. 2003, 'Money matters: when too much is finally enough', in 'Power Salaries: A Money Special Report', *Sydney Morning Herald*, 5 November, pp. 2–3.

Shields, J. 2005, 'Setting the Double Standard: Chief executive pay the BCA way', *Journal of Australian Political Economy*, no. 56, December, pp. 299–324.

—, O'Donnell, M. & O'Brien, J. 2003, *The Buck Stops Here: Private sector executive remuneration in Australia*, report prepared for the Labor Council of New South Wales, Sydney.

Sklair, L. 2001, *The Transnational Capitalist Class*, Blackwell, Oxford.

Smith, C. 1999, 'Progressing tax reform', in M. Carman and I. Rogers (eds), *Out of the Rut: Making Labor a genuine alternative*, Allen & Unwin, Sydney.

— 2004, 'For richer or poorer: recent trends in Australia's regional income dynamics', *Australasian Journal of Regional Studies*, vol. 10, no. 2, pp. 195–223.

Smyth P. & Wearing, M. 2002, 'After the Welfare State', in S. Bell (ed.), *Economic Governance and Institutional Dynamics*, Oxford University Press, Melbourne.

Soltow, L. 1972, 'The Census of Wealth of Men in Australia', *Australian Economic History Review*, vol. XII, no. 2, pp. 125–41.

Sorensen, T. 1994, 'The Folly of Regional Policy', *Agenda*, vol. 1, no. 1.

— 2002, 'Regional Economic Governance: States, markets and DIY', in S. Bell (ed.), *Economic Governance and Institutional Dynamics*, Oxford University Press, Melbourne.

Steketee, M. 2005, 'The inequality trap', *Weekend Australian Inquirer*, reproduced in J. Healey (ed.), *Wealth and Inequality, Issues in Society*, vol. 226, The Spinney Press, Thirroul.

Steven, R. 2000, 'White Settler Origins of Australia', *Journal of Australian Political Economy*, no. 46, December, pp. 40–70.

Stilwell, F. 1986, *The Accord and Beyond: the Political Economy of the Labor Government*, Pluto Press, Sydney.

— 1993, *Economic Inequality: Who gets what in Australia*, Pluto Press, Sydney.

— 1996, 'The Cul de Sac of Neoclassical Economics', in G. Argyrous and F. Stilwell (eds), *Economics as a Social Science: Readings in Political Economy*, Pluto Press, Sydney.

— 2000, *Changing Track: A new political economic direction for Australia*, Pluto Press, Sydney.

— 2001, 'Economic Inequality', in G. Argyrous and F. Stilwell (eds), *Economics as a Social Science: Readings in political economy*, Pluto Press, Sydney.

— 2003a, *Submission to the Productivity Commission Inquiry Into First Home Ownership*. Accessed online @ http://www.pc.gov.au/inquiry/housing/subs/sub212.pdf, 22 June 2004.

— 2003b, 'Refugees in a Region: Afghans in Young, NSW', *Urban Policy and Research*, vol. 21, no. 3, pp. 235–48.

— 2006, *Political Economy: the Contest of Economic Ideas*, 2nd edn, Oxford University Press, Melbourne.

— & Johnson, M. 1991, *Metropolitan and Non-Metropolitan Areas: Comparative economics*, Public Sector Research Centre, University of New South Wales, Sydney.

—— & Jordan, K. 2004, 'The Political Economy of Land: Putting Henry George in his place', *Journal of Australian Political Economy*, no. 54, December, pp. 119–34.

Strange, S. 1986, *Casino Capitalism*, Basil Blackwell, Oxford.

Stretton, H. 2005, *Australia Fair*, UNSW Press, Sydney.

—— 2006, 'Societal inequalities and corporate pay', *New Matilda*, 25 January. Accessed online @ http://www.newmatilda.com/policytoolkit/policydetail.asp?policyID=284, 10 March 2006.

Sydney Morning Herald 2003, 'Power Salaries: A Money Special Report', *Sydney Morning Herald*, 5 November.

—— 2006, 'Reaping rewards of capitalism: A share-owning nation', editorial, *Sydney Morning Herald*, 23 March, p. 10.

Tabb, W. 2004, *Economic Governance in the Age of Globalisation*, Columbia University Press, New York.

Tawney, R. 1964, *Equality*, George Allen & Unwin, Sydney.

Taylor, R., Page, A., Morrell, S., Carter, G. & Harrison, J. 2004, 'Socio-economic differentials in mental disorders and suicide attempts in Australia', *British Journal of Psychiatry*, vol. 185, December, pp. 486–93.

Thompson, E. 1994, *Fair Enough: Egalitarianism in Australia*, UNSW Press, Sydney.

Thomson, J. 2006, 'Gender Imbalance', *BRW Young Rich*, *Business Review Weekly*, 14 September–18 October, p. 18.

Thurow, L. 1996, *The Future of Capitalism*, Nicholas Brealey Publishing, London.

Tiffen, R. & Gittins, R. 2004, *How Australia Compares*, Cambridge University Press, Cambridge.

Toner, P. 1988, 'The Crisis of Equipment Investment in Australia', *Journal of Australian Political Economy*, no. 22, February, pp. 39–56.

Travers, P. 2005, 'Income and Wealth', in J. Spoehr (ed.), *State of South Australia: Trends and issues*, Wakefield Press, Adelaide.

Troy, P. N. (ed.) 1981, *Equity in the City*, Allen & Unwin, Sydney.

—— (ed.) 1999, *Serving the City: The crisis in Australia's urban services*, Pluto Press, Sydney.

—— (ed.) 2000, *Equity, Environment, Efficiency*, Melbourne University Press, Melbourne.

Turnbull, M. & Temple, J. 2005, *Taxation Reform in Australia: Some alternatives and indicative costings*, Office of Malcolm Turnbull, MP, Sydney, 29 August.

United Nations 2000, *Human Development Report*. Accessed online @ http://hdr.undp.org/reports/global/2000/en/, 24 March 2006.

—— 2000, *Human Development Report*. Accessed online @ http://hdr.undp.org/reports/global/2002/en/, 24 March 2006.

—— 2004, *Human Development Report*. Accessed online @ http://hdr.undp.org/reports/global/2004/, 22 September 2004

—— 2005, *Human Development Report 2005*. Accessed online @ http://hdr.undp.org/reports/global/2005/, 23 September 2005.

— 2006 *Human Development Report 2006.* Accessed online @ http://hdr.undp.org/
hdr2006/, 2 December 2006.

Vasta, E. & Castles, S. (eds) 1996, *The Teeth Are Smiling: the Persistence of Racism in
Multicultural Australia,* Allen & Unwin, Sydney.

Veblen, T. 1970, *The Theory of the Leisure Class,* Unwin Books, London (first published
by Macmillan, New York, 1899).

Veenhoven, R. 1984, *Conditions of Happiness,* Kluwer, Dordrecht, Netherlands.

Vinson, T. 1999, *Unequal in Life: The distribution of social disadvantage in Victoria and New
South Wales,* Ignatius Centre for Social Policy and Research, Jesuit Social Services,
Melbourne.

— 2004, *Community Adversity and Resilience: The distribution of social disadvantage in
Victoria and New South Wales and the mediating role of social cohesion,* Jesuit Social
Services, Melbourne.

—, Esson, K. & Johnston, K. 2002, *Inquiry into the Provision of Public Education in NSW,*
Pluto Press Australia in Conjunction with the NSW Teachers Federation, Sydney.

Wachtel, P. 1983, *The Poverty of Affluence: A psychological portrait of the American way of
life,* The Free Press, New York.

Wacjman, J. 2006, 'Technocapitalism Meets Technofeminism: Women and technology
in a wireless world', *Labour and Industry,* vol. 16, no. 3, April–May, pp. 7–20.

Wade, M. 2006, 'Mortgages now a lifelong debt', *Sydney Morning Herald,* Weekend Edition, 8–9 April, p. 3.

— 2004, 'Home Sweet Home – for $36 000 a year', *Sydney Morning Herald,* 12 March.

— 2006, 'South West First to Crack with Debt Load', *Sydney Morning Herald,* 28 September.

— & Cubby, B. 2006, 'Money Pit', *Sydney Morning Herald,* Weekend Edition, 1–2 April,
p. 25 and p. 33.

Walsh, J. 1999, 'Myths and Counter-Myths: An analysis of part-time female employees
and their orientations to work and working hours', *Work, Employment & Society,*
vol. 13, no. 2, pp. 179–203.

Walters, S. 2005, 'Making the Best of a Bad Job? Female part-timers' orientations
and attitudes to work', *Gender, Work and Organization,* vol. 12, no. 3, May,
pp. 193–216.

Waring, M. 1996, Three Masquerades: Essays on Equality, Work and Hu(man) Rights,
Allen & Unwin, Sydney.

Washington, S. 2006, 'Tell the Truth about CEO Pay: Reported Salary Totals Do Not
Reveal All', *Sydney Morning Herald: Business,* November 13.

Watson, I. 1998–99, *Proposals for a Wage Freeze and Tax Credits: Will subsidising low wage
jobs solve unemployment?,* Research Paper no. 29, Information and Research Service,
Department of the Parliamentary Library, Canberra.

— 2005, 'Contented Workers in Inferior Jobs? Re-assessing casual employment in
Australia', *Journal of Industrial Relations,* vol. 47, no. 4, December, pp. 371–92.

— & Buchanan, J. 2001, 'Beyond impoverished visions of the labour market', in R. Fincher and P. Saunders (eds), *Creating Unequal Futures? Rethinking poverty, inequality and disadvantage*, Allen & Unwin, Sydney.

Watts, M. 2000, 'The Dimensions and Costs of Unemployment in Australia', in S. Bell (ed.), *The Unemployment Crisis in Australia: Which way out?* Cambridge University Press, Melbourne.

Watts, R. 2006, 'Howard's Division for the Land of the Long Economic Boom', in *Advance Australia Fair: Building Sustainability, Justice and Peace*, proceedings of the 3rd National Now We the People Conference, Melbourne, 30–1 July, pp. 31–6.

Wealth Creator n.d., *Wealth Creator TV Show Website.* Accessed online @ http://www.wealthcreatormagazine.com.au/tv/index.php, 12 May 2005.

White, K. 2003, 'Women and Leadership in Higher Education in Australia', *Tertiary Education and Management*, vol. 9, no. 1, January, pp. 45–60.

White, R., Tranter, B. & Hanson, D. 2004 'Share Ownership in Australia: The emergence of new tensions?', *Journal of Sociology*, vol. 40, no. 2, pp. 99–120.

Whitehouse, G. 2003, 'Gender and Pay Equity: Future research directions', *Asia Pacific Journal of Human Resources*, vol. 41, no. 1, pp. 116–28.

— & Diamond, C. 2006, 'Gendered Dichotomies and Segregation Patterns in Computing Jobs in Australia', *Labour and Industry*, vol. 16, no. 3, April–May, pp. 73–90.

Wicks, D., Mishra, G. & Milne, L. 2001, 'Young Women, Work and Inequality: Is it what they want or what they get? An Australian contribution to research on women and workforce participation', paper for the British Sociological Association Jubilee Conference, 9–12 April.

Wikipedia 2005, *Happiness.* Accessed online @ http://en.wikipedia.org/wiki/Happiness, 25 May 2005.

Wilkinson, R. G. 1994, 'The Epidemiological Transition: From Material Scarcity to Social Disadvantage', *Daedalus*, vol. 123.

Wilkinson, R. G. 1996, *Unhealthy Societies: The afflictions of inequality*, Routledge, London and New York.

— 2005, *The Impact of Inequality: How to Make Sick Societies Healthier*, W. W. Norton, New York.

— & Marmot, M. (eds) 2003, *Social determinants of health: the solid facts*, 2nd edn, World Health Organization Regional Office for Europe. Accessed online @ http://www.euro.who.int/document/e81384.pdf, 20 February 2007.

— & Pickett, K. E. 2006, 'Income Inequality and Population Health: A review and explanation of the evidence', *Social Science and Medicine*, vol. 62, issue 7, April, pp. 1768–84.

Wilson, S., Gibson, R., Meagher, G., Denemark, D. & Western, M. 2006, *Australian Social Attitudes, 2005* (computer file), Australian Social Science Data Archive, Australian National University, Canberra.

Woldring, K. 1997, 'Exploring Old Paradigms: Worksharing as an alternative to government policies', in J. Tomlinson *et al.* (eds), *Unemployment: Policy and practice*, Australian Academic Press, Brisbane.

Wong, P. 2002, Maiden speech, Parliament, 21 August 2002. Accessed online @ http://www.pennywong.com.au/documents/WONG%20-%20Maiden%20Speech-%-20Reclaiming%20one%20Nation%20-%20210802.pdf, 20 February 2007.

Wooden, M. 2005, 'Minimum Wage Setting and the Australian Fair Pay Commission', *Journal of Australian Political Economy*, no. 56, December, pp. 81–91.

— & Warren, D. 2004, 'Non-standard Employment and Job Satisfaction: Evidence from the HILDA survey, *Journal of Industrial Relations*, vol. 46, no. 3, September, pp. 275–97.

Wynhausen, E. 2005, *Dirt Cheap: Life at the wrong end of the job market*, Pan Macmillan, Sydney.

Yates, J., Randolph, B. & Holloway, D. 2005, *Housing Affordability, Occupation and Location in Australian Cities and Regions*, Australian Housing and Urban Research Institute, Sydney.

— 2006, *Are Housing Affordability Problems Creating Labour Shortages?*, Australian Housing and Urban Research Institute, Sydney.

INDEX

CPSIA information can be obtained at www.ICGtesting.com
Printed in the USA
BVOW011757180413

318521BV00008B/162/P

9 780521 700320